INDUSTRIAL ORGANIZATION IN A DICHOTOMOUS ECONOMY

For my family, Jin-I and Chin

Industrial Organization in a Dichotomous Economy

The case of Taiwan

TEIN-CHEN CHOU
Institute of Economics
National Chung-Hsing University

Avebury
Aldershot · Brookfield USA · Hong Kong · Singapore · Sydney

© T. C. Chou 1995

All rights reserved. No part of this publication may be reproduced, stored in a retrieval system, or transmitted in any form or by any means, electronic, mechanical, photocopying or otherwise without the prior permission of the publisher.

Published by
Avebury
Ashgate Publishing Limited
Gower House
Croft Road
Aldershot
Hants GU11 3HR
England

Ashgate Publishing Company
Old Post Road
Brookfield
Vermont 05036
USA

British Library Cataloguing in Publication Data

Chou, Tien-Chen
    Industrial Organization in a
    Dichotomous Economy: Case
    of Taiwan
    I. Title
    338.0951249

ISBN 1 85972 049 8

Library of Congress Catalog Card Number: 94–74467

Typeset by
King Hwa Typewriting Co.
5F, No. 92, Huai Ning st., Taipei, Taiwan, R.O.C.

Printed and bound by Athenaeum Press Ltd., Gateshead, Tyne & Wear.

Contents

List of Figures vii
List of Tables viii
Acknowledgments xii
Introduction 1

Part I Industrialization, Growth Sources and Financial System 5

1 The Pattern and Strategy of Industrialization 7
2 Sources of Economic Growth and Structural Change: A Revised Approach 39
3 Financial Dualism and Economic Development 63

Part II Structure, Trade & Performance 115

4 The Evolution of Market Structure 117
5 Concentration, Profitability and Trade in A Simultaneous Equation Analysis 147
6 Concentration and Profitability in a Dichotomous Economy 171

Part III Large, Small and Foreign Firms 201

7 Aggregate Concentration Ratio and Business Groups 203
8 The Experience of SMEs' Development 225
9 American and Japanese Direct Foreign Investment in Taiwan 249

Appendix 2.1 Matbematical Inference Procedure 58

Appendix 5.1 Are In and Tm Close to An Identity? 165

Appendix 6.1 Sources and Definitions of Variables. 195

Appendix 7.1 Listing of the 17 Giant Firms and Their Related Business Groups, 1981 221

Appendix 8.1 Historical Review of the Government Assistance System to SMEs in Taiwan, 1954–1982 245

Appendix 9.1 Sources and Definitions of Variables 269

Index

List of Figures

Figure 1.1 The trend of real wages in manufacturing   22

Figure 3.1 The financial system in Taiwan   70

Figure 3.2 The allocation of funds under dualism   86

Figure 4.1 Aggregate price-cost margins in the manufacturing, 1961–1981   140

Figure 7.1 ACR 100 in terms of turnover, employment and assets, 1970–80   208

List of Tables

Table 1.1 Indicators of Taiwan's economy, 1953–81	8
Table 1.2 Sectoral shares and contributions to the growth of GDP, 1953–81	9
Table 1.3 Composition of manufacturing in terms of value added, 1953–81	11
Table 1.4 Comparison of manufactures concentration ratios for the World and Taiwan	14
Table 1.5 Sources of growth in manufacturing output, 1952–79	15
Table 1.6 Composition of trade, 1952–81	17
Table 1.7 Composition of manufactured exports, 1956–81	20
Table 1.8 The characteristics of industrialization phases in Taiwan	21
Table 1.9 The ratios of customs revenues to imports and tax revenues, 1953–82	25
Table 2.1 Sources of economic growth and structural change in Taiwan, 197–1984	51
Table 2.2 Comparison of sources of economic growth and structural change in manufacturing by different approaches	54

Table 3.1	Number of financial institutions	72
Table 3.2	Shares of financial institutions at end of year	73
Table 3.3	Number of banks and branches	75
Table 3.4	Loans of government and financial institutions	77
Table 3.5	Deposits of government financial institutions	78
Table 3.6	Stock market statistics	79
Table 3.7	Composition of business sector's financings from the financial system	81
Table 3.8	Household saving through the financial system, 1965–88	82
Table 3.9	Spread of bank interest rates	84
Table 3.10	Structure of bank loans by terms	92
Table 3.11	Distribution of bank loans and discounts	98
Table 3.12	Loans to small and medium sized enterprises	99
Table 3.13	Percentage share of export loans	99
Table 3.14	The distrbution of bank loans and value added by industry	100
Table 3.15	The distribution of bank loans and value added in manufacturing industries	101
Table 4.1	The structural change of ownership, 1951–1981	123
Table 4.2	Number of firms and their characteristics on manufacturing industries 1976	126
Table 4.3	The structure of top industrial & service enterprises in 1982	128
Table 4.4	Export intensity and export share of the top 500 enterprises and foreign firms, 1975–81	130
Table 4.5	Characteristics and size of domestic distributors in 1976	133
Table 4.6	Characteristics and size of import and export trading companies in 1976	136

Table 4.7	Aggregate concentration ratios in the manufacturing industry, 1970–1980	138
Table 5.1	Sources and definitions of variable	157
Table 5.2	Ordinary least squares estimates of our models	158
Table 5.3	Two-Stage least squares estimates of our models	161
Table 5.4	OLS and 2SLS estimates of the models without IN	166
Table 6.1	Characteristics of Taiwan's dichotomous market structure in 1976.	175
Table 6.2	Testing a two-regimes hypothesis in the concentration and profitability equation.	183
Table 6.3	Determinants of industry concentration in export-oriented and domestic-oriented sectors in 1976.	185
Table 6.4	Testing the existence of international linkages in the concentration equation (F-statistics).	187
Table 6.5	Determinants of industry profitability in export-oriented and domestic-oriented sectors in 1976.	189
Table 6.6	Testing the existence of international linkages in the profitability equation (F-statistics).	191
Table 7.1	Aggregate concentration ratios in the manufacturing industry	207
Table 7.2	Changes in the number of companies within 65 groups between 1972–76, and 50 groups between 1976–82	212
Table 7.3	Diversification of business groups, 1972 and 1978	213
Table 8.1	Criteria for small and medium enterprises in various periods	228–229
Table 8.2	Firm number and ratio of small and medium enterprises	230
Table 8.3	Value and share of output of small and medium enterprises	231

Table 8.4 Number and share of employees in small and
        medium enterprises   233

Table 8.5 Number and share of SMEs in manufacturing
        (1983, 1985, 1987)   235

Table 8.6 Export sales earnings of small and medium
        enterprises,1981–1985   236

Table 8.7 Shares of export and domestic sales in SMEs 781   237

Table 8.8 Export performance of manufacturing firms, 1985   240

Table 9.1 Direct foreign investment in Taiwan, 1953–85
        (on approval baiss)   251

Table 9.2 Some dimensions of Kojima's hypothesis   253

Table 9.3 American and Japanese direct investment in
        Taiwan by industry, 1953-85 (on approval basis)   255

Table 9.4 A comparison of some features between
        American and Japanese firms in Taiwan, 1983   256

Table 9.5 Ownership pattern of American and Japanese
        DFI in Taiwan, 1983   258

Table 9.6 Testing the difference between the American and
        Japanese profitability equations   262

Table 9.7 Determinants of profitability   264

Acknowledgments

I began my study of industrial economics while studying at Université Catholique de Louvain (UCL) in Belgium in 1981—85 under the direction of Professors Alexis Jacguemin and Marie-Paule Donsimoni. In 1989–90 I came back to UCL for a half year visiting. My days in Louvain-la-Neuve contributed greatly to the writing of this book. Moreover, my interest in the fields of economic development and industrialization was stimulated by professor Rong-I Wu during my first several years at the Department of Economics at Chung-Hsing University in Taiwan. Discussion with my colleagues has also been very instructive. Chapter 2 of the book was co-authored by professors Chin-lih Wang and Juh-luh Sun. All of these people have directly and indirectly contributed to this book.

The author's first book in English, *Industrial Organization in the Process of Economic Development: The Case of Taiwan*, was published in 1985. Over the past ten years, Chung-Hsing University and the National Science Council have provided research funding. Support for the core contents of Chapter 3 came from the East-West Center Program in the United States. The writing of this chapter was completed under the Visiting Scholar Program at Australian National University. I would like to thank all of these institutions for their assistance.

Most of the material in this book was previously published in journals, and their permission to use the material here is greatly appreciated. The journals include: *Hitotsubashi Journal of Economics, International Journal of Industrial Organization, Journal of Development Economics, Rivista Internazionale Di Scienze Economiche E Commerciali, Taiwan Economic Review, The Developing Economies, The Journal of Industrial Economics.*

Finally, the support of my family was of great help in the completion of this book. Thus, it is fitting that I dedicate this book to my wife and my daughter, with love and gratitude.

T.C. Chou
Taipei
November 1994

Introduction

There are several books and articles to discuss Taiwan's success in economic development and industrialization. This book tries to analyze the elements of this same story from the industrial organization's point of view. The impacts of foreign sector on Taiwan's industrialization and industrial organization are emphasized in the book. Here, the foreign sector includes foreign trade and foreign direct investment; besides concentration and price-cost margin, the elements of industrial orgnization include small-and-medium enterprises (SMEs), business groups, foreign enterprises and etc.

Chapter 1 attempts to review the pattern and strategy of Taiwan's industrialization over the last three decades. The facts concerning rapid growth, significant structural change, specialized industrialization, and exportations are presented first. Then the policy package instituted to support this exported development is examined. The discriminatory trade policy package has two sets of components: one embodies strict import controls, the other provides incentives for exports. The term "offsetting" implies that almost all the export incentive measures tend counter the barriers caused by the import controls component.

In chapter 2 we have developed a revised approach to analyze the sources of economic growth and structural change under an interindustry framework, with the key features of obtaining cross-terms separated from the combined source effects, which are derived from the Paasche approach as well as the Laspeyres approach. In comparison with the approaches based on the specific parameters and variables chosen, it is shown that some of the terms in the Chenery and Lewis-Soligo approaches are biased. Mainly because they absorb their own related cross-terms, these cross terms play a relatively important role in explaining economic growth and structural change in the industrialization process, both theoretically and empirically, and should be presented independently. Furthermore, this approach solves the confusing problem of selecting periods as a reference. In addition, this chapter also distinguishes the relationship and difference between the effects of economic growth and structural change.

Chapter 3 tries to explain how Taiwan's rapid economic growth was possible when the financial sector was so backward. In other words, the financial sector was highly regulated and oppressed. How could this help Taiwan's growth performance? Our empirical evidence shows that in loan decision-making, banks were conservative, and the efficiency of credit allocation was inefficient. The regression results show that both the collateral and the past relationship between the banks and firms, rather than the borrowers' profitability performance and the industry's business cycle, were important factors in rationing credit. In our theoretical model, we argue that if the informal sector can supplement the inefficient formal financial sector, then the economy can grow strongly. The reason is, on the one hand, the competitive export-oriented industries with a lot of small firms can obtain little credit allocated by the formal financial sector. But, fortunately, this active sector can develop very well by means of funds from the informal financial sector. On the other hand, the monopolistic, domestic-oriented industries with a few large firms received major loans from the formal sector. As a result, dichotomous market structure and the dual financial system are a twin system which facilitated Taiwan's economic development before 1985.

Chapter 4 tries to demonstrate the effects of economic development on market structure in the case of Taiwan. The ownership structure, aggregate concentration ratios and the degree of monopoly are examined. From our time-series analysis, we find that public enterprises showed a U trend of relative share, but foreign enterprises exhibited an inverted trend in the course of economic development. Examining the cross-section data, we find that: (1) in the domestic market, there were relatively large scale manufacturers with numerous small-scale distributors operating under a protective offsetting policy package; (2) in the export market, there were relatively small-scale firms with an enormous number of small-scale trading companies. This is the so-called dichotomous market structure: a monopolistic domestic market and a competitive export market exist simultaneously.

Chapter 5 is the first attempt to use a simultaneous four equation system to study the role of foreign trade in the analysis of market structure and performance, and the determinants of trade intensity in Taiwan. A cross-sectional analysis is carried out with the manufacturing censuses of 1976. The results indicate that public enterprises significantly influence market structures and performance. Also, import control mensures influence import intensity significantly and offset potential impacts of imports on concentration and on profitability. However, trade intensity is mainly explained by comparative advantage rather than market forces (concentration and profitability).

Chapter 6 is an attempt to apply a two-regime and a recursive structure-performance analysis to the case of Taiwan. A two-regime approach is employed because Taiwan's market structure is hypothesized as being dichotomous; the export-oriented sector being distinct with the domestic-oriented sector. A recursive system is used because industry concentration is not only a determinant of profitability but is itself determined by other variables.

Chapter 7 examines the market shares of the largest firms in the manufacturing sector, i.e. aggregate concentration ratios, in Taiwan. A non-increasing trend of aggregate concentration ratios emerged in the 1970's. This is different from an upward trend experienced by industrialized countries. To explain why this trend occurred, we go more deeply into the characteristics of industrial organization: conglomerate "business groups". It is found that entrepreneurs in Taiwan prefer a multi-companies group rather than a single multi-divisional corporation. This dispersed organization of large firms can understate the real figure of ACR calculated by the unit of individual firm.

In Chapter 8, we find that SMEs play a very distinguished role in Taiwan's export business. In 1985, 65% of manufacturing exports came from SMEs. In other words, in exports — the engine of Taiwan's rapid growth — more than 60% of industrial goods are produced by SMEs. Moreover, Taiwan's SMEs have a higher relative export intensity (i.e. 71% of their products were exported in 1985) than large firms and contribute with a higher percentage to total exports. This is a distinctive feature of Taiwan's economic development, and is contrary to the experience of many industrialized countries. We also find that, SMEs in Taiwan, by cooperating with Japanese general trading companies, multinational trading companies and foreign importers, have been able to avoid being restricted by economies of scale in international marketing, and still have managed to sell their manufacturing products in the whole world. This is also the fundamental driving force behind Taiwan's economic development with her export-led growth.

Several studies have in fact shown, by means of applying a structure-conduct-performance paradigm, that the differences in foreign ownership could lead to differences in the determinants of profitability. Accordingly, chapter 9 constructs a profitability equation and uses regression analysis to examine whether the determinants of the profitability of Japanese and American firms, respectively, are all the same. The empirical evidence for Taiwan, in contrast to the case of Korea, does not seem to support Kojima's hypothesis since both American and Japanese DFI in Taiwan are observed to be export-oriented. However, other results show that differences still remain with regard to the scale of operations, factor intensities and the balance of ownership between American and Japanese DFI in Taiwan.

Part I
Industrialization, Growth Sources and Financial System

Part I

1 The Pattern and Strategy of Industrialization*

Introduction

This paper attempts to review the pattern and strategy of Taiwan's industrialization over the last three decades. the facts concerning rapid growth, significant structural change, specialized industrialization, and export expansion are presented first. Then, the policy package instituted to support this export-led development is examined.

Due to an outward-oriented strategy from the early 1960s on, Taiwan's industrialization has been characterized by as pecialization pattern, with Taiwan becoming a heavy exporter of simple manufactured goods. One of the most important factors for this export-led industrialization is the import costs of the materials and unfinished goods which are to be reexported after additional processing. This study examines how the government controls these costs under its "offsetting" trade policy package. It points out how the policy discriminates against users serving the domestic market in favor of those producing goods for export. The discriminatory trade policy package has two sets of components: one embodies strict import controls, the other provides incentives for exports. The term "offsetting" implies that almost all the export incentive measures tend to counter the barriers caused by the import controls component.

---

*This paper was reproduced from *The Developing Economies*, Vol. 23, No. 2, June 1985, pp.138–157, with permission of the publisher.

Table 1.1

Indicators of Taiwan's economy, 1953–81

	Population	GNP	Per capita GNP	Exports	Imports
Average growth rate (%)					
1953–62	3.5	7.5	4.1	19.5	17.0
1963–72	2.9	10.8	8.1	29.9	23.5
1973–81	1.7	8.3	6.3	24.0	25.5
Index 1952=100					
1961	137	191	142	532	509
1971	185	507	291	5,614	2,919
1981	223	1,178	560	56,523	30,740

Sources: Executive Yuan, Council for Economic Planning and Development (CEPD), *Taiwan Statistical Data Book, 1982* (1982), Tables 1-1a and 1-1b.

Note: GNP is based on constant 1976 prices. The export and import figures are based on custom statistics and current prices.

The paper is organized as follows: the first section demonstrates the rapid growth performance and industrialization in Taiwan. The export-oriented specialization pattern is emphasized. In section II, based mainly on the composition of trade, industrializaton subphases are divided and the trend of real wages in the manufacturing is examined. the offsetting trade policy package is studied in section III. Concluding remarks are in section IV.

Specialization pattern of industrialization

Economic performance and structural change

Economic performance in Taiwan over the last three decades is presented in Table 1.1. The coincidence of high growth rates in both GNP and exports is a significant phenomenon. As we will see later, export expansion is the most important factor contributing to rapid economic development, i.e., it is the handmaiden of successful growth. GNP grew

Table 1.2

Sectoral shares and contributions to the growth of GDP, 1953–81

(%)

	Growth rates					Shares of GDP				Contribution ratios[a]			
	GDP	A	I	S	M	A	I	S	M/I[b]	A	I	S	M[b]
Average													
1953–62	7.5	4.8	11.7	7.5	12.5	32.1	20.9	47.0	66.1	20.5	32.6	46.9	70.6
1963–72	10.8	4.0	18.7	8.5	20.1	22.0	32.5	45.5	74.0	8.1	56.0	35.9	80.0
1973–81	8.4	2.1	11.0	7.6	10.9	12.1	43.5	44.4	76.9	3.0	57.0	40.0	76.2

Sources: CEPD, *Taiwan Statistical Data Book, 1982* (1982), Tables 1-1b and 3-7b.

Note: 1. The growth rates are based on constant 1976 prices, while the sectoral shares are based on current prices.

2. A, I, S, and M denote the agricultural, industrial, service, and manufacturing sectors.

a. Contribution ratios are product of the respective sectoral growth rates and shares of GDP divided by the growth rate of GDP.

b. The shares and contributions of manufacturing concern only the industrial sector.

rapidly over the period, with real average growth rates of 7.5 per cent in 1953–62, 10.8 per cent in 1963–72, and 8.3 per cent in 1973–81.

Another important phenomenon is the remarkable structural change involving the agriculture (A), industrial (I), and service (S) sectors. Although agriculture was not the major sector during 1953–62, it dropped 20 percentage points in terms of share GDP between 1953–62 and 1973–81. The industrial sector gained 22 percentage points during the same period, while the service sector maintained roughly the same share. As a consequence, during the period 1973–81 the share of agriculture was only 12.1 per cent while the industrial sector reached 43.5 per cent of GDP (Table 1.2). This structural change represents Taiwan's "industrialization."

Using the decomposition method to measure the sectoral contributions to the overall rate of growth of GDP, we find that the industrial sector contributed more than did the service sector after the 1960s. in the same way, we find that manufacturing's contribution to the growth of the industrial sector was vital, amounting to 71 per cent to 80 per cent over the period as a whole. Furthermore, the contribution ratios of manufacturing to growth of GDP (obtained by the product of the two contribution ratios–manufacturing to industry and industry to GDP) were respectively 23 per cent, 45 per cent, and 43 per cent in the three decades.

The figures presented suggest that industrialization is a function of both economic growth and structural change. Therefore, industrialization is used as a synonym for economic development hereafter. The structural change in manufacturing may be regarded as the core of the industrialization process.

Specialization in manufacturing

This subsection further examines the structural changes in manufacturing during the period 1953–81. There are many different indices to demonstrate such change.[1] The following one is simple, but useful. We can classify manufacturing industries into four groups: (1) food, beverages, and tobacco; (2) nondurable consumer goods; (3) intermediate goods industries; and (4) metal and machinery. The data on structural change in manufacturing can be obtained from table 1.3 which shows the relative share of each group (and industry) during the period. Over the last three decades, one outstanding characteristic of the structural change among these four groups was the replacing of the foodstuffs group, an agricultural raw-materials-based industry, by the metal and machinery group. The percentage changes in these two groups' shares were almost the same, namely, −21 per cent and +26 per cent respectively, between 1953 and 1981. The other two groups maintained relatively stable shares, amounting to 55 per cent to 60 per cent during the same period.

Let us now consider the evolution of individual industries. we find that there are some fast rising industries (those growing faster than the average), such as electrical and non-electrical machinery, clothing and footwear, leather and leather products, metal products, transport

Table 1.3
Composition of manufacturing in terms of value added, 1953–81

	1953	1956	1961	1966	1971	1976	1981
Food, beverages, and tobacco	33.2	34.6	29.8	22.0	14.2	12.2	12.0
Food	23.6	30.6	26.5	18.2	11.0	10.9	6.0
Beverages	0.5	0.6	0.6	0.8	0.5	0.6	0.6
Tobacco	9.1	3.4	2.7	3.0	2.7	0.7	5.4
Nondurable consumer goods	31.4	25.3	21.7	21.9	27.9	29.3	25.4
Textiles	20.4	14.8	11.3	13.1	12.8	12.1	9.2
Clothing and footwear	3.0	2.9	3.5	3.0	7.4	5.8	5.9
Furniture	1.0	1.1	1.1	1.1	0.6	0.6	0.6
Printing and publishing	3.9	4.1	4.4	2.8	2.3	2.3	2.1
Miscellaneous manufactures	3.1	2.4	1.4	1.9	4.8	8.5	7.6
Intermediate goods industries	28.3	29.3	33.5	35.7	32.1	29.4	29.8
Wood products	5.1	4.9	4.9	3.9	3.7	2.7	2.3
Paper and paper products	3.3	4.5	3.5	3.3	2.6	2.2	2.1
Leather and leather products	0.4	0.4	0.3	0.1	0.6	1.1	1.6
Rubber products	1.4	1.3	1.2	1.0	1.1	1.5	1.3
Chemicals	9.8	7.5	9.3	11.6	10.8	12.5	11.1
Petroleum and coal products	4.2	4.4	6.2	8.3	8.5	4.2	7.7
Nonmetallic mineral products	4.1	6.3	8.1	7.5	4.8	5.2	3.7
Metals and machinery	7.1	10.8	15.0	20.4	25.8	29.1	32.8
Metal products	0.9	2.7	4.1	2.4	3.1	4.3	6.2
Basic metals	2.0	2.2	3.1	3.3	2.9	3.8	3.3
Non-electrical machinery	1.7	1.1	2.7	3.8	3.5	3.8	3.2
Electrical machinery	1.1	2.4	2.3	6.2	11.1	11.7	12.4
Transport equipment	1.4	2.4	2.8	4.7	5.2	5.5	7.7
Total	100	100	100	100	100	100	100

Source: Executive Yuan, Directorate-General of Budget, Accounting and Statistics, *National Income of the Republic of China, 1982* (1982), Table 1.2.

Note: The value added is computed in terms of factor cost at current prices.

equipment, and chemicals. Later on, we will find (in Table 1.7) that aimost all these fast rising industries are also of rising importance in the exports field. Conversely, some industries are slow growing or even stagnant–such as food, tobacco, textiles, furniture, and paper products. These industries may be divided into two categories: one where export shares decrease–food and tobacco; the other where they do not–textiles, furniture, and wood products.

What is the meaning of this industrialization pattern? To answer this question, we can make a comparison with the general pattern throughout the world. Li (1979, pp.151–52) collects data from twenty-one large countries (those with populations over 20 million) and thirty-three small countries to show the worldwide industrialization pattern among four subgroups of countries, differentiated by income level. Because of differences in data sources, this comparison cannot be conducted strictly according to the classification of Table 1.3. However, it is still possible to compare the patterns in terms of Li's classification[2] at different income stages. Four years (1967, 1970, 1976, and 1981) are chosen for the comparison, because in those years Taiwan had income levels respectively equivalent to the four income stages of the amall countries group (see Table 1.4).[3] in order to show the degree of specialization, the share of the r largest industry groups in overall manufacturing output can be estimated to arrive at the "concentration ratio," C_r, which is similar to conventional industry or market concentration ratios, but at a more aggregated level. The ratios of Taiwan's C_r to those of other countries can then be compared.

Table 1.4 shows the measures of C_r in Taiwan and other countries for different income-level subgroups or stages. Here, r is denoted by the subscripts 1, 2, 3, and 4, respectively. The higher the ratio, the higher the degree of specialization. The declining trend of the manufactured concentration ratios, indicating diversification with increasing income levels, is significantly slower in Taiwan than in either the large or small countries groups. The difference in C_4 between the lowest and highest income stages was only 5 percentage points in Taiwan, whereas it was over 20 percentage points for both the large and small countries groups of Li's survey. Thus, it is clear that Taiwan tended to follow a specialization pattern during its industrialization process.

As the low share of the foodstuff industries in Taiwan could lead to a sharply understated concentration (specialization) level, we next exclude foodstuffs and recalculate the ratios, the figures within brackets, (C_r), representing the results. It is now more clear that Taiwan had considerably concentrated manufacturing output. After 1970, the four largest industries (excepting foodstuffs) in Taiwan accounted for 57 per cent of manufacturing output. The values of (C_4) in Taiwan were higher than those in the small countries group by from 10 to 21 percentage points at the various income stages. moreover, the gap between Taiwan and the small countries group in terms of (C_4) is increasing. If we divide the industries included in (C_4) into two categories–export-oriented (wearing apparel, electrical apparatus, and miscellaneous manufactures) and domestic-oriented (chemical and allied industries)–the export-oriented category accounts for around two-thirds of (C_4), that is, 37 per cent of overall manufacturing output. In fact, we find the increasing gap derives mainly from the export-oriented sectors. This suggests that Taiwan's manufacturing output is relatively concentrated in export-oriented industries, with the result that specialization emerges. This could be called an export-oriented and specialized industrialization pattern.

Sources of industrialization

Sustained economic growth requires a transformation of the structure of production that is compatible with both the evolution of domestic demand and the opportunities for international trade. Thus, the question of whether the source of growth in manufacturing output stems mainly from domestic or foreign demand is now studied. Using the Chenery decomposition technique, growth in manufacturing output can be linked

Table 1.4
Comparison of manufactures concentration ratios for the World and Taiwan
(%)

	Large-countries group				Small-countries group				Taiwan			
Income level stages	1	2	3	4	1	2	3	4	1967	1970	1976	1981
(Average income: U.S.$)	145	315	786	2,893	263	349	1,070	2,758	249	360	1,039	2,360
Number of countries	5	6	4	6	9	9	7	8				
C_1	34.6	27.4	16.2	15.2	37.0	34.1	24.9	17.1	23.3	22.2	19.0	20.1
					(14.3)	(17.0)	(14.7)	(12.1)	(21.0)	(22.2)	(19.0)	(20.1)
C_2	59.2	45.5	31.5	27.2	51.3	51.1	39.5	29.2	44.3	40.7	37.2	36.8
					(26.0)	(32.2)	(28.3)	(21.2)	(36.1)	(40.7)	(37.2)	(36.8)
C_3	69.8	64.1	44.8	37.6	63.0	66.1	53.1	38.3	59.4	57.3	49.4	49.2
					(33.4)	(37.8)	(35.2)	(30.0)	(43.0)	(51.4)	(48.9)	(49.2)
C_4	75.3	70.0	54.8	47.8	70.5	71.9	60.0	47.1	66.3	68.0	61.1	61.3
					(39.4)	(43.1)	(41.8)	(35.1)	(49.8)	(56.6)	(57.4)	(56.9)

Sources: Li [16, Table 3.3] and calculated from Table 1.3.
Notes: 1. Concentration ratios, $C_1 - C_4$, are calculated according to the classifications outlined in footnote 2.
2. Parentheses denote the concentration ratios with the foodstuffs group excluded.

Table 1.5

Sources of growth in manufacturing output, 1952–79

	Percent of total		
	Home demand	Export expansion	Import substitution
1953–61	80.9	12.1	7.0
1961–70	69.9	24.6	5.5
1971–79*	69.1	71.0	−52.8

Sources: The data for 1952–61 and 1961–70 are from Chen (1978, Tables 5 and 6); for 1971–79 from Sun (1981, Tables 8 and 9).

* The estimation for this period separates the effect of technological change (+12.7 per cent), which is not shown in the table.

to three main sources:[4] (1) expansion of home demand, (2) expansion of export demand, and (3) the effects of import substitution. The former two are divided from the respective increments in home demand and export demand between two periods. Negative values indicate decreases in the absolute value of each demand. The effect of import substitution is indicated by the difference in import shares (imports divided by "total supply" or domestic output plus imports). If the import share increases, the level of self-sufficiency decreases, the import substitution effect being negative.

Table 1.5 summarizes two studies employing this kind of estimation to indicate the evolution of sources of growth in manufacturing output during the period 1952–79. While the comparison of different studies calls for caution, the increasing importance of foreign demand cannot be doubted: 12.1 per cent of manufacturing output growth came from export expansion in the period 1952–61; the percentage doubled to 24.6 per cent in 1961–70, and then reached 71.0 per cent (to become the largest source of growth) in 1971–79. This confirms Taiwan's export-oriented industrialization.

Beside the growing importance of export expansion, table 1.5 also reveals a significant negative import substitution (−53 per cent) in the 1970s. As explained above, the negative import substitution effect indicates an increase in manufactured imports between 1971 and 1979. There are two possible explanations for this phenomenon, one of them being intra-industry trade and the other industrialization of the processing type in which unfinished goods are imported, to be later re-exported after additional processing. Consequently, imports increase as (though less than) exports grow. With intra-industry trade, manufactured imports stimulate competition with domestic products; with processing-type industrialization, manufactured imports are inputs for processed exports. While measurement of Taiwan's intra-industry trade is beyond the scope of this study, some evidence from the composition of imports (see Table 1.6) seems to support the importance of processing in Taiwan's industrialization.

Trade and phases of industrialization

Composition of trade

The composition of Taiwan's exports has changed significantly over the last three decades. Table 1.6-A shows that the export share of primary products (including agricultural products, minerals, food, beverages, and tobacco preparations) fell sharply from 84.7 per cent in the period 1952–61, to 40.8 per cent in 1962–71, and to a mere 13.7 per cent in 1972–81. The foreign exchange earned by exports of these products also decreased, from 52.1 per cent to 14.3 per cent of the amounts required to finance imports in thirty years (see Table 1.6-B). The importance of sugar and rice exports during the 1950s is quite evident. Exports of such agricultural and processed agricultural products characterize what has been called the primary import substitution phase (Pauuw and Fei, 1973). But the importance of industrial product exports rose rapidly. Over 60 per cent of exports came from industrial products

Table 1.6
Composition of trade, 1952–81

A. Percentage share of exports

(%)

	Agricultural products	(Rice)	Processed Agricultural products	(Sugar)	Industrial products	Primary products*
Average						
1952–61	18.6	(12.0)	63.6	(20.6)	17.8	84.7
1962–71	13.6	(3.3)	26.5	(12.7)	59.9	40.8
1972–81	5.0	(0.2)	7.6	(2.1)	87.4	13.7

B. Composition of imports and financing sources for imports

(%)

	Percent of total imports			Exports / Imports	Primary exports / Imports	Agricultural exports / Imports	Exports of rice & sugar / Imports
	Capital goods	Raw materials	Consumption goods				
Average							
1952–61	20.2	69.3	10.5	61.5	52.1	11.4	38.5
1962–71	28.9	65.6	5.5	90.6	37.0	12.3	14.5
1972–81	27.4	66.2	6.4	104.3	14.3	5.2	2.4

Sources: CEPD, *Taiwan Statistical Data Bood, 1982* (1982), Tables 10-7, 10-8, 10-9, and 10-12.

* Includes agricultural products (agriculture, forestry, hunting, and fishery), minerals, and food, beverages, and tobacco preparations.

after the early 1960s. This suggests that the industrialization process passed into a second, primary export substitution phase in the early 1960s. This means that the export of primary goods as the key source of foreign exchange was replaced, in the main, by exports of industial goods after that time. We will see that the changes in policy during the late 1950s from a "protective import substitution strategy" to the "offsetting policy package" to encourage exports was the most important factor leading to the transition from one phase to another at that time.

While significant changes were occurring in export composition, by contrast, the three-category composition of imports held constant during the period under observation. Two plausible explanations could be advanced. Firstly, due to the scarcity of resources, imported raw materials always amounted to over 65 per cent of all imports. This, it could be argued, suggests the possibility of a shortage of foreign exchange to finance suffcient materials imports, particularly in the 1950s. Indeed, foreign exchange earned from exports could only finance 62 per cent of Taiwan's imports in the 1950s.[5] On the other hand, the stable, low share of imported consumption goods could reveal a high degree of self-sufficiency or protection in those goods, an argument which would tend to support the processing industrialization claim. Again, the import policy on materials and capital goods is a determinate factor for this industrialization type.

In order to facilitate a further comparison, the composition of manufactured exports by industry is given in table 1.7, in which the trade data is converted from the Standard International Trade Classification (SITC) into Standard Industrial Classification (SIC).[6] Because of the difficulties inherent in classifying trade data precisely by industrial category, some reservation is appropriate in reading this table. Still, among the four largest contributors to total manufacturing output (shown in Table 1.6), wearing apparel, electrical apparatus, and miscellaneous manufactures were similarly outstanding in the export field. Exports of these products amounted to over 70 per cent of total exports after 1971.

The concentration ratios of manufactured exports can be calculated as in Table 1.4 to further reveal the characteristic concentration of manufactured exports. Though the figures are not presented here, we know that manufactured exports were much more concentrated than manufacturing output generally. The shares of the four largest industries in Taiwan's overall manufactured exports were 63 per cent, 82 per cent, 90 per cent, and 74 per cent in 1966, 1971, 1976, and 1981, respectively. The concentration of manufactured exports is probably related to concentrated export markets. The United States and Japan are the main export markets for Taiwan, accounting for 50 per cent of exports during the period 1953–81. The interaction between export commodity concentration and the conecntration of export markets is, however, beyond the scope of this study.

Industrialization phases

Mainly based on the composition of trade, we can further divide the industrialization process into different phases. As Pauuw and Fei (1973, pp.79–107) have shown, a series of data–composition of imports and exports, financing sources for imports (Table 1.6), manufacturing structure (Table 1.3), and the structure of manufactured exports (Table 1.7)– can be used to distinguish different industrialization phases. Following the staging method of Ranis (1981), we divide Taiwan's economic development transition phase, 1950–80, into four subphases: S_1 (traditional exports, pre-1953); S_2 (primary import substitution, IS, 1953–61); S_3 (primary export substitution, ES, 1961–75); and S_4 (secondary IS cum ES, post 1975).[7] Some characteristics of each phase are shown in Table 1.8. Because our study is concerned with the period after 1950, subphase S_1 is not a key topic here. The longest and most important subphase, S_3, may also be called the export expansion phase, which is why we devote much attention to export expansion below.

It is interesting to see the relationship between industrialization pattern and industrialization phases. Chou (1984, pp.12–131) has shown

Table 1.7
Composition of manufactured exports, 1956–81

%

	1956	1961	1966	1971	1976	1981
Food, beverages, and tobacco	48.7	13.5	11.1	0.7	0.2	0.2
Food	48.5	11.0	10.1	0.5	0.1	0.2
Beverages	0.2	0.2	0.1	0.0	0.0	0.0
Tobacco	0.0	2.3	0.9	0.2	0.1	0.0
Nondurable consumer goods	14.2	36.1	37.0	58.0	58.0	50.5
Textiles	9.4	28.1	19.9	14.6	14.0	10.1
Clothing and footwear	3.9	5.8	9.6	27.0	25.7	21.4
Furniture	0.0	0.0	0.1	0.5	1.3	2.0
Printing and publishing	0.0	0.0	0.2	0.1	0.1	0.1
Miscellaneous manufactures	0.9	2.2	7.2	15.8	16.9	16.9
Intermediate goods industries	26.3	36.3	29.6	14.1	12.3	13.1
Wood products	1.1	8.4	12.5	7.9	5.3	3.9
Paper and paper products	0.5	3.4	2.1	0.4	0.6	0.6
Leather and leather products	0.0	0.1	0.1	0.7	0.2	0.5
Rubber products	0.0	0.5	0.6	0.5	0.8	0.9
Chemicals	20.6	12.7	6.0	2.3	2.4	2.7
Petroleum and coal products	4.1	5.5	1.1	0.5	1.6	2.2
Nonmetallic mineral products	0.0	5.7	7.2	1.8	1.4	2.3
Metals and machinery	10.8	14.1	22.3	27.2	29.5	36.2
Metal products	2.8	1.3	3.0	2.5	3.4	5.0
Basic metals	7.7	10.0	6.6	3.3	1.7	2.4
Non-electrical machinery	0.3	0.9	4.0	4.1	4.7	5.1
Electrical machinery	0.0	1.7	8.1	15.9	17.0	19.6
Transport equipment	0.0	0.2	0.6	1.4	2.7	4.1
Total	100	100	100	100	100	100

Source: The data for 1956–71 are from Executive Yuan, Research, Development and Evaluation Commission, *Commodity Trade Statistics of the Republic of China, (SITC Reclassifications)* 1954–74 (Taipei: 1977); for 1976–81 form Ministry of Finance, Department of Statistics, *Monthly Statistics of Exports and Imports, the Republic of China,* December 1982.

Note: For methods of reclassification, see footnote 6.

Table 1.8 The characteristics of industrialization phases in Taiwan

Phases	Main manufactures (1)	Product differentiation (2)	Production technology (3)	Factor ratio (4)
Primary IS (1953–61)	Consumer nondurables	Little heterogenous	Easy/simple processing, low value-added	Raw-materials and land-intensive
Primary ES (1961–75)	Consumer nondurables	Homogenous abroad, but heterogenous at home	Easy/simple processing, low value-added	More labor-intensive
Secondary IS cum ES (post 1975)	Consumer durables & producer goods	Heterogenous and new product mix	Complicated, sophisticated, high-value-added	Capital-technology-, skilled-labor-intensive

Phases	Orientation of market (5)	Economics of scale (6)	Composition of trade* (7)	Scarcities (8)	Orientation of policy (9)
Primary IS (1953–61)	Domestic Market	Limited by domestic market	M: Producer goods E: Primary goods	Entrepreneurship & foreign exchange	Protection
Primary ES (1961–75)	Export market	Realized by exports	M: Producer goods E: Consumer nondurables	Trading network	Offsetting policy package
Secondary IS cum ES (post 1975)	Domestic and export markets	Very important	M: Producer goods & materials E: Consumer durables & Producer goods	Skilled-labor, sales-services, entrepreneurship	Turning point?

* M and E denote import and export respectively.

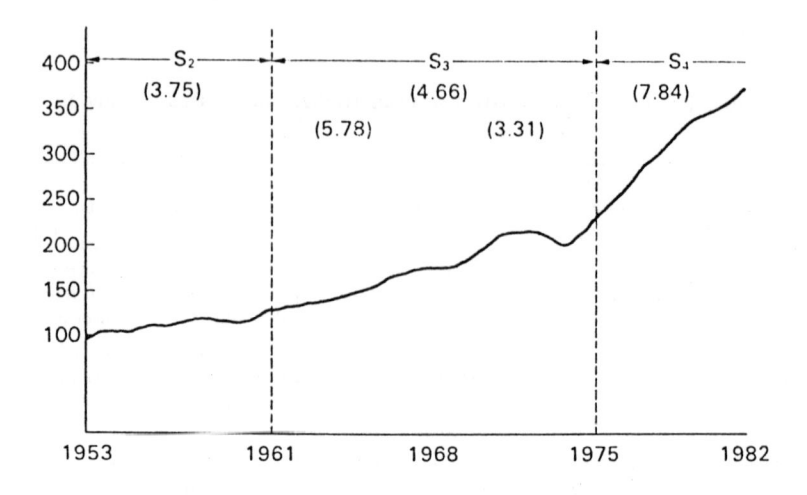

Sources: The data for 1953–72 were compiled by the author from Galenson (1979, Table 6.19); the consumer price index after 1972 may be found in CEPD, *Taiwan Statistical Data Book, 1983* (1983), Table 9-1, and monthly earning in manufacturing in CEPD, *Industry of Free China*, Vol. 57, No. 5 (may 1982), Table 17.

Note: Figures in parentheses are the average growth rates for the period concerned.

Figure 1.1   The trend of real wages in manufacturing (1953=100)

that specialization accompanies the export expansion phase through examining the trends of C_4 or (C_4) for both production and exports. we can confirm that after entering the secondary IS cum ES (S_4) phase, industrial structure alters toward diversification (i.e., C_4 and (C_4) decrease after S_4). In other words, during the last twenty years it was through export expansion that the specialization pattern emerged.

Causes for export expansion

We now further study the causes for export expansion. for a labor surplus economy, like that of Taiwan, the most advantageous factor in competing for export markets is the labor force. Slowly increasing real wages are the key factor in promoting exports. Figure 1 clearly shows that the increase of real manufacturing wages continued very slow during the phases S_2 and S_3 (1953–75), only doubling in twenty-three years. Though surplus labor was an important factor behind this trend beford the mid-1970s, a powerful government was another political and economic factor during that time. While the supply of abundant and cheap labor from the aguicultural sector, coupled with low living standards in the agricultural sector and a dispersed industrial pattern reinforced low non-agricultural wage level,[8] the government also, unlike in many other labor surplus LDCs (Leff 1979, p.54.), has resisted "bribing" labor by legislating artificially high wages (e.g., minimum wage requirements).[9]

Taiwan's abundant and cheap labor force, coordinated with simple processing techonlogy makes its labor-intensive, nondurable consumer goods industries (e.g., textiles, clothing, and electronic apparatus) very competitve in MDC markets. These industries led in the creation of an epoch of export expansion in Taiwan's industrialization during the 1960s and 1970s. From 1975 on, a rapid increase in real wages has induced the economy to enter the S_4 phase. Liang and Liang (1976, pp.216–21) have compared factor intensity among four groups of industries and find low capital (fixed assets)/labor ratios in export industries. Scott (1979, pp.355–57) also shows that Taiwan tends to export products which embody relatively little human and physical capital and to import those which embody relatively high proportion of both.[10]

Have the low wage levels been sufficient to support Taiwan's comparative advantage? The answer must be negative, for otherwise, how do we explain the fact that manufactured exports did not expand significantly during the S_2 phase (before 1961)? It has been shown that due to a scarcity of resources (particularly before the second IS phase), export processing required imported capital and raw materials (about 90 per cent of all imports, see Table 1.6). Scott (1979, pp.321–25) estimates the cost structure of some of Taiwan's export industries in 1971 and finds that the overall percentage of sales value represented by the cost of materials and equipment might be around 70 per cent to 75 per cent, or even more, for a typical exporter. If such an exporter is to export profitably at world prices without the benefit of any subsidy, he must be able to buy materials and equipment at world prices. This involves trade policy design, i.e., the package of protections, tariffs, and export incentives, a subject which will be studied in the next section.

The evolution of the offsetting policy package

The preceding section has shown that export expansion has been a crucial factor in determining Taiwan's industrialization pattern, and that exports are developed by low real wage costs and a policy package which influences the relative prices of imported materials and equipment. Here, we examine the offsetting trade policy package in some detail to illustrate the possibilities for and characteristics of export expansion during the S_3 phase.[11]

The main package: import controls cum tax rebates

There are two kinds of import restrictions: tariff and nontariff restrictions. A tariff structure that was designed for a completely different economy, that of the Chinese mainland, was adopted in Taiwan with the emergence of a bona fide need to impose foreign exchange controls in early 1951. In this initial tariff structure, rates for raw materials were frequently set at the same levels as, or even above, those for processed goods. The tariff schedule underwent major revisions in 1955, 1959, 1965, and 1974, but the continuing relatively high levels of duties on primary and intermediate goods served to maintain the relatively low levels of effective protection characteristic of the early 1950s.

Lee et al. (1975, pp.81–87) have calculated the effective protection and subsidy in Taiwan with 1969 input-output data and have shown that there were some redundant protections and even negative effects for downstream goods. The same conclusion can be found in many other studies, such as those by Hsing (1975), Lee (1971), and Lin (1973,

Table 1.9

The ratios of customs revenues to imports and tax revenues, 1953–82

(NT$ million)

Selected Year	Customs duties (1)	Harbor dues (2)	Customs revenues (3)=(1)+(2)	Imports values (4)	Tax & monopoly revenues (5)	Tariffs rate (%) (6)=(3)/(4)	Revenues rate (%) (7)=(3)/(5)
1953	575	68	643	2,754	2,964	23.3	21.7
1961	1,823	216	2,039	12,894	9,554	15.8	21.3
1975	23,527	4,621	28,148	226,460	97,504	12.4	28.9
1977	32,023	5,851	37,874	323,839	139,306	11.7	27.4
1982	56,323	12,568	68,891	763,084	338,087	9.0	20.4

Soruce: CEPD, *Taiwan Statistical Data Bood, 1982* (1982), Tables 8-5a and 10-4.

Note: Monopoly revenues derive from tobacco and wine monopoly revenues, which amounted to 590, 2,286, 13,125, 16,608, and 33,963 (NT$ million) in the years cited.

pp.90–95). Basically speaking, the tarff structure did not alter the characteristic bias against exports stemming from high import costs of materials during the last thirty years, even in the S_3 phase. moreover, this bias was augmented by other governmental measures: a defense surtax on tariffs (called a "temporary tax" after august 8, 1967), harbor dues levied on imported goods, and high import duties (called "duty-paying value").[12] The ratios of customs revenues to imports are presented in Table 1.9 and indicate the general level of protective tariffs. Chung (1980) indicates that this ratio for Taiwan ranked twenty-fourth among the ratios for eighty-two countries (even higher than those of the Republic of Korea and Singapore) in 1977. This suggests that, on the aggregate level, high import tariffs and biases against exports still exist.

To reduce the rates on materials and intermediate goods, it is necessary to increase the rates on finished goods by way of compensation because the government relies heavily upon customs revenues as a source of funds. Over 20 per cent of the government's tax and monopoly revenues derive from customs revenues (see Table 1.9) making this the biggest source of government income. In the study cited above, Chung points out that the ratio of Taiwan's customs revenues to overall government revenues stood at eighteenth among eighty-two countries in 1977. This poses difficulties for rectification of the tariff structures. On the one hand, reduction in the tariff rates on production goods will be resisted by the protected domestic firms; while on the other hand, increased rates on final goods will also be opposed by the users. Both financial and protection considerations impede the government's pursuit of a "rationalized" customs tariff system.

Under these circumstances, two questions present themselves: (1) Will the relatively low tariff on finished goods induce a lot of imports? and, (2) How are exports of processed goods possible? The former queston involves the issue of nontariff import barriers while the latter involves another policy package of export incentives. We now consider each in order.

At the beginning of the 1950s, for reasons both of balance of payments and protection, many commodities were placed on the list of import controlled items. At that time, the saving of foreign exchange was a much more important consideration than was protection.[13] Gradually, as the balance of payments improved, the aim of import controls shifted to protection and the justification of import controls on the basis of domestic availability became an important principle. The system of nontariff restrictions forms a powerful regulatory and protective instrument which compensates for the low effective protection level on finished goods to prevent import competition. Taiwan's protective scheme (high tariffs on intermediate goods and complex nontariff restrictions on finished goods) is very powerful even today. This explains why imported consumer goods continued to make up only a low share of total imports over the last thirty years (see Table 1.6).

High import costs of materials and equipment make the export of processed goods difficult, and thus another compensatory package of export incentives is a necessary condition for export expansion. Among such export incentives, tax rebates are the most important.[14] The tax rebates for exports comprise rebates of both customs duties and commodity taxes on imported raw materials. Scott finds that "unless these taxes were rebated, he (exporter) could not possibly export" (1979, p.325). Hsing states that "about two-thirds of 177 kinds of manufactures could not be exported or could be exported only with extreme difficulty" (1975, p.165). Lin (1973, pp.101–31) also reaches the same conclusion. The average ratio of tax refund for exports to overall tax revenues (in those categories) was 24.4 per cent during the preiod 1955 to 1982. It is evident that tax rebates significantly stimulated export expansion, because the tax refund ratios increased markedly at the S_3 phase.[15]

Tax rebates entail high administrative costs. Technical standards for tax rebates for each export good were set up on the basis of techincal data submitted by firms applying for such rebates, and the number of categories of manufactured inputs could reach one thousand or even more for a single finished product. Thus, the administrative work is very heavy both for the government and exporters, and although many technical improvements have been adopted, it is still time-consuming. Under the circumstances, reduced customs duties plus administrative costs or protected inefficiency are the costs of this offsetting policy package — import tariffs-cum-export rebates. Moreover, domestic consumers will be the final bearers of these costs. This is the situation described in the phrase "domestic sales subsidizing export sales," i.e., income from sales in the domestic market at higher monopolistic prices can be transferred to subsidize sales in the export market at lower, competitive prices through the above offsetting policy package.

Another offsetting package

The second form of offsetting policy package is "a lot of bureaucratic red-tape" cum "export-promotion facilities." There are many bureaucratic controls, such as registrations, import and export licensings, and supervision of foreign exchange transactions, the high administrative costs of which could not help but hurt price competition in the world market. To dismantle such impediments, the Taiwan government has taken certain measures such as (1) the establishment of a system of bonded factories and warehouses from 1965 on, and (2) the creation of Export Processing Zones where exporting firms could enjoy all of the tax benefits as well as a remarkable cutback in red-tape (also from 1965).[16]

Some organizations were also set up to promote exports. For instance, the China External Trade Development Council was founded in July 1970 to promote exports and conduct market research, many foreign business representative offices were built to handle trading affairs, and the China Export-Import Bank was established in 1979 to provide loans to foreign buyers to facilitate the purchase of domestically manufactured capital goods.

Finally, a system of low cost loans was initiated by the Bank of Taiwan in July 1957 to encourage exports. The export loans program helped to meet the short-term fund needs of manufacturers in their export operations—from raw materials procurement to finished goods delivery. The benefit of such loans to exporting firms has been appreciable. The loans were designed to offset the disadvantages of a weak private enterprise financial structure and one of the shortcomings of the state-owned banking system: the almost complete lack of a program for short-term operating funds.

Operation, effects, and prospects of the policy

It is clear that the compatibility of Taiwan's export expansion with its protective measures is dependent on the offsetting policy package. Two views of the operation of the offsetting policy could be advanced. On the one hand, it could support simple, labor-intensive processed export products in a very competitive market, making the prices of such exports very attractive. On the other hand, it could be seen as protecting the domestic market, thereby maintaining the high prices required to provide the subsidies to support export incentives through the tax systems, i.e., "domestic sales subsidizing export sales." It appears that the goal of protection in this operation is not the fostering of domestic upstream industries to provide inputs for processed exports. Otherwise, conflicts between the upstream industries and downstream exports would exist.

In any case, this policy package has two effects, one on the structure of production, and the other on organizational structure. Firstly, the operation of the offsetting policy package leads to an expansion of simple processing industries based on their advantage in labor costs. This is one of the most important factors in explaining Taiwan's successful export-led industrialization. Secondly, operation of the package stimulates small firms to engage in export business both through the direct effects of subsidies and through the indirect effects on production structure. Meanwhile, the maintenance of protective measures prevents import competition and induces protective monopoly in the domestic market.

Of course, the offsetting policy package is not without its limitations. Two conflicts, between producers and consumers and exporting producers and upstream producers may also be further discussed. On the one hand, more and more domestic consumers recognize the cost to their welfare under this policy package due to the high degree of protection. Hence the call for the government to dismantle import protection. The same request comes from the trade-deficit partners—in particular the United States (trade surplus from the United States amounted to U.S.$6.7 billion in 1983). On the other hand, inetrest-conflict between exporting and domestic upstream industries is also becoming more and more acute. The development of some upstream industries is normal when down-stream processing industries can provide a sufficient market. But under the offsetting policy package, exporting firms can meet their needs with imported materials and equipment with nearly no tariff costs through the tax rebate operation. Hence, domestic upstream industries must produce at least as efficiently as existing foreign firms, otherwise domestic processing firms will not use homemade materials. This would prove a serious barrier to the entry of domestic firms into these upstream industries, were it not for government protection. The attempt to satisfy both parties inevitably leads to contradictions berween export and protection policies, thus inducing additional regulations. Much debate surrounds the issue of whether this policy package should be altered.

From the first oil crisis (1973) on, there has been a wide divergence in "public opinion." One side in the debate has advocated that the government continue to play a central role in choosing, assisting, guiding, and directly investing in so-called "strategic" or "key" industries. The other side claims that the only role of government is to induce a more efficient market and efficient institutions, and that the offsetting policy package should be dismantled. The former choice, which is broadly reminiscent of Japan's industrial policy (see Kogiku, 1978), tends to protection, intervention, and regulation. The latter tends to create a laissez-faire atmosphere in which entrepreneurs carry out their own restructuring. In short, this is perhaps another one of those decisive moments, like the one at the end of the 1950s, for carefully considering how to improve the policy package so as to maintain a healthy climate for future develpoment.

Concluding remarks

Taiwan's rapid structural change and high growth in the last few decades have been demonstrated in this paper. Much evidence supports the contention that export expansion has been the most important source of growth in manufacturing output since the early 1970s. Therefore, the specialization pattern is a function of Taiwan's export-oriented growth strategy. Also, mainly on the basis of trade composition, we have shown that Taiwan's industrialization process can be divided into different phases, namely, the primary IS, the primary ES, and the second IS cum ES. While adducing the key facts of this economic performance, we also illustrate its chief causes. The success of export expansion is dependent on (1) a relatively cheap labor force and (2) the import of production goods at close to world prices. In the case of Taiwan, both conditions have been satisfied by government intervention. Each has been advanced in turn.

On the one hand, the government designed a very delicate institutional system to squeeze and transfer agricultural surplus from agricultural sector, the low level of rural living standards serving to hold down nonagricultural real wages before the mid-1970s. Both factors combined to ensure the abundant and cheap labor force necessary to expand labor-intensive exports since the S_3 phase.

On the other hand, import costs of production goods discriminate against users serving the domestic market in favor of those producing exports. This is ensured through an offsetting policy package: import controls cum tax rebates. Another offsetting package (e.g., inefficient banking services cum export loans) further discriminates between export-oriented and domestic-oriented firms. As a result, those firms processing exports can use imported materials and equipment obtained at close to world prices as well as benefit from various bureaucracy-skirting measures. This induces an export-led specialization pattern and results in "domestic sales subsidizing export sales."

However, it is arguable whether the offsetting trade policy can support Taiwan's industrialization toward the secondary IS cum ES phase. This matter requires further investigation.

Notes

1. For example, the Hoffman ratio (the relative share of consumer goods industries to capital goods industries) is normal. However, a serious problem in using this index is that the ratio will vary,

sometimes quite sharply, depending on how consumer and capital goods industries are differentiated.

2. Li classifies the twenty industries shown in Table 1.3 into five groups: foodstuffs (food, beverages, and tobacco); wearing apparel (textiles, leather products, and clothing and footwear); furniture and wood products; chemical and allied industries (rubber products, chemical products, and petroleum and coal products); and adds nine other industries. See Li (1979, Table 3.3).

3. Though the data are not presented here, in general, as with the small countries group, Taiwan's manufacturing output was concentrated in six industries throughout the four stages: 1. foodstuffs, 2. wearing apparel, 3. chemical and allied industries, 4. electrical machinery, 5. transport equipment, and 6. miscellaneous manufactures. But two characteristics may be noted in the case of Taiwan: (1) a significantly lower percentage share in foodstuffs (the percentage difference between Taiwan and small country group ranging from 5 per cent to 18 per cent, and (2) significantly higher shares in the other four groups (the differences amounting to 16 per cent to 27 per cent).

4. See Chenery (1960). For revisions of the method, see Morley and Smith (1970) and Chenery (1980), in which the effect of technological change is isolated from these three main sources.

5. Fortunately, foreign exchange constraints did not affect Taiwan's economic growth in that period due to timely U.S. aid. See Lee et al. (1975, p.84).

6. See Wang (1981, p.188). The SITC codes corresponding to the two-digit SIC industries are given in parentheses: food (04), beverages (11), tobacco (12), textiles (65), clothing and footwear (84, 85), furniture (82), printing and publishing (892), miscellaneous manufactures (81, 83, 86, 89 except 892), wood products (63), paper and paper products (64), leather and leather products (61), rubber products (62), chemical products (0.5), petroleum and coal

products (321, 332), nonmetallic mineral products (66), metals products (69), basic metals (67, 68), non-electrical machinery (71), electrical machinery (72), transport equipment (73).

7. Some authors, for instance Chen (1978), Ho (1981), and Schive and Gau (1981), divide Taiwan's industrialization process into four different subphases: S_1—pre-1949; S_2—1949–60 (the 1950s); S_3—1961–70 (the 1960s); and S_4—post 1970. These divisions give rise to over-lappings, particularly between S_3 and S_4. It could be argued that the primary ES phase (S_3) was continuing in the early 1980a, as some secondary IS industries were still being developed.

8. For the subsistence level of agricultural wage rates in Taiwan, see Wu (1971, pp.104–20). For data concerning the dispersed industrial pattern, see Chou (1984, Appendix A).

9. An exception might be public enterprises with their artificially high institutional wage structure before the mid-1970s. In general, the labor market in Taiwan is "unprotected," i.e., there are very low minimum wages and an absence of collective bargaining (Wu 1971, pp.123–26).

10. However, Lin (1973, pp.131–37) and Liang and Liang (1976, p.221) show that Taiwan's exports to LDCs are relatively more capital intensive than those to MDCs. This suggests a "dual" trade structure. Also, they recognize that many considerations other than factor intensities are important in determining trade patterns—transport costs, trade policies, tariffs and protectionism, etc.

11. For an overview of Taiwan's policy evolution during the 1950s and 1960s and its background, see Chou (1984, pp.16–20).

12. The "duty-paying value" was 120 per cent of the c.i.f. import costs before February 1980, after which time the ratio was cut to 115 per cent, and then to 110 per cent in May 1983. The defense surtax on customs tariffs was imposed in April 1958. The rate was a homogeneous 20 per cent on the tariff of all imported goods till July 1968, after which it was changed to a multiple system. This

surtax was terminated in 1973. The rate of harbor dues on traded goods was first levied at 1.5 per cent on both imports and exports (in August 1974), then at 2 per cent from December 1950. From November 1958 it was levied only on imports, first at 3 per cent, then at 3.75 per cent (from August 1967) and later at 4 per cent (from December 1971). In order to reduce the costs of exporting, the harbor dues levied on imported materials intended for exports was cut to 1 per cent from June 1973 on.

13. For the same conclusion, see Yin (1962, p.4), Hsing (1975, p.145), Tu (1976, p.90), and Scott (1979, p.378).

14. In addition to tax rebates there are other tax incentives aimed at encouraging exports in the Status for Encouragement of Investment, e.g., (1) exemption from business and related stamp taxes; (2) a deduction of 2 per cent of annual total export earnings from taxable income; and (3) a 10 per cent tax reduction for manufacturing, mining, or handicrafts enterprises that export more than 50 per cent of their output. The latter allowance (3) was terminated in December 1970.

15. The average ratios of tax refund and tax reduction for exportation to the overall concerned tax revenues were: 3.84 per cent for the 1955–60 fiscal year, 25.73 per cent for the 1961–75 fiscal year, and 23.39 per cent for the 1976–82 fiscal year (see Ministry of Finance, *Yearbood of Tax Statistics, R.O.C. in 1982* (1983), Table 21).

16. Exports in 1980 from the three existing zones amounted to U.S.$1,424 million, while imports were U.S.$1,005 million, 7.2 per cent and 5.1 per cent respectively of total annual exports and imports. About 4.4 per cent of Taiwan's manufacturing employment (80,761 people) was in the zones in 1980. Scott (1979, pp.336–40) provides a cost-benefit analysis for the EPZs; Schive (1981) studies the local content behavior of firms in the EPZs; the historical background for the establishment of the Kaohsiung EPZ can be found in Li (1979, pp.352–58).

References

Chen, C.S. (1978), Import substitution and industrialization in Taiwan: Theory and empirical evidence, *Economic Essays*, 8, pp.121–173. (in Chinese)

Chenery, H.B. (1960), "Patterns of Industrial Growth," *American Economic Review*, 50 (3), pp.624–654.

──── (1980), "Interactions between Industrialization and Exports," *American Economic Review*, 70 (2), pp.281–287.

Chou, T.C. (1984), "Strategy and Pattern of Industrialization in Taiwan, 1960–80—Offsetting Policy and Specialization of Manufacturing," *Études et documents*, Université Catholique de Louvain, April.

Chung, S.P. (1980), Analysis of tariff and harbor dues in Taiwan, *Quarterly Bank of Taiwan*, 31 (4), pp.23–39, (in Chinese).

Doanges, J.B. and J. Riedel (1977), "The Expansion of Manufactured Exports in Developing Countries: An Empirical Assessment of Supply and Demand Issues," *Weltwirtschaftliches Archiv*, 113 (1), pp.58–87.

Fei, J.C.H. and G. Ranis (1964), *Development of the Labor Surplus Economy: Theory and Policy*, Richard D. Irwin, Homewood.

Galenson, W. (1979), ed. *Economic Growth and Structural Change in Taiwan: The Postwar Experience of the Republic of China*, Cornell University Press, Ithaca.

Ho, B.Y. (1981), Study of the development of secondary import substitution industries in Taiwan, in *Proceedings of a conference on Taiwan's foreign trade*, ed. Academia Sinica, Institute of Economics Taipei, pp.405–447. (in Chinese)

Hsing, M. (1975), Taiwan's industrialization and foreign trade policies in retrospect, in *Essays on the foreign trade of Taiwan*, ed. C. Sun Lianjian-chubanshe, Taipei.

Kogiku, K.C. (1978), "Japan's Industrial Structure Policy," *Revista internationale di scienze economiche e commerciali*, 20 (8–9), pp.677–708.

Kuznets, S. (1979), "Growth and Structural Shifts," in *Economic Growth and Structural Change in Taiwan*, ed. M. Galenson, Cornell University Press, Ithaca.

Lee, T.H. (1971), *Intersectoral Capital Flows in the Economic Development of Taiwan*, 1895–1960, Cornell University Press, Ithaca.

Lee, T.H., K.S. Liang, C. Schive and R.S. Yeh (1975), "The Structure of Effective Protection and Subsidy in Taiwan," *Economic Essays*, Taipei, No. 6, November.

Leff, N.H. (1979), "Entrepreneurship and Economic Development: The Problem Revisited," *Journal of Economic Literature*, 17 (1), pp.46–64.

Li, C.K. (1979), Study on Taiwan's industrial structure, 1951–1977, *Economic Study*, 22, pp.109–156. (in Chinese)

Li, K.T. (1976), *The Experience of Dynamic Growth of Taiwan*, Mei Ya Publications, Taipei.

Liang, K.S. and C.I. Liang Hou (1976), "Exports and Employment in Taiwan," in *Proceedings of a conference on Taiwan's population and economic development*, ed. Academia Sinica, Institute of Economics, Taipei.

Lin, C.Y. (1973), *Industrialization in Taiwan, 1946–72: Trade and Import-substitution Policies for Developing Countries*, Praeger Publishers, N.Y.

Morley, S.A. and G.W. Smith (1970), "On the Measurement of Import Substitution," *American Economic Review*, 60 (4), pp.728–735.

Paauw, D.S. and J.C.H. Fei (1973), *The Transition in Open Dualistic Economies: Theory and Southeast Asian Experience*, Yale University Press, New Haven.

Ranis, G. (1981), "Prospects for Taiwan's Economic Development," paper presented at a conference on economic development in Taiwan, mimeographed.

Schive, C. (1981), Local content of foreign firms in Taiwan, in *Proceedings of a conference on Taiwan's foreign trade*, ed. Academia Sinica, Institute of Economics, Taipei.

―――― and T. Gau (1981), The measurement and empirical analysis of secondary import-substitution in Taiwan, in *Proceedings of the Chinese economic association's annual conference*, ed. Chinese Economic Association, Taipei.

Scott, M. (1979), "Foreign Trade" in *Economic Growth and Structural Change in Taiwan*, ed. W. Galenson, Cornell University Press, Ithaca.

Sun. G.L. (1981), Measurement of economic structural change in Taiwan, 1961–1979, *Jingji yanjiu*, Taipei, 23, pp.57–108. (in Chinese)

Tu, W.T. (1976), Industrialization and industrial protective policy, in *Essays on the industrial development of Taiwan*, ed. W.T. Tu, Lianjing-chubanshe, Taipei.

Wang, I.Y. (1981), Trade patterns and comparative advantage in Taiwan, in *Proceedings of a conference on Taiwan's foreign trade*, ed. Academia Sinica, Institute of Economics, Taipei.

Wu, R.I. (1971), *The Strategy of Economic Development: A Case Study of Taiwan*, Vander, Louvain.

Yin, K.T. (1962), *My view on the economy of Taiwan*, 3rd vol. Executive Yuan, Council for U.S. Aid, Taipei (in Chinese).

2 Sources of Economic Growth and Structural Change: A Revised Approach*

Introduction

Industrialization is a major goal of economic development in many developing counties. In the process of industrialization, economic growth should be accompanied by structural change where the relative share of different sectors changes over time. In order to analyze the sources of economic growth and structural change from the demand side,[1] Chenery and his collaborators have quantitatively provided a tractable and powerful approach. They use the concept of non-proportionate growth to decompose sources into four components, namely, the effects of final demand, export expansion, import subsitiution and technological change.[2] Their approach is referred to as an important analytical tool in understanding and analyzing the patterns of development in the industrialization process. In addition, Lewis and Soligo (1965) have also provided another important method to analyze the sources of economic growth-under the concept of first difference on the production growth of sectors. We refer to the former as Chenery's approach, and the latter as Lewis-Soligo's approach.

---

*This paper was reproduced from *Journal of Development Economics*, 38, 1992, pp.383–401, with permission of the publisher. Two co-authors are Chin-Lih Wang who is the professor, Department of Economics, National Chung-Hsing University, and Juh-Luh Sun who is the professor, Department of Public Finance, National Chung-Hsing University.

However, there is a vital shortcoming in their approaches in that the cross-terms of different decomposition sources are neglected.[3] As a result, these neglected cross-terms are absorbed by related source effects, in accordance with the specific reference basis relating to the parameters and variables chosen. Under these circumstances, there exist at least three essential problems: (1) if the cross-terms are relatively important, we shall lose important information for policies. (2) If the cross-terms are completely distributed into other related source effects, follwing problem (1), we shall be misled into taking inadequate development policies. (3) It is difficult and confusing to choose adequate parameters and variables referring to different chosen periods, since different period parameters and variables chosen as a reference result in some decomposed source effects being overestimated or else underestimated. Therefore, in this paper we attempt to mathematically develop a revised measure to show the role of cross-terms, solve the confusing problem of periods chosen, and then test it empirically. Besides, it is common to apply either the Chenery or the Lewis-Soligo approach, both of which are for analyzing sources of economic growth and structural change. However, these two concepts are very similar yet different. Thus, in this paper we also try to clearly and rigorously distinguish the relationship and difference between them.

In section 2, the models in which Chenery's and Lewis-Soligo's approaches are revised will be constructed to decompose sources of economic growth and structural change, and also to distinguish between these two concepts, In section 3, the decomposed results based on different chosen periods are compared and related to our revised approach. In section 4, the case of Taiwan provides an empirical analysis to verify our approach. Finally, concluding remarks are given in section 5.

Models of economic growth and structural change

The basic equation for an open economy within the Leontief input-output framework can be stated as follows:

$$X_i = W_i + D_i + E_i - M_i (i = 1, 2, \ldots, n) \tag{1}$$

where X_i is total domestic production in sector i and W_i, D_i, E_i and M_i represent intermediate use, domestic final demand, exports and imports, respectively. The function for intermediate use is commonly illustrated as

$$W_i = \sum_j a_{ij} X_j, \tag{2}$$

where a_{ij} are input-output coefficients. Now if we let Z_i stand for the total supply of sector i from domestic and foreign sources, and U_i for the proportion of supply produced domestically,[4] the basic eq. (1), after handling, can be thus rewritten in matrix notation as

$$X = R\hat{U}(D + E), \tag{3}$$

where X, D and E represent the vectors of production, domestic final demand and exports, respectively. A $\wedge$ over variable U denotes a diagonal matrix, and $\hat{U}$ is the matrix of the proportion of domestic supply. $R = (I - \hat{U}A)^{-1}$, where A is the matrix of the input-output coefficients and $\hat{U}A$ is an approximation to the matrix of the domestic coefficients. So R is the inverse of the matrix relating to the domestec coefficient. $\hat{U}(D+E)$ represents final demand to be supplied from domestic production. Eq. (3), developed by Syrquin (1976) and Chenery and Syrquin (1980), is the basic framework used here to analyze sources of economic growth and structural change.[5]

It is common for economic growth in the industrialization process to be accompanied by structural change. Economic growth is referred to as the expansion of commodities produced domestically by each sector, or as the entire economy in the certain interval period when structural change reveals that some sectors of the economy are growing faster than others, so that the relative shares of the sectors can be changed. The implications of these two concepts are quite different, and highly relevant. Thus the effects of economic growth and structural change should be distinguished rigorously. In order to do this adequately under an interindustry framework, the assumption of proportionate growth, following Chenery (1960), is used. Hence the effects of growth in sector i can be decomposed into two parts: one illustrates the 'slanting effect' which indicates the deviations from proportionate expansion, and the other is the 'synchronous effect' that describes the results of proportionate growth, say in matrix notation:

$$\mathrm{d}X = \delta X + \partial X,$$

where

$$\mathrm{d}X = X^2 - X^1, \quad \delta X = X^2 - \lambda X^1, \quad \partial X = \lambda X^1 = X^1, \qquad (4)$$

where the superscripts refer to time periods, $\delta X = X^2 - \lambda X^1$, the slanting effect, denotes the difference between domestic supply in period 2 and the proportionately growing domestic supply of period 1. It represents structural change for every sector in the whole economy. Chenery's approach is based on this effect of analyzing the sources of industrialization. $\partial X = \lambda X^1 - X^1$, the synchronous effect, denotes the difference between the proportionately growing domestic supply of period 1 and the actual domestic supply in period 1. It represents every sector expanding at the same proportionate rate. In other words, the economic system doesn't change structurally, but grows proportionately. $\mathrm{d}X$, the gross effect, denotes the difference in domestic supply between periods 2 and 1. It represents actual economic growth in every sector. Lewis-Soligo's approach is based on this effect of analyzing the sources of industrialization. It is obvious that the difference between these two approaches lies in the synchronous effect.

The rate of proportionate growth (λ) used here is defined as

$$\lambda = \sum X_i^2 / \sum X_i^1. \tag{5}$$

This definition is considerably different from Chenery's.[6] The main reason for this is that this definition is consistent with interindustry relations.

In order to avoid selecting periods relating to parameters and variables as a reference basis when analyzing sources of economic growth and structural change, we use the formulation whereby parameter and variable in period 2 in eq. (3) can be broken down by illustrating period 1, and adding the change between periods 1 and 2. For example: $R^2 = R^1 + (R^2 - R^1) = R^1 + dR$. Therefore, the decomposed slanting effect indicating the sources of structural change can be shown as

$$\begin{aligned}\delta X &= R^2 \hat{U}^2 (D^2 + E^2) - \lambda R^1 \hat{U}^1 (D^1 - E^1) \\ &= R^1 \hat{U}^1 \delta D + R^1 \hat{U}^1 \delta E + R^1 d\hat{U}(\lambda D^1 + \lambda E^1) + dR\hat{U}^1(\lambda D^1 - \lambda E^1) \\ &\quad + dRd\hat{U}(\lambda D^1 + \lambda E^1) + R^1 d\hat{U} \delta D + R^1 d\hat{U} \delta E + dR\hat{U}^1 \delta D \\ &\quad + dR\hat{U}^1 \delta E + dRd\hat{U} \delta D + dRd\hat{U} \delta E. \end{aligned} \tag{6}$$

There are 11 terms of source effects, in the right-hand side of eq. (6), that express the sources of the slanting effect, namely the deviations of production in each sector from proportionate growth between the two periods. The first four terms represent the source effects of deviations in domestic demand, export expansion, import substitution and technological change, respectively. The remaining terms are the effects of cross products, which result from the interaction of two or three of the former four terms. The fifth term, $dRd\hat{U}(\lambda D^1 + \lambda E^1)$ for example, is the cross-effect of technological change and import substitution. Therefore, it is obvious that the cross-terms are not properly attributable to any one of the first four terms, and should be presented independently.

The synchronous effect indicating the results from proportionate growth is then:

$$\partial X = \lambda R^1 \hat{U}^1 (D^1 + E^1) - R^1 \hat{U}^1 (D^1 + E^1)$$
$$= R^1 \hat{U}^1 \partial D + R^1 \hat{U}^1 \partial E. \tag{7}$$

This equation shows that when production growth between periods 1 and 2 in all sectors is in the same proportionate rate λ, the source effects can only be decomposed into two parts; namely, the two absolutely separate and synchronously expanded effects of domestic demand and export expansion. Under these circumstances, structural change in the economy will not occur. That is, the economy only grows when every sector is expanding at the same rate.

By definition, the sources of the gross effect of economic growth in all sectors are equivalent to the sum of eqs. (6) and (7):

$$\begin{aligned} \mathrm{d}X &= \delta X + \partial X \\ &= R^1 \hat{U}^1 \mathrm{d}D + R^1 \hat{U}^1 \mathrm{d}E + R^1 \mathrm{d}\hat{U}(D^1 + E^1) + \mathrm{d}R\hat{U}^1(D^1 + E^1) \\ &\quad + \mathrm{d}R\mathrm{d}\hat{U}(D^1 + E^1) + R^1 \mathrm{d}\hat{U}\mathrm{d}D + R^1 \mathrm{d}\hat{U}\mathrm{d}E + \mathrm{d}R\hat{U}^1\mathrm{d}D \\ &\quad + \mathrm{d}R\hat{U}^1\mathrm{d}E + \mathrm{d}R\mathrm{d}\hat{U}\mathrm{d}D + \mathrm{d}R\mathrm{d}\hat{U}\mathrm{d}E. \end{aligned} \tag{8}$$

In a way that is similar to the analysis of the source effects of structural change, the sources of economic growth between time periods in each sector can be expressed as the sum of 11 terms in which the first four terms, respectively, are the effects of increases in domestic demand and export expansion, and the change in import substitution and technological change, while the remaining terms are the effects of their cross products.

By comparison, the first two terms on the right-hand side of eq. (8) are the sum of those in eqs. (6) and (7). The sum of the remaining terms of eq. (8) is identical to that of eq. (6). However, because the term $(\lambda D^1 + \lambda E^1)$ can be completely divided into $(D^1 + E^1)$ and $(\partial D + \partial E)$, the former three remaining terms in eq. (8) can be viewed as the parts of those of eq. (6). Furthermore, the residual of those terms in eq. (6) may be combined with corresponding cross-terms, and finally expressed as in eq. (8).[7] Hence each term of the source effects of these two equations is strictly different. We must distinguish between them in the analysis of development patterns.

The problem of the periods chosen

Now we turn our attention to comparing the source effects decomposed from the above model with those based on different periods chosen. In particular, we focus deeply on the role of the cross-terms. There are two forms for selecting periods as a reference basis: one is the Paasche form expressed in the parameters (coefficients) in period 2 and variable (weights) in period 1, and the other is the Laspeyres form expressed in the parameter in period 1 and variables in period 2.[8]

The Paasche form

The source effects of structural change, proportionate and actual growth in all sectors with parameters based on period 2 and variable on period 1 can be first shown in the matrix notation as

$$\delta X = R^2\hat{U}^2\delta D + R^2\hat{U}^2\delta E + R^2 \mathrm{d}\hat{U}\lambda Z^1 + R^2\hat{U}^2\mathrm{d}A\lambda X^1, \quad (9)$$

$$\partial X = R^2\hat{U}^2\partial D + R^2\hat{U}^2\partial E + (1-\lambda)R^2\mathrm{d}\hat{U}Z^1$$
$$+ (1-\lambda)R^2\hat{U}^2\mathrm{d}AX^1, \quad (10)$$

$$\mathrm{d}X = R^2\hat{U}^2\mathrm{d}D + R^2\hat{U}^2\mathrm{d}E + R^2\mathrm{d}\hat{U}Z^1 + R^2\hat{U}^2\mathrm{d}AX^1. \quad (11)$$

In comparison with our revised approach discussed in section 2, the terms on the right-hand side of eq. (9) with relation to the counterparts of eq. (6) can be expressed as

$$R^2\hat{U}^2\delta D = R^1\hat{U}^1\delta D + R^1\mathrm{d}\hat{U}\delta D + \mathrm{d}R\hat{U}^1\delta D + \mathrm{d}R\mathrm{d}\hat{U}\delta D, \quad (12a)$$

$$R^2\hat{U}^2\delta E = R^1\hat{U}^1\delta E + R^1\mathrm{d}\hat{U}\delta E + \mathrm{d}R\hat{U}^1\delta E + \mathrm{d}R\mathrm{d}\hat{U}\delta E, \quad (12b)$$

$$R^2 \mathrm{d}\hat{U}\lambda Z^1 = R^1 \mathrm{d}\hat{U}(\lambda D^1 + \lambda E^1) + \mathrm{d}R\mathrm{d}\hat{U}(\lambda D^1 + \lambda E^1) + R^2 \mathrm{d}\hat{U}\lambda W^1, \tag{12c}$$

$$R^2 \hat{U}^2 \mathrm{d}A\lambda X^1 = \mathrm{d}R\hat{U}^1(\lambda D^1 + \lambda E^1) - R^2 \mathrm{d}\hat{U}\lambda W^1. \tag{12d}$$

As shown above, the sources of structural change interpreted by eq. (9) were only decomposed into four terms, while eq. (6) had 11 terms containing seven cross-terms. The sum of all terms for these two equations is identical. So, some terms of eq. (6) must absorb the cross-terms. According to eq. (12), the first two terms of eq. (9) represent the source effects of deviations from domestic demand and export expansion, and absorb their own related cross-terms in eq. (6). The remaining one, $\mathrm{d}R\mathrm{d}\hat{U}(\lambda D^1 + \lambda E^1)$, is absorbed by the effect of import substitution. Besides, the source effects of import substitution and technological change may be adjusted in relation to each other with the term $R^2 \mathrm{d}\hat{U}\lambda W^1$. Therefore, the first terms on the right-hand side of eq. (12) can be viewed as pure (revised) effects. The combined effects on the left-hand side of eq. (12) are the sum of the pure effects and the cross-terms.

The above results are analogously applied for the comparative analysis of the sources of economic growth. Similarly, we can also illustrate the relationship between the combined and pure effects in accordance with the terms of eqs. (11) and (8) in the following:

$$R^2 \hat{U}^2 \mathrm{d}D = R^1 \hat{U}^1 \mathrm{d}D + R^1 \mathrm{d}\hat{U}\mathrm{d}D + \mathrm{d}R\hat{U}^1 \mathrm{d}D + \mathrm{d}R\mathrm{d}\hat{U}\mathrm{d}D, \tag{13a}$$

$$R^2 \hat{U}^2 \mathrm{d}E = R^1 \hat{U}^1 \mathrm{d}E + R^1 \mathrm{d}\hat{U}\mathrm{d}E + \mathrm{d}R\hat{U}^1 \mathrm{d}E + \mathrm{d}R\mathrm{d}\hat{U}\mathrm{d}E, \tag{13b}$$

$$R^2 \mathrm{d}\hat{U} Z^1 = R^1 \mathrm{d}\hat{U}(D^1 + E^1) + \mathrm{d}R\mathrm{d}\hat{U}(D^1 + E^1) + R^2 \mathrm{d}\hat{U} W^1, \tag{13c}$$

$$R^2 \hat{U}^2 \mathrm{d}A X^1 = \mathrm{d}R\hat{U}^1(D^1 + E^1) - R^2 \mathrm{d}\hat{U} W^1. \tag{13d}$$

To sum up, the decomposed source effect of growth and structural change on the Paasche form, one of the popular measures developed and used in the literature, is a kind of combined effect. It is the result of joining cross-terms to the related pure effect.

The Laspeyres form

We now change the analysis from the Paasche form to the Laspeyres form. The different concepts of the source effects, namely, the sources of structural change, proportionate growth and actual economic growth, can be expressed as

$$\delta X = R^1 \hat{U}^1 \delta D + R^1 \hat{U}^1 \delta E + R^1 \mathrm{d}\hat{U} Z^2 + R^1 \hat{U}^1 \mathrm{d} A X^2, \quad (14)$$

$$\partial X = R^1 \hat{U}^1 \partial D + R^1 \hat{U}^1 \partial E, \quad (15)$$

$$\mathrm{d} X = R^1 \hat{U}^1 \mathrm{d} D + R^1 \hat{U}^1 \mathrm{d} E + R^1 \mathrm{d}\hat{U} Z^2 + R^1 \hat{U}^1 \mathrm{d} A X^2. \quad (16)$$

As shown above, the source effects of proportionate growth based on the Laspeyres form equal our approach's results. According ro eq. (4), the first two terms of eq. (14), adding the corresponding terms of the synchronous effects, are equal to those of eq. (16). Therefore, it is shown that the last two tems of these two equations, the so-called source effects of important substitution and technological change, are identical.

The source effects shown in eqs. (14) and (16) have only four terms which is less than our 11 terms in eqs. (6) and (8). Since the former two terms are the same as each other and the associated sum of all terms is identical, the last two terms of eqs. (14) and (16), shown as the combined source effects, naturally absorb all the remaining cross-terms in eqs. (6) and (8). Their corresponding relationship can be stated as follows:

$$\begin{aligned}
R^1 \mathrm{d}\hat{U} Z^2 &= R^1 \mathrm{d}\hat{U}(\lambda D^1 + \lambda E^1) + R^1 \mathrm{d}\hat{U} \delta D + R^1 \mathrm{d}\hat{U} \delta E + R^1 \mathrm{d}\hat{U} W^2 \\
&= R^1 \mathrm{d}\hat{U}(D^1 + E^1) + R^1 \mathrm{d}\hat{U} \mathrm{d} D + R^1 \mathrm{d}\hat{U} \mathrm{d} E \\
&\quad + R^1 \mathrm{d}\hat{U} W^2, \quad (17a) \\
R^1 \hat{U}^1 \mathrm{d} A X^2 &= \mathrm{d} R \hat{U}^1 (\lambda D^1 + \lambda E^1) + \mathrm{d} R \mathrm{d}\hat{U}(\lambda D^1 + \lambda E^1) \\
&\quad + \mathrm{d} R \hat{U}^1 \delta D + \mathrm{d} R \mathrm{d}\hat{U} \delta D + \mathrm{d} R \hat{U}^1 \delta E + \mathrm{d} R \mathrm{d}\hat{U} \delta E \\
&\quad - R^1 \mathrm{d}\hat{U} W^2
\end{aligned}$$

$$= \mathrm{d}R\hat{U}^1(D^1 + E^1) + \mathrm{d}R\mathrm{d}\hat{U}(D^1 + E^1)$$
$$+ \mathrm{d}R\hat{U}^1\mathrm{d}D + \mathrm{d}R\mathrm{d}\hat{U}\mathrm{d}D + \mathrm{d}R\hat{U}^1\mathrm{d}D + \mathrm{d}R\hat{U}^1\mathrm{d}E$$
$$+ \mathrm{d}R\mathrm{d}\hat{U}\mathrm{d}E - R^1\mathrm{d}\hat{U}W^2. \tag{17b}$$

The so-called technological change (combined) effect, i.e., the last term of eqs. (14) and (16), absorbs five cross-term effects. However, if it is based on the Paasche form, it absorbs nothing. Furthermore, the import substitution (conbined) effect that absorbs the remaining two cross-terms is different from that based on the Paasche form. On the contrary, it is found that the cross-terms are almost absorbed by the domestic demand effect and the export expansion effect, based on the Paasche form.

It is recognized that the estimated sources of economic growth and structural change of these two forms are strikingly different from ours. Our approach shows the role of the cross-terms, but the approaches chosen with specific periods as bases do not. That is, our approach can distinguish between pure effects and cross-terms independently, whereas their approaches do not have this function because their decomposed source effects are combined ones in which the cross-terms enter into a combination with the pure effects.

Besides, the approaches based on both the Paasche form and the Laspeyres form have the following shortcomings: (1) If the cross-terms to be interpreted as the sources of economic growth and structural change are relatively important, we will lose important information for policy implications. (2) If all the values of the cross-terms are positive, it naturally follows that technological change effects derived from the Laspeyres form are overestimated, as are the combined effects of domestic demand and export expansion derived from the Paasche form. Therefore, no matter how the period is chosen concerning the parameters and variables, sources of economic growth and structural change decomposed only into four terms without cross-terms will produce more or less biases. The cross-terms are the result of interactions. Naturally, they are not attributable to any specific term (pure source effect) and are presented independently. (3) The corresponding estimated combined effects from different periods as a base are different and inconsistent. Under these circumstances, there is a confusing problem as to which criteria should be used to select which formula and which period for analyzing the patterns of development. In using our approach, there exist no such problems and the approach is capable of finding out and checking the variation sources of the corresponding terms of the Paasche form and the Laspeyres form.

However, it is clear that the cross-term problem does not occur when using differentials. It is a problem of finite differences with long gaps. Fane (1971, 1973) and Dervis and Robinson (1980) have used a different approach to decomposing time changes by specifying the driving variables in the analysis explicitly as continuous functions of time. They then integrate these functions and decompose the total change over a finite period into various components, with no need to consider cross terms. This approach, however, requires the specification of the explicit time-dependent functions. When considering driving variables such as changes in input-output coefficients or import coefficients, the specification of such functions requires explicit information about the underlying economic process at work.[9]

A numerical example of Taiwan's case

In order to test whether the cross-terms are relatively important in explaining the sources of economic growth and structural change, we take Taiwan's economic experience as an example. The sources of data used here are the interindustry relations, tables in 1979 and 1984. For simplicity in illustrating our approach, the category of industries is classified into seven sectors. The figures for each term in eqs. (6) and (8) in each sector and in the economy are presented in table 2.1. The differences between the source effects of final demand and export expansion are the synchronous effects, with the value in parentheses being its relative contribution.

The proportionate growth rate in the economy for the time periods under consideration was 1.9615. Agriculture, mining, construction and transportation illustrated the negative slanting effect as their shares declined. This was mainly because these sectors expanded less than the average for the whole economy. In comparison with the effect of economic growth and structural change, table 2.1 shows that the gross effects of actual growth in each sector is greater than the slanting effect, and the corresponding figures for the source effects and the values of the relative contributions are strikingly diffierent.

The sum of the cross-terms for each sector is shown in the sixth row of table 2.1. The relative contributions of these cross-terms in all sectors range from −72.91%. to 45.54%. These figures show well enough that the cross-terms play an important role in explaining the sources of economic growth and structural change, and in analyzing the patterns of development. Besides, the importance of each cross-term, represented by the value of its relative contribution, is still more or less outstanding. For example, the total contribution of the cross-terms, the last column presented in table 2.1, is 6.81% which is higher than the important-substitution effect and the technological change effect, 2.11% and 5.21$, respectively. According to the chosen parameters and variables in different periods, the positive relative contribution of each cross-term in the whole economy may indicate that some of the terms in eqs. (11) and (16) would apparently have overestimated results. In other words, the respective domestic demand effect and export expansion effect, with respect to the Paasche form, have additional relative contributions of 1.58% and 5.01%, while the import substitution effect and the technological change effect, based on the Laspeyres form, also have additional contributions of 2.41% and 4.40%. These interpretations of the whole economy are applied identically for the illustration of the source effects of economic growth, and the structural change in

Table 2.1
Sources of economic growth and structural change in Taiwan, 1979-1984 (Unit: NT$ 1 billion).[a]

Sector		Agricultural		Mining		Manufacturing		Construction	
		S.E.	G.E.	S.E.	G.E.	S.E.	G.E.	S.E.	G.E.
Total		−86.27	106.82	−18.30	9.82	95.94	1,760.02	−85.05	91.61
(1)	Demand	−38.72 (44.88)	101.35 (94.88)	−4.74 (25.90)	13.97 (142.26)	−321.71 (−335.32)	551.02 (31.31)	−86.48 (101.68)	86.58 (94.51)
(2)	Exports	−32.66 (37.85)	20.36 (19.06)	1.17 (−6.39)	10.58 (107.74)	91.87 (95.76)	883.22 (50.18)	−0.19 (0.22)	3.41 (3.72)
(3)	Import substitution	1.72 (−1.99)	0.88 (0.82)	0.60 (−3.28)	0.31 (3.16)	90.57 (94.40)	46.18 (2.62)	0.46 (−0.54)	0.23 (0.25)
(4)	Technological change	−18.12 (21.00)	−9.24 (−8.65)	−15.46 (84.48)	−7.88 (−80.24)	238.78 (248.88)	121.73 (6.92)	1.08 (−1.27)	0.55 (0.60)
(5)	Sum of cross-terms	1.51 (−1.75)	−6.53 (−6.11)	0.13 (−0.71)	−7.16 (−72.91)	−3.57 (−3.72)	157.87 (8.97)	0.08 (−0.09)	0.84 (0.92)
(5.1)	(1), (3)	−0.04 (0.05)	0.40 (0.37)	0.63 (−3.44)	0.61 (6.21)	−7.50 (−7.82)	11.26 (0.64)	−0.04 (0.05)	0.09 (0.10)
(5.2)	(2), (3)	−0.40 (0.46)	0.00	0.13 (−0.71)	0.44 (4.48)	17.22 (17.95)	42.86 (2.44)	0.05 (−0.06)	0.15 (0.16)
(5.3)	(1), (4)	1.31 (−1.51)	−4.46 (−4.18)	−0.04 (0.22)	−5.37 (−54.68)	−36.43 (−37.97)	24.51 (1.39)	−0.05 (0.06)	0.35 (0.38)
(5.4)	(2), (4)	0.61 (−0.70)	−2.51 (−2.35)	−0.29 (1.58)	−2.54 (−25.87)	11.71 (12.21)	67.82 (3.85)	0.07 (−0.08)	0.20 (0.22)
(5.5)	(3), (4)	0.09 (−0.11)	0.05 (0.05)	−0.29 (1.58)	−0.15 (−1.53)	10.08 (10.51)	5.14 (0.29)	0.04 (−0.05)	0.02 (0.02)
(5.6)	(1), (3), (4)	−0.02 (0.02)	0.02 (0.02)	0.01 (−0.05)	−0.06 (−0.61)	−0.69 (−0.72)	1.12 (0.06)	0.01 (−0.01)	0.02 (0.02)
(5.7)	(2), (3), (4)	−0.04 (0.04)	−0.03 (−0.03)	−0.02 (0.11)	−0.09 (−0.92)	2.04 (2.13)	5.16 (0.29)	0.00	0.01 (0.01)

[a]S.E. and G.E. represent the slanting effect of structural change and the gross effect of industrial growth, respectively. The value in the parentheses is its relative contribution. In the first column, (5.1), for example, is the cross-effect of demand and import substitution where (1) stands for the demand term, and (3) is the import substitution term.

Table 2.1 (continued)

Sector		Utilities S.E.	Utilities G.E.	Transportation S.E.	Transportation G.E.	Services S.E.	Services G.E.	Whole economy G.E.
Total		27.76	91.83	−2.13	111.87	85.12	661.31	2,833.28
(1)	Demand	−2.73 (−9.83)	42.20 (45.95)	−18.82 (883.57)	62.11 (55.52)	42.36 (49.77)	498.10 (75.32)	1,355.34 (47.84)
(2)	Exports	1.87 (6.74)	21.01 (22.88)	3.75 (−176.06)	36.81 (32.90)	−18.21 (−21.39)	102.24 (15.46)	1,077.64 (38.04)
(3)	Import substitution	2.57 (9.26)	1.31 (1.43)	10.11 (−474.65)	5.16 (4.61)	11.29 (13.26)	5.76 (0.87)	59.82 (2.11)
(4)	Technological change	28.12 (101.30)	14.33 (15.60)	3.80 (−178.40)	1.94 (1.73)	51.37 (60.35)	26.19 (3.96)	147.63 (5.21)
(5)	Sum of cross-terms	−2.07 (−7.46)	12.96 (14.11)	−0.97 (45.54)	5.85 (5.23)	−1.69 (−1.99)	29.02 (4.39)	192.85 (6.81)
(5.1)	(1), (3)	−0.16 (−0.58)	0.40 (0.44)	−0.86 (40.38)	2.55 (2.28)	−0.44 (−0.52)	2.56 (0.39)	17.86 (0.63)
(5.2)	(2), (3)	0.34 (1.22)	1.05 (1.14)	0.45 (−21.13)	2.01 (1.80)	1.26 (1.48)	3.79 (0.57)	50.30 (1.78)
(5.3)	(1), (4)	−3.59 (−12.93)	4.03 (4.39)	−1.26 (59.15)	−1.41 (−1.26)	−5.77 (−6.78)	7.84 (1.19)	25.49 (0.90)
(5.4)	(2), (4)	0.59 (2.13)	6.75 (7.35)	0.35 (−16.43)	2.36 (2.11)	1.38 (1.62)	12.95 (1.96)	85.04 (3.00)
(5.5)	(3), (4)	0.62 (2.23)	0.31 (0.34)	0.29 (−13.62)	0.15 (0.13)	1.60 (1.88)	0.81 (0.12)	6.33 (0.22)
(5.6)	(1), (3), (4)	−0.03 (−0.11)	0.08 (0.09)	−0.02 (0.93)	0.04 (0.04)	−0.08 (−0.09)	0.24 (0.04)	1.46 (0.05)
(5.7)	(2), (3), (4)	0.16 (0.58)	0.34 (0.37)	0.08 (−3.76)	0.15 (0.13)	0.36 (0.42)	0.83 (0.13)	6.38 (0.23)

each sector. Although is some sectors the sum of cross-terms is so relatively small (see table 2.1), the individual cross-terms may be still large enough to bias the measurement of noncross-terms.[10] Therefore, in theoretical base we emphasize the independently separated individual cross-term has its own meaning and implication for a sector's structure change and growth.

Furthermore, we select the manufacturing sector presented in table 2.2 to show the variation between the pure effects and the combined effects. No matter how we consider industrial growth or structural change, the pure effects of final demand and export expansion derived from our approach are less than the combined ones from the Paasche form because the latter absorbs almost all the cross-terms, while those derived from the Laspeyres form have the same figures as ours. However, the situation of the import substitution effect and the technological change effect is shown to be another story. The pure effect of technological change accounts for a significantly higher relative share than that of important substitution in our approach. On the contrary, the combined effect of technological change accounts for a significntly lower relative share than that of import substitution in the Paasche form as well as the Laspeyres form. In the meantime, owing to the import substitution and technological change derived from the Laspeyres form absorbing all the cross-terms, there are larger shares in the field of industrial growth (positive values of the cross-terms) and smaller shares in the field of structural change than in those from the Paasche form.

As shown above, the figures of the source effects of industrial growth and structural change using different approaches are shown to have outstanding different results. Our approach can decompose the combined effects into the pure effects and cross-terms. The important role of the cross-terms has been quantitatively revealed. Furthermore, we can get an absolutely pure contribution of various sources of the demand side on industrial growth and structural change.

Table 2.2
Comparison of sources of economic growth and structural change in manufacturing by different approaches (Unit: NT$ 1 billion).[a]

		The revised approach		The Paasche approach		The Laspeyres approach	
		S.E.	G.E.	S.E.	G.E.	S.E.	G.E.
Total		95.94	1,760.02	95.94	1,760.02	95.94	1,760.02
(1)	Demand	−321.71 (−335.32)	551.02 (31.31)	−366.33 (−381.83)	587.91 (33.40)	−321.71 (−335.32)	551.02 (31.31)
(2)	Exports	91.87 (95.76)	883.22 (50.18)	122.84 (128.05)	999.06 (56.76)	91.87 (95.76)	883.22 (50.18)
(3)	Import substitution	90.57 (94.40)	46.18 (2.62)	250.87 (261.48)	127.90 (7.27)	244.47 (254.82)	244.48 (13.89)
(4)	Technological change	238.78 (248.88)	121.73 (6.92)	88.56 (92.30)	45.15 (2.57)	81.31 (84.74)	81.30 (4.62)
(5)	Sum of cross-terms	−3.57 (−3.72)	157.87 (8.97)				
(5.1)	(1), (3)	−7.50 (−7.82)	11.26 (0.64)				
(5.2)	(2), (3)	17.22 (17.95)	42.86 (2.44)				
(5.3)	(1), (4)	−36.43 (−37.97)	24.51 (1.39)				
(5.4)	(2), (4)	11.71 (12.21)	67.82 (3.85)				
(5.5)	(3), (4)	10.08 (10.51)	5.14 (0.29)				
(5.6)	(1), (3), (4)	−0.69 (−0.72)	1.12 (0.06)				
(5.7)	(2), (3), (4)	2.04 (2.13)	5.16 (0.29)				

[a]S.E. and G.E. represent the slanting effect of structural change and the gross effect of industrial growth, respectively. The value in the parentheses is its relative contribution. In the first column, (5.1), for example, is the cross-effect of demand and import substitution where (1) stands for the demand term, and (3) is the import substitution term.

Concluding remarks

The sources of economic growth and structural change can be used to understand and analyze the process of industrialization in developing countries. On the basis of the interindustry model, we have developed a revised approach in which the important features of the cross-terms are revealed and the pure source effects of industrial growth and structural change are able to be derived in this paper. These results are quite different from those chosen specific parameters and variables that are chosen in different periods as a reference. The latter approach reveals that some terms estimated by these approaches which only have four decomposed combined source effects may be overestimated or underestimated because these terms absorb some of the cross-terms shown by our approach. The empirical results for the case of Taiwan have revealed sufficiently that the cross-terms might play a relatively important role in interpreting the sources of economic growth and structural change in the industrialization process. Thus the cross-terms should be presented independently.

Economic growth in a system is usually associated with structural change. In this paper we have also rigorously distinguished their effects. With the assumption of proportionate growth, the gross effect of economic growth is the sum of the slanting and synchronous effects. Since the slanting effect expresses the sources of structural change, the synchronous effect is the main source of the difference between the Chenery approach and the Lewis-Soligo approach.

Notes

1. To study the sources of growth, another important measurement referred to as supply-side analysis uses the production function approach. In this field, works include Denison (1967), Robinson 1971) and others.

2. The direct type of decomposition was first developed by Chenery (1960). It has been incorporated into the explicit interindustry framework the study of Japanese industrialization by Chenery, Shishido and Watanabe (1962), and has been further revised by Syrquin (1976). Besides the above, the works which study this approach, or use it, include Chenery (1979, 1980), Chenery and Syrquin (1980), Celasun (1983) and Kubo, Robinson and Syrquin (1986).

3. Eysenbach (1969) first discovered the impact of the cross-terms on the effect of the source components. He mentioned that Lewis-Soligo's approach (1965) could result in the import-substitution effect being overestimated because it absorbs the cross-terms.

4. Another important treatment of import substitution is the ratio, U_{di}, which stands for domestic production to total domestic demand. Under this condition, eq. (3) can be rewritten as $X_d = R_d(\hat{U}_d D + E)$. Furthermore, this treatment can be classified into two components: the proportions of intermediate and of final demand produced domestically.

5. Generally speaking, the forms of the material balance equations of the input-output accounts are dependent upon the treatment of the $I - 0$ linkage and import substitution. Eq. (3) is one of these. For simplicity, this paper only employs the form to illustrate our concept and methodology. But the results of eq. (3) discussed here can be similarly applied to any form of material balance equation.

6. The proportionate growth rate defined by Chenery is the ratio of GNP in period 2 to GNP in period 1. Here, we use the ratio of the two periods' total output as a proportionate growth. If every sector grows with the same proportionate rate, then its structure would not change in two periods:

$$S_i^2 = X_i^2 / \sum X_i^2 = \lambda X_i^1 / \sum \lambda X_i^1 = X_i^1 / \sum X_i^1 = S_i^1,$$
$$\lambda = \sum X_i^2 / \sum X_i^1 = \bar{X}^2 / \bar{X}^1$$

(ratio of two periods' output mean value).

If $\sum X_i^2 = \lambda \sum X_i^1$ and $X_i^2 \neq \lambda X_i^1$, then $S_i^1 \neq S_i^2$, here we get a structure change in the sector $i(S_i^t$: the structure of i sector in period t).

7. The slanting effect, or Chenery's approach, measures the effects that deviate from a balanced growth path. Thus the source effects are expressed on the basis of balanced growth or measured in terms of deviated figures. However, the gross effect, or Lewis-Soligo's approach, measures the effects expanded from the absolute first difference between two periods. So the source effects are expressed on the basis of the base period, or measured in terms of the first difference figures.

8. These forms were named by Chenery (1979). To avoid an arbitrary choice between them, Chenery suggested that the calculations of the source effects use an average of the two, or it is possible to define an appropriate Divisia index by specifying the time path of the different variable (Fane (1971, 1973)). But these mean weights method may not avoid the biasedness of each term.

9. We thank one referee to provide this paragraph and to explain the cross-term problem in this way.

10. In our table 2.1 of the 14 sums of cross-terms (seven sectors and two types of decomposition), there are between 0 and 1% (in absolute value), two are between 1 and 3% two are between 3 and 5%, four are between 5 and 10%, one is between 10 and 15%, leaving the two remaining extreme cases (which are referred to in the text above) of -72.91% and 45.54%. Clearly for a number of sectors the sum of cross-terms is so relatively small that it can be safely ignored in practice if not in theory. We would like to thank another referee to mention this point.

Appendix

Appendix 2.1   Mathematical inference procedure

The procedures for the mathematical inference of eqs. (12), (13) and (17) can be in details indicated as below:

$$\begin{aligned}
R^2\hat{U}^2\delta D &= (R^1 + \mathrm{d}R)(\hat{U}^1 + \mathrm{d}\hat{U})\delta D \\
&= R^1\hat{U}^1\delta D + R^1\mathrm{d}\hat{U}\delta D + \mathrm{d}R\hat{U}^1\delta D + \mathrm{d}R\mathrm{d}\hat{U}\delta D. \quad (12\mathrm{a})\\
R^2\hat{U}^2\delta E &= (R^1 + \mathrm{d}R)(\hat{U}^1 + \mathrm{d}\hat{U})\delta E \\
&= R^1\hat{U}^1\delta E + R^1\mathrm{d}\hat{U}\delta E + \mathrm{d}R\hat{U}^1\delta E + \mathrm{d}R\mathrm{d}\hat{U}\delta E. \quad (12\mathrm{b})
\end{aligned}$$

$$\begin{aligned}
R^2\mathrm{d}\hat{U}\lambda Z^1 &= R^2\mathrm{d}\hat{U}\lambda(D^1 + E^1 + W^1)\\
&= R^2\mathrm{d}\hat{U}\lambda(D^1 + E^1) + R^2\mathrm{d}\hat{U}\lambda W^1\\
&= (R^1 + \mathrm{d}R)\mathrm{d}\hat{U}(\lambda D^1 + \lambda E^1) + R^2\mathrm{d}\hat{U}\lambda W^1\\
&= R^1\mathrm{d}\hat{U}(\lambda D^1 + \lambda E^1) + \mathrm{d}R\mathrm{d}\hat{U}(\lambda D^1 + \lambda E^1)\\
&\quad + R^2\mathrm{d}\hat{U}\lambda W^1. \quad (12\mathrm{c})
\end{aligned}$$

$$\begin{aligned}
R^2\hat{U}^2\mathrm{d}A\lambda X^1 &= R^2\hat{U}^2(A^2 - A^1)\lambda X^1\\
&= R^2\hat{U}^2 A^2\lambda X^1 - R^2\hat{U}^2 A^1\lambda X^1\\
&= R^2\hat{U}^2 A^2\lambda X^1 - R^2\hat{U}^2 A^1\lambda X^1\\
&\quad + R^2(I - \hat{U}^2 A^2)\lambda X^1 - \lambda X^1\\
&= R^2\hat{U}^2 A^2\lambda X^1 - R^2\hat{U}^2 A^1\lambda X^1 + R^2\lambda X^1\\
&\quad - R^2\hat{U}^2 A^2\lambda X^1 - \lambda X^1\\
&= R^2\lambda X^1 - R^2\hat{U}^2 A^1\lambda X^1 - \lambda X^1\\
&= R^2\lambda\hat{U}^1(D^1 + E^1 + W^1) - R^2\hat{U}^2\lambda W^1\\
&\quad - \lambda R^1\hat{U}^1(D^1 + E^1)\\
&= R^2\hat{U}^1(\lambda D^1 + \lambda E^1) + R^2\hat{U}^1\lambda W^1 - R^2\hat{U}^2\lambda W^1\\
&\quad - R^1\hat{U}^1(\lambda D^1 + \lambda E^1)\\
&= (R^2 - R^1)\hat{U}^1(\lambda D^1 + \lambda E^1) - R^2(\hat{U}^2 - \hat{U}^1)\lambda W^1\\
&= \mathrm{d}R\hat{U}^1(\lambda D^1 + \lambda E^1) - R^2\mathrm{d}\hat{U}\lambda W^1. \quad (12\mathrm{d})
\end{aligned}$$

$$\begin{aligned}
R^2\hat{U}^2 \mathrm{d}D &= (R^1 + \mathrm{d}R)(\hat{U}^1 + \mathrm{d}\hat{U})\mathrm{d}D \\
&= R^1\hat{U}^1\mathrm{d}D + \mathrm{d}R\hat{U}^1\mathrm{d}D + R^1\mathrm{d}\hat{U}\mathrm{d}D + \mathrm{d}R\mathrm{d}\hat{U}\mathrm{d}D. \quad (13\mathrm{a}) \\
R^2\hat{U}^2 \mathrm{d}E &= (R^1 + \mathrm{d}R)(\hat{U}^1 + \mathrm{d}\hat{U})\mathrm{d}E \\
&= R^1\hat{U}^1\mathrm{d}E + R^1\mathrm{d}\hat{U}\mathrm{d}E + \mathrm{d}R\hat{U}^1\mathrm{d}E + \mathrm{d}R\mathrm{d}\hat{U}\mathrm{d}E. \quad (13\mathrm{b}) \\
R^2\mathrm{d}\hat{U}Z^1 &= R^2\mathrm{d}\hat{U}(D^1 + E^1 + W^1) \\
&= R^2\mathrm{d}\hat{U}(D^1 + E^1) + R^2\mathrm{d}\hat{U}W^1 \\
&= (R^1 + \mathrm{d}R)\mathrm{d}\hat{U}(D^1 + E^1) + R^2\mathrm{d}\hat{U}W^1 \\
&= R^1\mathrm{d}\hat{U}(D^1 + E^1) + \mathrm{d}R\mathrm{d}\hat{U}(D^1 + E^1) \\
&\quad + R^2\mathrm{d}\hat{U}W^1. \quad (13\mathrm{c})
\end{aligned}$$

$$\begin{aligned}
R^2\hat{U}^2 \mathrm{d}AX^1 &= R^2\hat{U}^2(A^2 - A^1)X^1 \\
&= R^2\hat{U}^2 A^2 X^1 - R^2\hat{U}^2 A^1 X^1 \\
&= R^2\hat{U}^2 A^2 X^1 - R^2\hat{U}^2 A^1 X^1 + R^2(I - \hat{U}^2 A^2)X^1 - X^1 \\
&= R^2\hat{U}^2 A^2 X^1 - R^2\hat{U}^2 A^1 X^1 + R^2 X^1 - R^2\hat{U}^2 A^2 X^1 - X^1 \\
&= R^2 X^1 - R^2\hat{U}^2 A^1 X^1 - X^1 \\
&= R^2\hat{U}^1(D^1 + E^1 + W^1) - R^2\hat{U}^2 W^1 - R^1\hat{U}^1(D^1 + E^1) \\
&= R^2\hat{U}^1(D^1 + E^1) + R^2\hat{U}^1 W^1 - R^2\hat{U}^2 W^1 \\
&\quad - R^1\hat{U}^1(D^1 + E^1) \\
&= (R^2 - R^1)\hat{U}^1(D^1 + E^1) - R^2(\hat{U}^2 - \hat{U}^1)W^1 \\
&= \mathrm{d}R\hat{U}^1(D^1 + E^1) - R^2\mathrm{d}\hat{U}W^1. \quad (13\mathrm{d})
\end{aligned}$$

$$\begin{aligned}
R^1\mathrm{d}\hat{U}Z^2 &= R^1\mathrm{d}\hat{U}(D^2 + E^2) + R^1\mathrm{d}\hat{U}W^2 \\
&= R^1\mathrm{d}\hat{U}[(D^1 + E^1) + (\mathrm{d}D + \mathrm{d}E)] + R^1\mathrm{d}\hat{U}W^2 \\
&= R^1\mathrm{d}\hat{U}(D^1 + E^1) + R^1\mathrm{d}\hat{U}\mathrm{d}D + R^1\mathrm{d}\hat{U}\mathrm{d}E \\
&\quad + R^1\mathrm{d}\hat{U}W^2. \quad (17\mathrm{a}) \\
R^1\mathrm{d}\hat{U}Z^1 &= R^1\mathrm{d}\hat{U}(D^2 + E^2) + R^1\mathrm{d}\hat{U}W^2 \\
&= R^1\mathrm{d}\hat{U}[(\lambda D^1 + \lambda E^1) + (\delta D + \delta E)] + R^1\mathrm{d}\hat{U}W^2 \\
&= R^1\mathrm{d}\hat{U}(\lambda D^1 + \lambda E^1) + R^1\mathrm{d}\hat{U}\delta D + R^1\mathrm{d}\hat{U}\delta E
\end{aligned}$$

$$+R^1 \mathrm{d}\hat{U}W^2. \qquad (17a)$$

$$\begin{aligned}
R^1\hat{U}^1\mathrm{d}AX^2 &= R^1\hat{U}^1(A^2 - A^1)X^2 \\
&= R^1\hat{U}^1 A^2 X^2 - R^1\hat{U}^1 A^1 X^2 \\
&= R^1\hat{U}^1 A^2 X^2 - R^1\hat{U}^1 A^1 X^2 + X^2 - R^1(I - \hat{U}^1 A^1)X^2 \\
&= R^1\hat{U}^1 A^2 X^2 - R^1\hat{U}^1 A^1 X^2 + X^2 - R^1 X^2 + R^1\hat{U}^1 A^1 X^2 \\
&= R^1\hat{U}^1 A^2 X^2 + X^2 - R^1 X^2 \\
&= R^1\hat{U}^1 A^2 X^2 + X^2 - R^1\hat{U}^2(D^2 + E^2 + W^2) \\
&= R^1\hat{U}^1 W^2 + R^2\hat{U}^2(D^2 + E^2) - R^1\hat{U}^1(D^2 + E^2) \\
&\quad - R^1\hat{U}^2 W^2 \\
&= (R^2 - R^1)\hat{U}^2(D^2 + E^2) - R^1(\hat{U}^2 - \hat{U}^1)W^2 \\
&= \mathrm{d}R\hat{U}^2(D^2 + E^2) - R^1\mathrm{d}\hat{U}W^2 \\
&= \mathrm{d}R(\hat{U}^1 + \mathrm{d}\hat{U})[(D^1 + \mathrm{d}D) + (E^1 + \mathrm{d}E)] \\
&\quad - R^1\mathrm{d}\hat{U}W^2 \\
&= \mathrm{d}R\hat{U}^1(D^1 + E^1) + \mathrm{d}R\mathrm{d}\hat{U}(D^1 + E^1) \\
&\quad + \mathrm{d}R\hat{U}^1\mathrm{d}D + \mathrm{d}R\mathrm{d}\hat{U}\mathrm{d}D + \mathrm{d}R\hat{U}^1\mathrm{d}E + \mathrm{d}R\mathrm{d}\hat{U}\mathrm{d}E \\
&\quad - R^1\mathrm{d}\hat{U}W^2. \qquad (17b)
\end{aligned}$$

$$\begin{aligned}
R^1\hat{U}^1\mathrm{d}AX^2 &= \mathrm{d}R\hat{U}^2(D^2 + E^2) - R^1\mathrm{d}\hat{U}W^2 \\
&= \mathrm{d}R(\hat{U}^1 + \mathrm{d}\hat{U})[(\lambda D^1 + \lambda E^1) + (\delta D + \delta E)] \\
&\quad - R^1\mathrm{d}\hat{U}W^2 \\
&= \mathrm{d}R\hat{U}^1(\lambda D^1 + \lambda E^1) + \mathrm{d}R\mathrm{d}\hat{U}(\lambda D^1 + \lambda E^1) \\
&\quad + \mathrm{d}R\hat{U}^1\delta D + \mathrm{d}R\mathrm{d}\hat{U}\delta D + \mathrm{d}R\hat{U}^1\delta E + \mathrm{d}R\mathrm{d}\hat{U}\delta E \\
&\quad - R^1\mathrm{d}\hat{U}W^2. \qquad (17b)
\end{aligned}$$

References

Celasun, M. (1983), "Sources of Industrial Growth and Structural Change: The Case of Turkey," *World Bank Staff Working Paper*, no. 614, World Bank, Washington, DC.

Chenery, H.B. (1960), "Patterns of Industrial Growth," *American Economic Review*, 50, pp.624–54.

——— (1979), *Structural Change and Development Policy*, Oxford University Press, Oxford.

——— (1980), "Interactions between Industrialization and Exports," *American Economic Review, Papers and Proceedings*, pp.281–87.

——— and M. Syrquin (1980), "A Comparative Analysis of Industrial Growth," in: R.O.C. Matthews, ed., *Economic Growth and Resources*, Vol.2, Macmillan, New York, pp.223–57.

———, Shuntaro Shishido and Tsuenhiko Watanabe (1962), "The Pattern of Japanese Growth, 1914–1954," *Econometrica*, 30, pp.98–139.

Denison, E. (1967), *Why Growth Rates Differ: Post War Experience in Nine Western Countries*, The Brookings Institution, Washington.

Dervis, K. and S. Robinson (1990), "The Sources and Structure of Inequality in Turkey (1950–1973)," in: E. Ozbudun and A. Ulusan, eds., *The Political Economy of Income Distribution in Turkey*, Helmes and Meier, New York.

Eysenbach, M.L. (1969), "A Note on Growth and Structural Change in

Pakistan's Manufacturing Industry 1954–1964," *The Pakistan Development Revew*, 9 (1), pp.58–65.

Fane, G. (1971), "Import Substitution and Export Expansion: Their Measurement and An Example of Their Application," *The Pakistan Development Review*, 11 (1).

────── (1973), "Consistent Measures of Important Substitution," *Oxford Economic Papers*, 25 (2).

Kubo, Y., S. Robinson and M. Syrquin (1986), "The Methodology of Multisector Comparative Analysis," in: H.B. Chenery et al., eds. *Industrialization and Growth: A Comparative Study*, Oxford University Press, Oxford, pp.121–47.

Lewis, S. R., Jr. and R. Soligo (1965), "Growth and Structural Change in Pakistan's Manufacturing Industry, 1954–1964," *The Pakistan Development Review*, 5 (1), pp.94–113.

Robinson, S. (1971), "The Sources of Growth in Less Developed Countries: A Cross-Section Study," *Quarterly Journal of Economics*, Aug., pp.392–408.

Syrquin, Moshe (1976), "Sources of Industrial Growth and Change: An Alternative Measure," *Paper presented at the European Meeting of the Econometric Society*, Helsinki.

3 Financial Dualism and Economic Development

Introduction

For more than four decades, Taiwan's economic performance has been remarkable. Rapid economic growth has been achieved with price stabilization and full employment. The average real GNP growth rate has been 8.9 per cent per annum; except for two brief periods of oil crises, inflation rates have hovered round 3 per cent per annum; for the past two decades, unemployment rates have been as low as 2 per cent. As a result of these achievements, per capita income has increased from US$100 in the immediate postwar period to US$8,000 in in 1990. Not only has income multiplied, but the industrial structure has also been radically transformed.[1]

However, in contrast with the outward-oriented and rapid industrialization, Taiwan's financial sector has been surprisingly closed and heavily protected. This paper will attempt to provide a theoretical and empirical explanation for such an apparent contradiction. How could a rapidly developing real sector co-exist with such a backward financial sector? How were these two features related?

To answer these questions, we need to start with a succinct review of Taiwan's financial development during the past four decades. History clearly indicates that the formation and change of Taiwan's financial sector, financial market and financial structure have been a function of government policy. Business and operational conditions of any financial institution require government approval. The pricing of financial services had been standardized. In the 1980s interest rates for deposits and loans were gradually deregulated. But even after deregulation[2], interest rates continue to deviate from market equilibrium rates and are characteristic of "collusive pricing" due to insufficient competition in the financial sector. This collusive market structure is constructed under the control of entry barriers and ownership of banks by the government. Hence financial repression, a phenomenon so prevalent in developing countries, is still a feature of Taiwan's financial sector.[3]

Under financial repression, financial demand of the community necessarily exceeds credits allocated through the organized financial market.[4] In other words, whenever financial prices are restrained and financial competition is insufficient, loanable funds that the organized financial sector are able to raise will be inadequate to meet the financial needs of the community - a condition of overdemand and undersupply at existing prices. Unorganized financial markets (or kerb markets) are developed to fill the gap. The co-existence of organized (or formal) and unorganized (or informal) financial markets is described as a "dual financial system". The dual system certainly indicates financial backwardness compared with the western industrialized countries. But the key question is whether this dual system hinders economic and social development? Tsiang (1956) and Shaw (1973) argue that under some conditions, informal financial sector augments total loanable funds, hence are conducive to economic growth. Such a proposition basically regards organized and unorganized financial markets as complementary rather than mutually displacing. The policy implication of such a view is clear: financial policy should not aim at suppressing the kerb market but rather should promote the development of the organized market. However, if organized and unorganized financial markets displace rather than complement each other, then the correct financial policy would be geared towards eliminating kerb markets. The discussion on the relationships between organized and kerb markers as such can shed light on the puzzle. This paper examines the coexistence of economic performance and financial backwardness, whether the two financial markets are complementary, and whether non-suppression of the kerb market facilitates economic development. Kerb markets then become a solution to the problem of inadequate intermediation in the organized market.

Is Taiwan's financial sector a complementary dual system? Empirical studies testing this hypothesis will be a major exercise of this paper. If Taiwan has a complementary dual financial system, then is this system positively correlated with the efficiency of the credit allocation in the organized market? If the correlation is positive, then loanable funds of the whole community may expand as a result of the dual financial system. If the correlation is negative, then loanable funds are not increased. Obviously, in the former case, improving the credit allocation function of the organized financial market will benefit economic growth. In the latter case, it will be better for an economy to tolerate inefficient credit allocation in the organized financial market.

It is clear that we need to test the efficiency of credit allocation of Taiwan's state-owned banks. In such a test, we will also have to study the loan-approving behaviour of the banks. We will construct a "risk-utility model" to analyse the decision-making process of credit-allocators. Such a model should endogenize the abovementioned distinct features of Taiwan's financial sectors; for example, the market structure of this sector would be one of collusive monopoly. From this model, we can assess whether credit allocators approve loans based on the efficiency of using capital. According to our theoretical model, the answer is probably negative. Is this hypothesis empirically sustainable?

To explain the relationship between economic development and the financial sector, we need to start with some premises.

- Taiwan's economic performance has been remarkable.
- Taiwan's financial sector is backward, primarily due to government controls and the resulting collusive monopoly.

- As a result of government control, a dual financial system has evolved.
- Because of the collusive monopoly of state-owned banks, credit allocators will be, from either theoretical or empirical perspective, conservative in their lending behaviour, hence reducing the efficiency of credit allocation.

From the above premises, we can infer that Taiwan's dual financial system is one of complementarity rather than displacement. Also, the efficiency of credit allocation in organized financial markets is negatively related to the complementary dual financial sector. Such an analytical framework implies that backward financial dualism and financial repression can go hand in hand with rapid economic growth, and that low efficiency of the organized financial market is not a hindrance to economic growth. However, once the financial sector is deregulated and liberalized, the major premise of this model may not be tenable. That is, in a liberalized and deregulated financial sector, the dual financial system may turn into one of displacement and competition rather than complementarity between the two markets. The conclusion that this paper will reach may not be applicable to the post-liberalization period.

The second section of the paper reviews the course of Taiwan's financial development in the past forty years so that we can understand the change from tight credit control to the beginning of liberalization. We will also provide a quantitative description of the structure of the dual financial system. The third section explores the relationship between organized and unorganized financial markets. The forth section attempts to construct a decision-making model to analyze the lending behaviour of credit allocators. The fifth section describes banks' credit allocation and uses regression analysis to test the decision-making model constructed in the previous section. The analysis reveals the inefficiency of the conservative credit allocation of state-owned banks. The final section draws several conclusions from the analysis.

Taiwan's dual financial system and its development

A review

After half a century of Japanese colonial rule, Taiwan was returned to the government of the Republic of China in 1945. Japanese colonial enterprises, land and houses were mostly nationalized, making the Nationalist government - which relocated itself to Taiwan in 1949 - the largest owner of public land, enterprises, and banks. Because hyperinflation and financial instability were major reasons for the government's debacle on the mainland, the leadership was very discreet, even conservative, in managing the financial sector.

Cheng (1991) gives a chronological description of Taiwan's financial development between 1945 and 1991. Basically it covers the establishment of financial institutions and financial markets, as well as policy changes affecting exchange rates and interest rates. History shows that the state-dominated financial sector was derived from the confiscation and reorganization of Japanese banks and insurance companies into provincial government-controlled banks, as well as the gradual installation of banks relocated from the mainland. Savings and loan companies and credit cooperatives managed by Chinese during the colonial period continued to be in private hands. Between 1976 and 1978, savings and loan companies, however, were transformed into enterprise banks serving small and medium-sized companies.

The Taiwan authorities, despite four decades of requests to open up the financial sector, not only from nationals but also from overseas Chinese and foreign governments, have displayed a mentality of resistance and conservatism. Under strong pressure from all sides, some concessions were made, mostly politically motivated (see Cheng's analysis in more detail on this view).

- Special permission was granted for the establishment of insurance (1962) and trust and investment companies (1970–72). Licences were limited, so was their duration. The policy for extending special permission can only be understood in the political context.

- Farmers' associations and fishermen's associations, both playing an important role in local elections, have been permitted to form credit divisions, which have become a critical link in grass-roots financial activities. These credit divisions were also privileged to extend their branches to rural areas.

- Due primarily to American pressure, many foreign banks and insurance companies have been established in Taiwan, especially during the 1980s. By the end of the 1990, there were thirty-five branches of foreign banks, exceeding the number of domestic banks. As to foreign insurance companies, permits have been issued to Americans only. So far eight branch offices of American life insurance companies have reached the market, rivalling an equal number of local companies.

State-owned banks (including commercial and specialized banks), private banks, small and medium regional enterprises (SME) banks, and local financial institutions (credit cooperatives and credit divisions of farmers' and fishermen's associations) are "monetary institutions" in that they can accept cheque (or demand) deposits. In contrast, trust and investment companies, postal savings, and insurance companies fall into the category of "other financial institutions". All these financial institutions, except insurance companies, primarily perform the function of intermediation between savers and fund users - the latter may include families, enterprises, and even the government. Financial intermediation as such facilitates so-called "indirect finance".

Direct finance goes through the capital market (bonds and stocks) and the money market. A formal capital market started in 1961, following the formation of the Taiwan Stock Exchange. The emergence of the Fu Hua Stock Financial Company in 1980 legalized lending for stock exchanges. The advent of newly admitted security companies since 1988 coincided with the massive monetary supply released after the large-scale appreciation of the New Taiwan dollar (NT$), creating an explosively hectic stock market - at one point, the turnover surpassed any other market in the world. Upon the recommendation of renowned scholars, the money market came into being in 1976, and has developed into a significant market where three bills' exchange companies trade treasury bills and other financial instruments.

Apart from the creation of financial markets and institutions, other factors also affect the efficiency of the financial sector, including the number of firms in the financial sector, the scope of their business operation, the enforcement of financial regulations, the difficulty of financial innovation, and the degree of freedom of price adjustment. Taking all these factors into account, Taiwan has a highly regulated financial industry. However, currency appreciation (from US$1 to NT$38 to 1:27 ratio) since 1986, as a result of long-term trade surpluses (especially vis-a-vis the United States) has begun to impact on Taiwan's financial sector. Financial liberalization has accelerated, including the deregulation of interest rates. Nearly all restrictions on interest rates were lifted (see footnote 2), but the rates are still not at the market equilibrium level, primarily due to inadequate competition among financial institutions. Other restrictions, including the bans on new institutions, new branches, and new business lines, as well as the over-regulation of state-owned banks (details below), still remain. However, a breakthrough was recently recorded. The Ministry of Finance has ratified fifteen applications for new banks which are expected to enter the market in 1992. Meanwhile, a policy allowing trust and investment companies to transform themselves into banks seem to be under way. These new policy measures will certainly leave deep imprints on the financial sector. However, for the present, the dual financial system (see Figure 3.1) continues to function, because of the various restrictions detailed above.

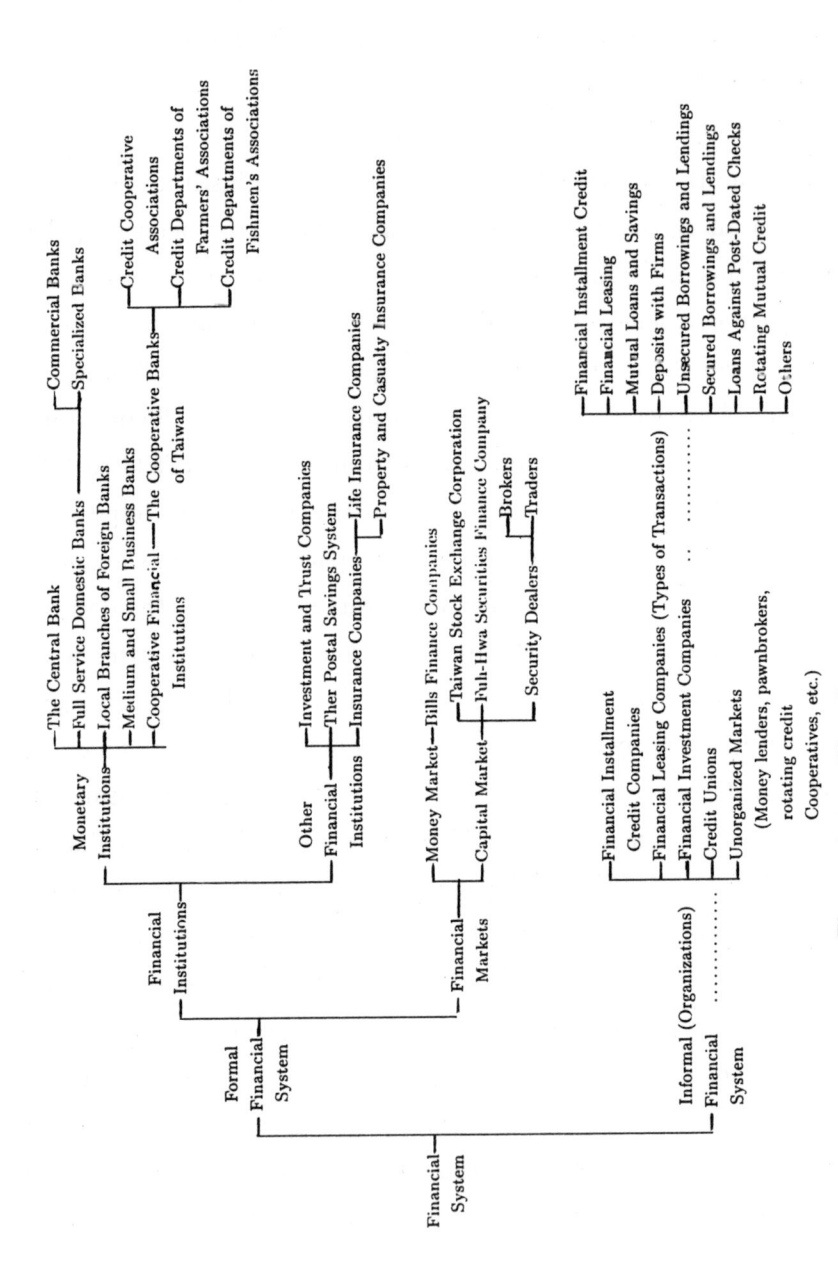

Figure 3.1 The financial system in Taiwan

The structure of financial dualism

According to Figure 3.1, the organized financial system consists in financial institutions and financial markets. Although financial instalment credit companies and financial leasing companies are legally organized, they are not permitted to do financing business which requires a Ministry of Finance licence. Therefore, these organizations are categorized into an "informal financial system" in Figure 3.1. Table 3.1 shows the numbers of various financial institutions; the units in this table are branches. Postal savings branches are widespread across the island, accounting for one-third of financial institutions in 1980. The percentage dropped in the 1980s, but still stood at 29.9 per cent in 1990. Next to postal savings are banks, including domestic ones (18.4 per cent in 1990), branches of foreign banks (about 1.1 per cent), SME banks (about 6.9 per cent), with a subtotal of 26.4 per cent. Third in terms of the number of branches is the category of the credit division of farmers' and fishermen's associations. Fourth is credit cooperatives. Postal savings branches redeposit the capital they raise in the Central Bank. Hence these institutions perform the saving function rather than the function of rationing credit.[5] Therefore banks that mediate between savers and borrowers have the most units among the financial institutions.

Certainly the number of branches does not necessarily identify the structure of the financial sector, for the obvious reasons that branches are of different scale. Table 3.2 spells out the relative structure of the financial sector in terms of assets, loans and investment, and deposits of various types of institutions. The share of domestic banks, while decreasing, is still the largest,[6] their share in total financial assets was 53.5 per cent 1990, the figures for loans and investment, and deposits were about one-third and 46.3 per cent, respectively. This reveals that domestic banks are important players in the sector, while "non-banks" are not that significant.

Table 3.1
Number of financial institutions[a]

	Total		Domestic banks		Local branches of foreign banks		Medium and small business banks		Credit cooperative associations		Credit departments of farmers' and fishermen's associations		Investment and trust companies		Postal savings system		Insurance companies	
	Units	%	Units	%	Units	%	Units	%	Units	%	Units	%	Units	%	Units	%	Units	%
1961	1,359	100.00	260	19.13	1	0.07	84	6.18	153	11.26	385	28.33	1	0.07	451	33.19	24	1.77
1970	1,827	100.00	394	21.57	7	0.38	118	6.46	222	12.15	393	21.51	6	0.33	610	33.39	77	4.21
1980	2,830	100.00	536	18.94	21	0.74	165	5.83	274	9.68	724	25.58	26	0.92	952	33.64	132	4.66
1990	4,020	100.00	741	18.43	43	1.07	279	6.94	473	11.76	1,052	26.17	53	1.32	1,205	29.98	174	4.33

Sources: Shea (1990: 4, Table 1): Ministry of Finance. *Yearbook of Financial Statistics of the ROC*, 1990.

[a]The Central Bank of China and the Central Reinsurance Corporation which do not have financial business with the general public are excluded.

Table 3.2

Shares of financial institutions at end of year[a]

	Total assets				Loan and investment[b]				Total deposits[c]			
	1961	1970	1980	1990	1961	1970	1980	1990	1961	1970	1980	1990
Domestic banks	80.22	70.48	64.53	53.48	81.95	76.42	67.52	62.61	75.57	65.75	55.58	46.25
Local branches of foreign banks	0.88	2.95	5.49	2.93	0.40	3.05	7.58	3.38	0.03	1.54	0.32	1.10
Medium-and-small business banks	3.09	4.37	3.71	7.37	3.76	4.92	4.82	9.18	4.90	5.24	4.55	7.42
Credit cooperative associations	7.52	7.97	6.84	9.22	7.06	7.10	7.03	8.47	10.13	10.54	10.65	11.50
Credit department of farmers' and fishmen's associations	5.21	5.08	5.02	6.87	4.66	4.35	4.71	5.80	5.91	5.42	6.96	8.26
Investment and trust companies	1.33	1.44	4.29	4.36	1.58	1.98	6.32	5.50	—	—	6.20	5.34
Postal saving system	0.84	5.80	8.33	11.70	0.32	0.47	0.17	0.17	3.38	9.70	13.65	14.90
Insurance companies	0.91	1.91	1.79	4.07	0.27	1.71	1.85	4.89	0.08	1.81	2.09	5.23
Total	100.00	100.00	100.00	100.00	100.00	100.00	100.00	100.00	100.00	100.00	100.00	100.00

Sources: Shea (1990: A5, Table 2): the Central Bank of China, *Financial Statistics Monthly Taiwan Districts. ROC*, various issues.

[a]The Central Bank of China is excluded.

[b]Loans and investments include loans, discounts, portfolio investments and the holdings of real estate.

[c]Total deposits include deposits held by enterprises and individuals, government deposits, trust funds, and life insurance reserves.

Particularly noteworthy is the contrast between state-owned banks and private banks regarding the number of branches. Thirteen state-owned or state-controlled banks (including six commercial and seven specialized banks) have 725 branches, three times as many as those belonging to private banks, which have 228 sub-units (Table 3.3). Moreover, saving and loans are still the major intermediation function performed by Taiwan's financial institutions, which have a very low level of securitization. Tables 3.4 and 3.5 list the share of public and private banks in total deposits and loans. In terms of lending, state-owned financial institutions accounted for 80 per cent of total lending in 1963. The corresponding figure for 1988 dropped to 66.5 per cent, but this percentage is still twice as much as that for private financial institutions. Regarding deposits, state-owned financial institutions continued to attract 65.2 per cent, while private institutions absorbed 34.8 per cent only. Of the public institutions, three provincial government-owned commercial banks (the First, Hua-Nan, and Chang-Hwa), in combination, commanded 23 per cent of total loans and 25 per cent of total deposits in the financial sector.[7] However, low concentration ratios in the banking industry should not be misunderstood as a competitive market structure, high entry barriers in such an industry enable Taiwan's banks to enjoy monopoly power.

The money market and the capital market have significantly expanded in recent years. The discounted bills in the money market amounted to NT$7.4 billion in 1976, or 1.06 per cent of GNP and 1.66 per cent of total loans and advances from financial institutions that year. By 1989, the corresponding figures reached NT$580.3 billions, 14.65 per cent and 13.27 per cent, respectively (Shea 1990: A8, Table 4). Regarding the capital market, bond-trading is still quite limited, at NT$0.88 billion in 1961, or 1.26 per cent of GNP and 4.59 per cent of total loans and advances from financial institutions that year. The size of the bond market only grew to NT$254.1 billion or 6.41 per cent of GNP and 5.81 per cent of total loans and advances in 1989 (Shea

Table 3.3

Number of banks and branches

Year	Government-owned specialized banks — Number of banks	Government-owned specialized banks — Total number of branches	Government-owned commercial banks — Number of banks	Government-owned commercial banks — Total number of branches	Private-owned banks — Number of banks	Private-owned banks — Total number of branches	Local branches of foreign banks — Number of banks	Local branches of foreign banks — Total number of branches
1962	5		4		1		1	1
1965	5		4		2		4	4
1970	6		5		2		6	6
1975	6		5		4		12	12
1978	6	198	5	340	9	105	13	13
1979	7	207	5	346	11	112	13	13
1980	7	216	5	347	11	115	21	21
1981	7	230	5	363	11	121	24	24
1982	7	242	6	366	11	128	25	25
1983	7	243	6	370	11	133	28	28
1984	7	243	6	371	11	145	31	31
1985	7	248	6	386	11	154	32	32
1986	7	257	6	389	11	167	32	32
1987	7	282	6	391	11	196	32	33
1988	7	293	6	406	11	204	32	35
1989	7	301	6	424	11	228	33	38
1990	7	311	6	433	11	252	35	43

Source: Yang (1990), Table 3, p.54.

1990:A8, Table 5). It is evident that the bond market is much smaller than the money market. Corporate debentures usually do not exceed 15 per cent of total bonds, indicating that private firms until now do not really use this instrument to raise capital.

Of all direct financial markets, the stock market has experienced the most rapid expansion and change. Table 3.6 characterizes this dramatic change. Trading value reached a record, US$970 billion in 1989. Due to the limited number of listed companies - a total of 181 only that year, the turnover rate stood as high as 590.2. A total of 307 security houses and 4.20 million investors are involved. All these features denoted the volatility of Taiwan's stock market.[8] From the viewpoint of direct finance, the stock exchange is the most critical market. Initial issues and the supplementary issues of public corporations indicate the amount of capital raised from the stock market. In 1990, nineteen new companies went public, adding NT$20.5 billion (US$774 million) market value of stock to the market. The market value for 164 additional issues from the existing public corporations were NT$77.7 billion (US$2.91 billion). Combining these two categories gave a total of NT$100 billion, which indicated the amount of capital raised by 199 corporations via the capital market in 1990. But capital thus raised accounted for only 2.2 per cent of total loans and advances from financial institutions; and this amount was even lower than the trading value in bond and money markets. In other words, while the trading value of Taiwan's stock exchange closely trailed that in Tokyo and New York[9], the capital raised from this market remained limited. While the funding amount for individual public corporations is not small, the total amount for the corporate world was negligible, indicating that Taiwan's stock market still has great potential to expand.

Thus far we have described only the organized financial system. The question still remains as to the size of private lending. We can examine this issue from two angles, the demand side - the structure of corporate capital, and the supply side - the contribution of household savings to

Table 3.4

Loans of government and financial institutions (NT$ million)

Year	Government financial institutions Amounts	Share(%)	Three major commercial banks Amounts	Share(%)	Private financial institutions Amounts	Share(%)	Total
1963	17,421	79.939	4,647	21.32	4,372	20.061	21,793
1964	21,166	77.951	5,418	19.95	5,987	22.049	27,153
1965	25,905	77.690	6,420	19.25	7,439	22.310	33,344
1966	29,807	76.844	7,847	20.23	8,982	23.156	38,789
1967	36,040	77.301	11,231	24.09	10,583	22.699	46,623
1968	45,610	78.776	15,449	26.68	12,288	21.224	57,898
1969	57,050	79.436	20,653	28.76	14,769	20.564	71,819
1970	68,806	80.434	24,268	28.37	16,737	19.566	85,543
1971	81,260	76.245	30,656	28.76	25,318	23.755	106,578
1972	99,254	74.165	38,868	29.04	34,575	25.835	133,829
1973	145,128	71.202	48,845	23.96	58,698	28.798	203,826
1974	203,275	72.738	61,452	21.99	76,187	27.262	279,462
1975	272,193	73.793	81,743	22.16	96,668	26.207	368,861
1976	335,385	73.461	112,631	24.67	121,162	26.539	456,547
1977	414,191	72.691	144,434	25.35	155,608	27.309	569,799
1978	530,342	68.730	204,231	26.47	241,244	31.270	771,636
1979	613,039	68.095	220,436	24.49	287,226	31.905	900,265
1980	714,859	66.390	240,115	22.30	361,897	33.610	1,076,756
1981	763,864	62.884	251,103	20.67	450,851	37.116	1,214,715
1982	920,367	64.760	271,144	19.08	500,840	35.240	1,421,207
1983	1,104,117	66.081	322,034	19.27	566,733	33.919	1,670,850
1984	1,249,630	66.402	357,661	19.01	632,298	33.598	1,881,928
1985	1,360,256	66.881	376,686	18.52	673,598	33.119	2,033,854
1986	1,508,406	67.399	463,011	20.69	729,606	32.601	2,238,012
1987	1,750,963	66.574	560,348	21.31	879,130	33.426	2,630,093
1988	2,358,877	66.584	824,944	23.02	197,400	33.416	3,583,277

Source: Yang(1990), Table 4, p.55.

Table 3.5
Deposits of government financial institutions[a] (NT$ million)

Year	Government financial institutions Amounts	Share(%)	Three major commercial banks Amounts	Share(%)	Private financial institutions Amounts	Share(%)	Total
1967	42,702	77.805	16,796	30.21	12,896	23.195	55,598
1968	50,134	77.277	19,995	30.82	14,742	22.723	64,876
1969	58,907	78.108	24,735	32.80	16,510	21.892	75,417
1970	68,838	78.326	28,479	32.40	19,049	21.674	87,887
1971	85,296	77.075	36,236	32.74	25,370	22.925	110,666
1972	116,270	76.310	48,265	31.68	36,096	23.690	152,366
1973	152,678	72.818	59,773	28.51	56,993	27.182	209,671
1974	188,631	73.353	69,249	26.93	68,523	26.647	257,154
1975	238,893	73.147	83,813	25.66	87,701	26.853	326,594
1976	431,237	77.548	139,786	25.14	124,852	22.452	556,089
1977	557,008	65.703	174,541	20.59	290,760	34.297	847,768
1978	726,135	73.862	241,502	24.57	256,956	26.138	983,071
1979	700,588	71.886	233,799	23.99	274,000	28.114	974,588
1980	521,221	66.845	218,671	23.53	308,120	33.155	929,341
1981	727,715	65.848	251,906	22.79	377,423	34.152	1,105,138
1982	880,230	64.888	277,662	21.74	476,309	35.112	1,356,539
1983	1,098,571	64.016	373,853	21.79	617,508	35.984	1,716,079
1984	1,316,574	63.043	444,118	21.27	771,800	36.927	2,088,374
1985	1,608,014	65.208	546,826	22.18	857,948	34.792	2,465,762
1986	1,955,664	66.617	683,339	23.28	980,023	33.383	2,935,687
1987	2,383,964	66.073	841,426	23.32	1,124,090	33.927	3,608,054
1988	2,917,980	65.183	1,118,839	24.99	1,558,565	34.817	4,476,435

Source: Yang(1990), Table 5, p.56.

[a] Postal agencies and insurance companies are excluded.

Table 3.6

Stock market statistics (NT$ million)

Year	Number of brokers, dealers & brokers branches (Brokers)	Client account Number (1000 persons)	Client account As a % of population	Number of listed companies	Total per value of listed stocks Amounts	Total per value of listed stocks As a % of total loans and discounts of financial institutions	Total markets value Amounts	Total markets value As a % of GNP	Total trading value Amounts	Total trading value As a % of GNP	Stock price index (1966=100)	Turnover rate
1962	—	—	—	18	5,940	23.09	6,840	8.88	447	0.58	—	—
1970	—	—	—	42	8,450	8.95	19,970	8.82	10,866	4.8	134.08	159.81
1980	68 (27)	362	1.88	102	108,659	10.62	219,053	14.71	162,113	10.8	546.91	107.84
1986	67 (28)	474	2.44	130	240,882	11.98	548,436	18.75	675,655	23.09	944.74	162.11
1987	67 (28)	634	3.22	141	287,346	11.87	1,386,065	42.14	2,668,633	81.14	2,135.03	267.47
1988	149 (102)	1,606	8.07	163	343,579	10.24	3,383,280	94.37	7,868,023	219.45	5,202.21	332.63
1989	307 (247)	4,208	20.15	181	421,300	9.63	6,174,164	155.66	25,407,964	640.56	5,616.14	590.24
1990	453 (373)	5,033	—	199	506,430	—	2,681,910	—	19,031,300	—	6,775.31	506.04

Source: Shea (1990). Table 7, p.A9.

capital. Table 3.7 shows that between 1964 and 1988, 53.7 per cent of capital for business was derived from financial institutions, 7.1 per cent from the money market, 14 per cent form the capital market, and 25.1 per cent from the kerb market. Table 3.8 shows the structure of household savings on the average between 1965 and 1988. The figures in this table reveal 87.4 per cent of household saving through financial institutions, while 12.4 per cent was through the kerb market; the size of the "kerb market" being 14.2 per cent of the size of "financial institutions". Household saving in financial institutions accounted for 59.7 per cent of total capital sources in the community; household saving in the kerb market amounting to 8.5 per cent; again the size of the latter being 14.2 per cent of the size of the former. In other words, viewed from the supply of funds, the size of private lending is about 14.1 per cent of the size of the financial institutions; viewed from demand for funds, lending from the kerb market is about 25.1 per cent of total lending, and about 46.8 per cent of lending from formal institutions. If a household saves $100 in financial institutions, then $14.1 flows to the kerb market. If a corporation borrows $100 from financial institutions, then $46.8 is from the kerb market. These two numbers fully characterize the dualistic nature of Taiwan's financial system. Moreover, the kerb market as a source of corporate capital financing remains as important in the 1986–88 period, indicating that the financial dualism still exists in that time.

Distinct features of Taiwan's financial system

From the above, we can observe financial repression and dualism in Taiwan's financial sector, largely as a result of the government's conservatism. To facilitate statistical analysis in the subsequent section, we shall summarize the distinct features of Taiwan's financial system as follows:

Table 3.7

Composition of business sector's financings from the financial system

Year	Financial institutions Amount	%	Money markets* Amount	%	Capital market** Amount	%	Kurb market Amount	%	Total Amount	%
1964–70	29,892	57.10	0	0.00	8,211	15.68	14,251	27.22	52,354	100.00
1971–75	138,532	67.40	28	0.01	20,071	9.76	46,917	22.83	205,548	100.00
1976–80	372,024	57.16	29,240	4.49	90,730	13.94	158,808	24.40	650,803	100.00
1981–85	789,964	52.16	160,318	10.59	210,713	13.91	353,555	23.34	1,514,550	100.00
1986–88	1,211,237	51.65	140,628	6.00	345,846	14.75	647,341	27.60	2,345,052	100.00
1964–88	413,822	53.73	54,793	7.11	108,103	14.03	193,527	25.13	770,245	100.00

Source: Shea (1990). Table 8, p.A10.

Table 3.8

Household saving through the financial system, 1965–88

	As a % of saving	As A % total sources of funds
Financial Institutions[b]	87.43	59.74
Money Market[c]	0.89	0.61
Bond Market[d]	1.71	1.17
Curb Market[e]	12.44	8.50
Total	102.47	70.02

Source: Shea (1990), Table 14, p.A18.

The relative proportion of the kerb market to the formal financial institutions is very significant in Taiwan's dualistic financial system. From the supply side of funds, the size of the kerb market is about 14.1 per cent of financial institutions; from the demand side of funds, the size of the kerb market is about 46.8 per cent of financial institutions.

Direct finance is far short of indirect finance. Domestic banks are the most important medium for indirect finance, indicating the low level of securitization and dis-intermediaton of Taiwan's financial institutions. Non-banks play a non-significant role. Traditional deposits and loans through commercial banks are still the major mode of financial intermediation. To understand the links between credit allocation and economic development, banks should be our central focus.

Until new banks join the industry, state-owned banks by any measure - number of branches, deposits, loans, and assets - will continue to be the mainstay of the banking sector. Hence the government is in a position to affect credit allocation either directly via the management of its own banks or indirectly via restrictive regulation of private banks.

So far, the overall thrust of government banking regulations remains the suspension of granting new bank licences, the application of strict criteria and reviewing processes for the formation of new branches, and the approval item by item of business operations. Moreover, staff of state-owned banks are classified as civil servants, hence personnel management, budgeting, and business management are under government regulation, practically stripping them of any managerial autonomy. The most consequential regulation pertaining to lending decisions are the ratio of non-performing loans in total loans, as well as the revenue that banks have to render to the government.

Multi-layer restriction and regulation leads to the inadequate competition among banks. Moreover, because of similar ownership structures and regulatory environments, there is a strong tendency for collusive pricing. Under this sort of collusive monopoly, interest rates do not attain the equilibrium level under a competitive market. Interest rate rigidities still exist despite the fact that the rates were largely deregulated. Table 3.9 points out the interest rate discrepancies during the period 1968–88. The gap was still as wide as 3.14 per cent on average between 1983 and 1987, and still stood at 3.36 per cent in 1988, a level higher than that in many industrialized countries of the 1960s. The gap may shrink after new banks join the market. In the absence of competition, banks in collusive monopoly have no incentive to induce savings, and have every reason to be conservative in lending. This may explain why a high proportion of capital demand, as described above, was not met by banks or financial institutions. Given this kind of market structure in the banking sector, it is a reasonable conjecture that kerb markets and financial institutions are complementary to each other in their function of meeting capital demand, an issue which we shall turn to below. Under the repression of the formal financial sector, it could intuitively deduce a benign policy to the

Table 3.9
Spread of bank interest rates (NT$ million)

Year	Interest revenue of banks [1]	Interest cost of banks [2]	Total deposits [3]	Total loans [4]	Interest rate on loans (%) [5]	Interest rate on deposits (%) [6]	Interest rate spread (%) [7]	
1968	5,964	3,880	50,576	43,277	13.78	7.67	6.11 –	
1969	7,296	4,510	59,483	54,640	13.35	7.58	5.77	
1970	9,022	5,623	70,282	67,216	13.42	8.00	5.42	– 5.11
1971	10,813	7,033	76,129	82,134	13.17	9.24	3.93	
1972	12,799	8,575	102,882	101,180	12.65	8.33	4.31 –	
1973	17,247	11,089	150,539	138,703	12.43	7.37	5.07	
1974	33,174	23,087	192,739	199,809	16.60	11.98	4.62	
1975	40,024	27,476	244,608	271,179	14.76	11.23	3.53	– 4.81
1976	45,935	28,802	387,855	347,373	13.22	7.43	5.80	
1977	44,045	30,072	579,172	430,416	10.23	5.19	5.04 –	
1978	48,946	32,665	749,669	530,954	9.22	4.36	4.86 –	
1979	76,406	44,101	859,862	664,940	11.49	5.13	6.36	
1980	102,329	61,915	846,080	813,580	12.58	7.32	5.26	– 5.28
1981	138,419	83,369	896,474	937,497	14.76	9.30	5.47	
1982	146,568	103,784	1,122,877	1,071,090	13.68	9.24	4.44 –	
1983	136,301	104,873	1,406,265	1,246,494	10.93	7.46	3.48 –	
1984	142,728	126,221	1,707,486	1,421,807	10.04	7.39	2.65	
1985	158,100	145,363	2,096,471	1,558,817	10.14	6.93	3.21	– 3.14
1986	144,374	140,472	2,584,975	1,712,740	8.43	5.43	3.00	
1987	152,105	139,259	3,168,125	1,961,519	7.75	4.40	3.36 –	
1988	178,016	146,221	3,841,859	2,483,031	7.17	3.81	3.36	

Source: Yang (1990), Table 2.2. p.75.

operation of the kerb financial market. Otherwise, the repressed financial market should hurt Taiwan's economic development.

Financial dualism and economic development

Allocation of funds under the dualism framework

As explained above, financial dualism is obviously found in the financial system of Taiwan. The main cause of this dualism is the extreme regulations by the government: the financial-demanders (seekers) cannot be satisfied from the formal (official) channels, they are forced to seek from other sources. On the other hand, when the official interest rates are lower than the market rates, and the rates in the formal sector are higher, this will attract some financial suppliers to draw out from the formal sector and turn to the other more profitable sector. This section discusses the relationship between the demanders and the suppliers in the dualistic financial system, and the relationship between this dualism and economic development.

As illustrated in Figure 3.2a, in an unregulated situation, the equilibrium transaction volume is OQ_0, the equilibrium interest rate is R_0. When the government intervenes in the market and fixes the interest rate $\bar{R}(< R_0)$, the financial demand of the whole community will be increased from OQ_0 to OQ_2, but the loanable funds are reduced to OQ_1, leading to an excess demand $Q_1 Q_2$.

If government strictly forbids the illegal financial activities, then the loanable funds in the community are limited to OQ_1, and the distribution of loanable funds is confined within this formal sector. The consequence is, when interest rates are under regulation and when the informal underground financial system does not exist, the social welfare loss due to this situation will be $\triangle ABE$.[10]

If the government tolerates underground activities, then as can be seen from Figure 3.2a, viewed from the demand side, the excess-demand $Q_1 Q_2$ will be absorbed partially by the informal sector. Viewed from

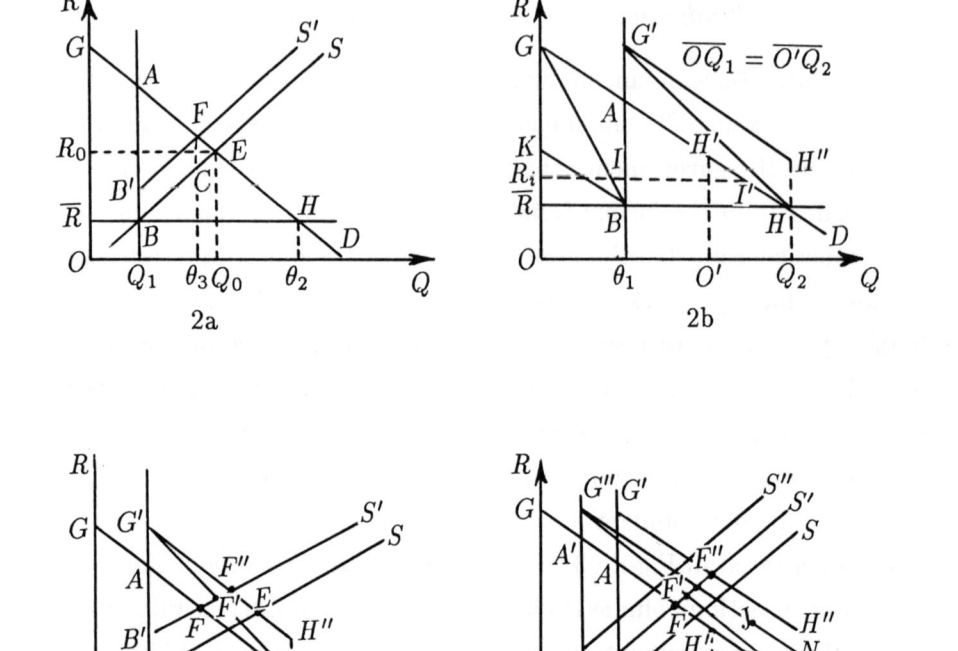

Figure 3.2 The allocation of funds under dualism

the supply side, when the deposit interest rate is restricted to $\bar{R}$, only OQ_1 loanable funds will remain in the informal sector. Naturally, risks in the informal sector are higher than in the legal sector, so that the supply curve of the informal financial sector will be BS plus a certain degree of risk premium, such as $B'S'$.

Similarly, owing to the existing of the informal financial sector, the excess demand can be satisfied from the informal sector by Q_1Q_3, so that the whole financing volume is increased to OQ_3. This is still lower than the unrestricted OQ_0, but is higher than OQ_1 (when the informal sector is forbidden). Also, social welfare loss is reduced from $\triangle ABE$ to $\triangle CEF$.

It is clear from the analysis that when the informal financial sector (kerb market) is allowed, either from the point of view of financial demand or financial supply, the two sectors (formal and informal) are in a complementary relationship rather than a mutually displacing one.

The co-existence of the dual sectors implies the underdevelopment of the financial sector, but when the two sectors are under the complementary relationship, the existence of the informal sector does not hinder economic development. On the contrary, it favours economic development. Of course, the above statement assumes financial repression; if the formal financial sector is not repressed by the government (there is no excess demand for funds in this case) the informal sector does not play such a positive role. Although the complementary relationship needs to be proven by further empirical evidence, Taiwan's sound economic performance and dual financial system seems to support this complementary relationship.[11]

If the existence of this relationship between the two financial sectors is acknowledged, one would like to understand how this mechanism functions. In fact, Figure 3.2a is an extreme case. The condition for the informal sector to attain its equilibrium point F is that the formal sector allocates credit to the fund demander whose capital efficiency is GA. In other words, the credit allocation of the formal sector is very efficient.

However, this condition could not be guaranteed in the real world. As we will see, this efficiency would influence the complementarity of the two sectors and total financing funds.

To conclude, the degree of supplementarity between the two sectors depends on the financial allocative efficiency of the formal sector. Hereunder, the analysis is on the financial allocative efficiency of the formal sector and the degree of its supplementarity with the informal sector. Three cases are discussed: (i) when the allocation is very efficient; (ii) when it is very inefficient; and (iii) when it is modestly efficient.

Allocation efficiency of the financial institution

Case 1: very efficient. As Figure 3.2b shows, suppose the loanable funds under government regulation are OQ_1 (as in Figure 3.2a). When the formal sector allocates funds very efficiently to the demander of GA, the demanders whose efficiency is between OR and Q_1A are obliged to seek their funds in the informal sector. Therefore, in the case of very efficient allocation, the demand curve of the underground financial market is AH.

Case 2: very inefficient. One can find a point O' on OQ of Figure 3.2b, and let $O'Q_2 = OQ_1$. If the formal sector allocates its resources to the demanders of HH', then this implies that the resources are allocated to the least efficient finance users. In this case, demanders whose efficiency is above $O'H'$ are forced to seek their funds in the informal sector. In such cases, the demand for the funds "crowded" into the informal sector is $G'H''$.

Case 3: modestly efficient. The above two cases are unlikely, extreme ones. In the real economy, the efficiency of the formal sector must lie between the two extreme points. Combinations within this line are countless, and for simplicity's sake, we present a representative case to illustrate the mechanism.

Supposing that anyone whose financial efficiency is above $O\bar{R}$ will obtain equal loan opportunities from the financial institutions, then when the interest rate is fixed at $\bar{R}$, one knows from Figure 3.2b that the lenders whose financial efficiency lies between $O\bar{R}$ and OG, have an average probability OQ_1/OQ_2 of receiving loans.

Also from Figure 3.2b, only R_i funds are to be allocated to the demanders whose efficiency is over OR_i so there will be $R_iI' - R_iI (= II')$ demand for funds to be crowded into the informal sector. That means the distance between GB and OG is the amount that can be obtained from the formal sector. The distance between GH and GB is the quantity "crowded" into the informal sector. Consequently, in the case of modest efficiency, the demand curve for funds in the informal sector is $G'H$.

To summarize: the demand curves for funds of the above three cases (very efficient, very inefficient and modestly efficient) are $AH, G'H''$ and $G'H$ respectively. Recall that these three curves are valid only when the government tolerates the existence of the informal financial sector.

With this understanding, now we are able to combine Figure 3.2a and Figure 3.2b into Figure 3.2c. This figure shows that when the interest rate is fixed at R, and the informal sector is allowed, we can obtain three equilibrium points, F, F' and F'', that represent the three efficiency cases as discussed above, the excess demand for funds is not satisfied in the formal sector and in turn find their needs in the informal sector. This explains the supplementing between the formal and informal sectors: when the formal sector is inefficient, it can be compensated by another informal sector; this reduces the disadvantages of the inefficiency of the formal sector. Further, this leads to a negative correlation between the complementarity of the two sectors and the efficiency credit allocation of the formal sector. This result could be intuitively understood when the more efficient fund users are crowded into the informal sector, the more easily they can find financing from the informal sector.

Discussion on the dis-intermediation effect

When the interest rate in the informal sector is higher than that in the formal sector, some financial funds should be absorbed into the informal sector. As a result, the financing intermediation function of the formal sector would decrease. This phenomenon is defined as the "dis-intermediation effect". In Figure 3.2d, we can explain how this effect works. If the financing funds $O''Q_1$ are shifted from the formal sector to the informal one, the vertical line for the informal sector is also shifted to $O''G''$. Corresponding to three cases of financial allocated efficiency (very efficient, very inefficient and modestly efficient), the demand curves for funds are $AH, G''N$ and $G''H$ respectively. Among them, $G''H$ is demand for financing funds under modest credit allocation efficiency with the disintermediation effect. Comparing it with the case without the disintermediation effect, we find that the more inefficient the credit allocation is, the more the dis-intermediation effect is. As a result, the total financing funds of the community will decrease in such cases. However, as shown in Figure 3.2d, unless the dis-intermediation effect is complete (the funds being totally absorbed by the informal sector), the above conclusion that the existence of the informal sector can augment the total loanable funds is still true. (Unless $O''Q_1 = OQ_1, F'' = F$, otherwise when $O''Q_1 < OQ_1$, then F'' should be to the right of F.)

Three conclusions can be drawn:

- In the process of economic development, the formal and informal financial sectors are complementary, rather than displacing each other.

- The degree of complementarity depends on the financial allocative efficiency in the formal sector. When the formal sector is efficient, the complementary function of the informal sector is low; and vice versa.

- The existence of the dis-intermediation effect will mitigate this complementary effect; the less efficient is the allocation, the higher is the dis-intermediation effect. However, if the dis-intermediation effect is not complete, the informal sector could still augment total loanable funds.

Bank loan decision model

Features of the banking industry in Taiwan

As explained above, banks make up the bulk of the institutions in the financial system in Taiwan. Except for a few cases, banking licences were frozen between 1950 and 1990. This highly protected industry was fully under government control, including personnel. Collusion, oligopoly, social welfare losses etc. are the expected consequences.

There are two further peculiarities.

- The main business activities of the banks are deposits and loans. Both activities are about 50 per cent of banks' assets, and have grown steadily.

- Banks prefer to lend to public enterprises and large businesses in the form of short-run loans, mortgages, etc.; lending to small and medium sized enterprises, and long-run loans, account for a small share of their operations.

These two characteristics show that Taiwan's banking activities are not very diversified, owing to very conservative policies. The oligopoly profit of this industry was on average 13 per cent during 1977 and 1988.[12] The main source of this high profit is the interest rate margin between deposits and loans which are generally over 3 per cent (Table 3.10).

With this background in mind, we will discuss the loan decisions of Taiwan's banking industry. One peculiarity in the banking industry is that the government pays special attention to bad loans with very rigid measures and auditing. Another is that the profits of the banks are determined by the government and banks' profitability is an important criterion to evaluate the managers.

Table 3.10

Structure of bank loans by terms

Year	TL(NT$ M.)	LL/TL(%)	TS/TL(%)	SS/SL(%)	LS/LL(%)
1960	9,600	27.80	63.98	27.80	55.55
1965	26,601	29.30	61.09	29.30	72.31
1970	75,284	25.68	62.43	25.68	77.32
1975	315,684	30.91	56.92	30.91	62.52
1980	680,232	38.72	56.92	38.72	61.85
1985	1,196,462	60.11	57.52	60.11	65.28
1990	3,129,496	65.88	61.19	65.88	67.79

Source: Ministry of Finance, *Yearbook of Financial Statistics of the ROC*, 1990.

TL: Total loan = LL + SL.
LL: Long-term loan.
SL: Short-term loan.
TS: Total secured loan = SS + LS
SS: Short-term secured loan.
LS: Long-term secured loan.

The basic model

A representative bank-loan decision-maker's utility (U) is a function of his initial wealth (W_0) and the changes in wealth (ΔW) due to his loan decision:

$$U = U(W_0 + \Delta W) \qquad (1)$$

His loan decision will make profits or losses to the bank and affect his own wealth (ΔW) and utility.

Let the amount of collateral be D under the loan Q, then the possible bad loan is $N = Q - D$. In the case when the loan fails, the changes in the lender's wealth would be negative and in proportion to N. The interest spread is δ, then the net interest revenue from the lending loan Q is δQ. In the case when the loan is successful, the changes in the lender's wealth is positive and in proportion to δQ.

For simplicity, we know

$U_b = U_1(\delta Q), U_1' > 0$, when the loan is successful,

and

$U_c = U_2(Q - D), U_2' < 0$, when the loan fails.

Therefore, the determinants of U_b, U_c are two factors: one is the incentive system in banks and the other is the utility function. The incentive system determines the transformation of δQ (or $Q - D$) into the changes of the lender's wealth (ΔW). The specification of the utility function determines the transformation of ΔW into utility.

Suppose his expected loan failure rate is π, from the subjective aspect, the expected utility of the loan decision is:

$$\bar{u} = \pi U_c + (1 - \pi) U_b \qquad (2)$$

When U_b and U_c are known, then $\bar{u}$ is dependent on π, and

$$\pi_c = U_b / (U_b - U_c) \qquad (3)$$

where π_c is defined as a critical rate of expected failure which is derived from the condition of $\bar{u} = 0$.

Alternatively, π is a conditional expectation, i.e. the lender collects all the borrower's information in order to decide an expected loan failure value.[13] Therefore, from the objective aspect, the related information on the borrower's credit is as follows. Let FS be the financial statement demonstrating the borrower's financial situation, i.e. profit and financial ratios, Q the amount of the loan, BC as the business cycle indicating the economic or industrial environment. RE is the relationship with the bank, then

$$\pi = \pi(\underset{-}{FS}, \underset{+}{Q}, \underset{-}{BC}, \underset{-}{RE}) \qquad (4)$$

(signs under the variables indicate their relationship with π). It is easy to say that a sound financial statement and good industrial situation would reduce probability of default. The credit relationship, the learning effect, has a cumulative formation. Therefore, FS, BC and RE have the negative sign.

FS is a key variable to represent the borrower's credit condition. Unfortunately, as shown by Patrick (1990), the lack of credit information has been the most severe difficulty in the financial development of Taiwan. Because the credit information collection is very costly and with significant economies of scale, this should be constructed in a cooperative manner by the whole banking industry and cannot be done well by an individual bank. However, even until now, owing to the existing excess-demand in the loan market, there is not any pressure to push Taiwan's banking industry to cooperatively construct this credit information system. Therefore, there is no faith in the financial statements provided by private enterprises, on the one hand. And, on the other hand, it is customary that private enterprises prepare two or even three editions of the financial statements for the tax authority, the banks, and the owners, respectively. Because of the lack of access to the financial statements, the expected value of π would be very high in general. In such a case, the banks emphasize collateral in deciding their credit rationing.

The branches of foreign banks in Taiwan have experienced a relatively high ratio of non-performing loans,[14] when they try to make a loan decision according to the borrower's financial statement and without asking for collateral. After this experience foreign banks in Taiwan also changed their loan policies. Therefore, collateral is the most important factor in the loan policy.

From the above discussion, one can construct a flow chart of the decision-making process of bank loans:

```
Credit information  →  FS   →  π  →  ū = πU_c + (1 − π)U_b
    system             Q
                       BC
                       RE
```

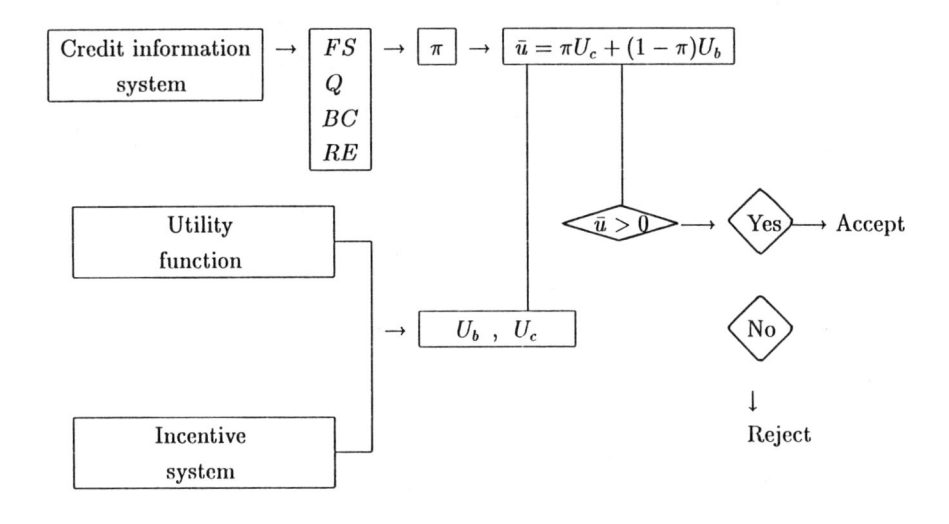

Figure 3.3   The flow chart of credit allocation

Regulation of bad loans and profits

As shown above, the incentive system of the banks is a crucial factor in the decision-making process of bank loans. For most of the government-owned banks, two requirements are very important tools in the incentive system. One is the regulation of bad-loan ratios, and the other is the minimum profit requirement. The ratio of bad loans or overdue loans is a criterion not only for management performance, but also for a necessary condition to open new branches. For example, in June 1984, this ratio was set at less than 2 per cent for new branches. Because of the highly protected banking industry and the government's entry barriers, every branch can enlarge its market share and earn excess profit. Therefore, this regulation is effective, even private banks need to control bad-loan ratios seriously.

If the required bad-loan ratio is set at $\bar{t}$, the expected bad-loan ratio for a decision maker, N_e is

$$N_e = \pi(Q - D) \leq \bar{t}Q \tag{5}$$

After rearrangement, we obtain

$$D \geq (1 - \bar{t}/\pi)Q \tag{6}$$

Let the minimum collateral requirement D_{m1} be

$$D_{m1} = (1 - \bar{t}/\pi)Q \tag{7}$$

From equation (7), we know: the higher Q is, the higher π is; and (ii) the lower $\bar{t}$ is, the more collateral is required. In other words, the regulation on the bad-loans ratio in Taiwan's banking industry leads to a high requirement for collateral. Also, a high expected value of π due to the lack of credit information enlarges the requirement of collateral.

The profit of government-owned banks is an important source of government revenue, therefore a minimum profit requirement is a very effective tool for examining management performance. The excess profit over the required profit is a criterion to decide bonuses to all employees. The following exercise tries to present how this incentive system affects the collateral requirement. Let the minimum required profit be $\overline{PR}$, then the *ex post* relationship is

$$\delta Q - N \geq \overline{PR} \tag{8}$$

However, the required profit to influence decision making should be *ex ante*. That is, the expected profit should be

$$(1 - \pi)\delta Q - \pi(Q - D) \geq \overline{PR} \tag{9}$$

Rearranging equation (9), we get

$$D = (1 + \delta - \delta/\pi)\delta Q + (1/\pi)\overline{PR} \tag{10}$$

Equation 10 shows when the profit is required with the other things (δ, π, Q) being equal, the more collateral is also required. Again, we can define the minimum collateral requirement as:

$$D_{m2} = (1 + \delta - \delta/\pi)Q + (1/\pi)\overline{PR} \qquad (11)$$

It is easy to prove equation (7) is identical to equation (11).[15] Therefore, we know, the regulation on the bad-loan ratio has the same collateral requirement as the minimum required profit system.

In summary, the credit information system, incentive system of banks and subjective utility of lenders together determine the rationing of loanable funds. The lack of a credit information system, the strict regulation of the bad-loan ratio and the required profitability of banks lead to a very conservative behaviour in lending decisions, i.e. to require a very high ratio of collateral. This decision-making process on bank loans seems not to consider the efficiency and productivity of the borrower's use of the capital. This is the subject of the following section.

Efficiency of bank credit allocation

Credit allocation in the banks

As shown above, over 50 per cent of banking business in Taiwan is still on conventional lending rather than innovative activities, e.g. securitization of providing funds. Therefore, the intermediation function of Taiwan's banks mainly relies on lending activities; the efficiency of credit allocation could be examined. There are two angles to observe in a bank's loan allocation: one is the terms of loans, i.e. long-term vs. short-term loans and secured loans vs. unsecured loans; the other is the characteristics of borrowers, i.e. individuals, enterprises and government, large vs. small sized enterprises, different market orientation of firm borrowers, and loan allocations among different industries.

First, Table 3.10 shows the structure of banks' loans according to different lending terms, i.e. short-term vs. long-term and short-term

Table 3.11

Distribution of bank loans and discounts

Year	Total NT$ million	Government enterprises (%)	Private enterprises (%)	Individuals & others (%)	Government agencies (%)
1960	10,101	37.57	53.00	7.99	1.44
1965	27,737	24.47	56.75	15.20	3.58
1970	78,064	17.52	63.95	12.68	5.85
1975	319,596	18.90	65.92	11.12	4.07
1980	693,599	24.38	50.89	22.65	2.09
1985	1,221,410	18.72	43.69	34.43	3.16
1990	3,141,678	8.30	40.64	41.85	9.20

Source: Ministry of Finance, *Yearbook of Financial Statistics of the ROC*, 1990.

secured vs. long-term secured. The borrowers of short-term loans need to pay interest only, but long-term borrowers pay by instalment. Hence it is more welcome to arrange a short-term loan for Taiwan's private enterprises whose working capital is generally limited. For the banks, an expected failure of short-term loans is less important than a long-term loan. Therefore, the lower share of short-term loans is only to be expected. However, this trend has been dramatically changed since 1985 as a result of a huge increase in the money supply. It is impressive that the ratio of secured loans to total bank loans has been around 57–64 per cent, in the period 1960–90. This also reveals the banks conservatism in rationing funds.

Second, Tables 11–15 describe the characteristics of bank borrowers. These findings can be summarized below.

Private enterprises received 41–66 per cent of banks' loans in the period 1960–90; the share of loans borrowed by public enterprises fluctuated in the same period (see Table 3.11). However, the government borrowed less than 10 per cent of bank loans in that period. If we want

Table 3.12

Loans to small and medium sized enterprises

Year	Loans to SMEs (NT$ millions)	Shares of total loans (%)
1972	21,739	22.71
1975	60,797	21.64
1980	214,617	31.92
1985	488,822	35.72
1989	1,220,707	35.88

Source: Small Business Integrated Assistance Centre, *Annual Report of Small Business Finance*.

Table 3.13

Percentage share of export loans

Year	EL NT$ million	EL/TL (%)	EL/SL (%)	EL/SS (%)	Export/GNP (%)
1971	5,196	5.36	7.44	13.09	31.27
1975	8,000	2.50	3.67	6.74	34.36
1980	13,367	1.93	3.21	5.96	47.83
1985	19,195	1.57	4.02	8.78	48.63
1990	18,047	0.57	1.69	3.49	41.45

Source: Ministry of Finance, *Yearbook of Financial Statistics of the ROC*, 1990.

TL: Total loans.

EL: Export loans.

SL: Short-term loans.

SS: Short-term secured loans.

Table 3.14

The distribution of bank loans and value added by industry

Year	Agricultural Loan[a]	Agricultural VA	Mining Loan	Mining VA	Manufacturing Loan	Manufacturing VA	Electricity gas & water Loan	Electricity gas & water VA	Construction of buildings Loan	Construction of buildings VA	Commercial Loan	Commercial VA	Transportation Loan	Transportation VA	Others Loan	Others VA
1960	—	32.67	—	2.57	—	21.84	—	1.90	—	4.45	—	17.57	—	5.39	—	13.62
1965	—	27.23	—	2.13	—	25.68	—	2.43	—	4.58	—	18.26	—	6.19	—	13.50
1970	—	18.08	0.69	1.57	67.61	34.11	0.00	2.84	1.56	4.54	18.03	16.93	5.70	7.03	6.41	14.90
1975	—	14.73	0.23	1.43	82.84	35.80	0.00	2.97	0.63	6.10	12.56	15.31	2.86	6.97	0.88	16.69
1980	—	8.61	0.12	1.06	79.45	40.36	0.00	2.82	1.27	7.01	14.44	14.73	2.27	6.70	2.45	18.17
1985	—	6.37	0.12	0.62	70.74	41.43	0.22	4.41	2.21	4.55	17.39	15.18	5.31	7.07	4.02	20.37
1990	—	4.31	—	0.40	—	54.02	—	2.26	—	6.60	—	11.70	—	5.12	—	15.59

Source: Ministry of Finance, *Yearbook of Financial Statistics of the ROC*, 1990.

[a] Loan to agricultural sector is excluded.

Table 3.15

The distribution of bank loans and value added in manufacturing industries

Year	Food VA	Food Loan	Textiles VA	Textiles Loan	Wood VA	Wood Loan	Papers VA	Papers Loan	Chemicals VA	Chemicals Loan	Non-metallic products VA	Non-metallic products Loan	Basic metallic products VA	Basic metallic products Loan	Metallic products VA	Metallic products Loan	Others VA	Others Loan
1960	41.51	—	14.91	—	4.26	—	7.20	—	11.07	—	7.15	—	4.39	—	1.46	—	8.04	—
1965	32.29	—	15.19	—	4.31	—	5.37	—	18.56	—	6.48	—	3.02	—	1.90	—	12.88	—
1970	22.98	—	16.23	—	4.30	—	4.33	—	22.37	—	4.71	—	2.89	—	2.03	—	20.15	—
1975	16.83	14.56	16.06	30.88	3.76	5.86	4.22	3.30	21.83	19.66	4.64	5.10	3.95	4.87	2.32	14.65	26.39	1.10
1980	12.33	13.73	16.40	20.85	2.92	5.25	4.61	3.86	21.07	17.99	4.58	4.56	6.49	5.95	3.90	26.18	27.70	1.63
1985	12.65	10.74	16.80	30.88	2.29	3.67	3.99	3.83	22.31	16.77	3.76	4.25	5.89	5.08	4.78	29.20	27.52	2.52
1990	10.87	—	12.19	—	1.67	—	4.40	—	22.50	—	3.00	—	6.93	—	5.17	—	33.29	—

Source: Ministry of Finance, *Yearbook of Financial Statistics of the ROC,* 1990.

to judge credit allocation among different economic agencies, it is meaningful to compare the share structure of value-added with the share of banks' loans. We found that the value-added share of public firms in the whole economy was 18.4 per cent in 1960 and 14.3 per cent in 1985, but they received bank loans of 40.8 per cent and 28.6 per cent of total loans, respectively. On the contrary, the value-added share of private enterprises was higher than their loans share. One important reason for the banks preference for public enterprises is that the government guarantees them against bankruptcy, so there is no risk of failure.

Small and medium enterprises (SMEs) in Taiwan play a very distinguished role in production, job creation and exportation, i.e. 60 per cent of employment, 45 per cent of production and 60 per cent of exports (Chou 1992). However, Table 3.12 shows the share of SMEs' borrowing as less than 30 per cent before 1980, around 30–35 per cent in 1981–85, and slightly more than 35 per cent in 1986–89. Additionally, the share of short-term loans to SMEs is over 90 per cent, but around 70 per cent in large firms (Chou 1988b, Table 10, p.34), Liu (1988, Table 4, p.9) used 1983 private firms' data to demonstrate the distribution of bank loans among different sized firms. He found the ratio of bank loans to assets on the smallest size group (the value of assets less than NT$1 million) is only 5 per cent, but the ratio in the largest sized group (with assets of more than NT$1 billion) is 28.6 per cent. On the contrary, the share of lending from the kerb market is 42.6 per cent in the smallest sized group and 4.2 per cent in the largest sized group.

Although exports are an engine for Taiwan's economic development, the share of export loans is small (see Table 3.13). Therefore, the interest rate subsidy in export loans is quite small. The lack of the banks lending to exporters leads exporters to rely on financing from the informal financial sector.

From comparing the value-added share of different industries with their share of bank lending, we find that the manufacturing industry gets a relatively high share of loans (Table 3.14). This coincides with government priorities for industrial development policy. Disaggregate industrial data is shown in Table 3.15.

In sum, the above data shows that banks prefer to lend to public enterprises, and big enterprises in the form of short-term loans. However, loans to SMEs and exporters formed a low percentage of the total. Hence it is reasonable to infer that the kerb market plays an active and important role in supporting SMEs and exporters development. The government's benign attitude towards the operation of the kerb market is a very important condition for Taiwan's dual financial system.

Testing the efficiency of credit allocation

The above descriptive data show that credit allocation by Taiwan's banks seems to be inefficient. However, this is an indirect deduction, and not supported by regression analysis.

In this empirical test, we chose the Bank Loan/External Funds ratio (BL) as the dependent variable, to test the following null hypothesis:

H_0: credit allocation is inefficient

or

H_1: credit allocation is efficient.

The model to be tested is as follows:

$$BL = a_0 + a_1 SA + a_2 PS + a_3 GR + a_4 FA + a_5 FL \; a_6 BL_{t-1} \qquad (12)$$

where

BL = bank loans/external funds

SA = sales/assets

PS = profits/sales

GR = industry's growth rate

FA = fixed assets/total assets

FL = fixed assets/external funds

BL_{t-1} is a proxy for relationships between the lender and the bank.

Every explanatory variable is expected to generate positive signs. If a_1, a_2 and a_3 are significant, then we confirm that banks are making loan decisions upon the performance, profitability and business cycles of the industry. In this case, the null hypothesis could not be accepted. If a_4 and a_5 are significant, then we confirm that bank loan decisions are conservative: more safety-oriented. In this case, the null hypothesis could not be rejected.

We used census data from *The Statistics of Revenue and Financial Structural Changes in Taiwan's Main Industries*, published by Joint Credit Information Centre, Association of Banking Industry in Taipei. The cross-section, data for one year (1986) covering seventy-nine industries are used to test the hypothesis. Using the ordinary least square technique, we obtained the following results:[16]

$$BL = \underset{(3.44)}{1.02} - \underset{(2.30)}{5.58}\,SA - \underset{(1.28)}{0.18}\,PS - \underset{(0.68)}{0.03}\,GR + \underset{(3.78)}{0.26}\,FA + \underset{(2.59)}{0.001}\,FL$$
$$+ \underset{(10.86)}{0.74}\,BL_{t-1}$$
$$R^2 = 0.8963,\ \bar{R}^2 = 0.8877 \tag{13}$$

The result shows that the former three variables (industry performance-oriented) generate unexpected negative signs, and two of the three are insignificant.[17] The other three variables (safety-oriented) generated expected positive signs and are statistically very significant. Overall, the results cannot reject the null hypothesis; in other words, bank credit allocations are not efficient in Taiwan. This is consistent with the results obtained by Shea (1990), who pooled 1965–88 data to test a similar hypothesis.

Financial dualism and market structure dichotomy

The above analysis confirms the existence of financial dualism: the co-existence of formal and informal financial sectors. What is more important is that this relates to the dichotomous market structure (DMS). DMS means that the market structure of export-oriented industries and the market structure of domestic market-oriented industries are quite distinct.[18] Export-oriented industries are mainly small to medium sized firms, market competition is quite keen, barriers to entry are low; domestic market-oriented industries are mainly large enterprises, with a higher degree of monopoly and higher barriers to entry. We try to show that export-oriented industries obtained fewer funds from the banking system, and the percentage of loans from the informal sector are significantly higher than for the domestic-oriented industries.

This phenomenon also explains why DMS exists. Bank preferences for credit allocation to favoured large, domestic-oriented industries cause the export-oriented industries to seek their funds from the informal sector, at higher interest rates. However, as everyone knows, these small, export-oriented industries contribute greatly to Taiwan's economic growth, which was paradoxically supported more by the informal sector than from the formal sector.[19] Of course, the large firms not only provide final products for domestic needs but also provide intermediate inputs to small export-oriented firms. However, the best situation to SME is that the price of these intermediate inputs are competitive with imports; even in some cases, the prices are higher than imported ones due to the protected industrial development policies toward capital-intensive large firms. Hence, there is an absence of subsidies from domestic-oriented large firms to export-oriented small firms.

Nevertheless, since 1986 the New Taiwan Dollar has been appreciatively strongly against the US dollar, and the labour movement and environment protection movement created an impact on the DMS: export-oriented industries gradually moved to other developing countries and to Mainland China; the liberalization movement in Taiwan also made previously favoured industries face the pressure of foreign competition. The banking industry has been open to free competition since 1991; fifteen new bank licences have been granted, and it is expected that the formal financial sector will gradually take over the informal sector, providing more competition and lower profits. It would be expected that the structural changes in DMS will be reinforced by structural changes in the dual financial system. Both changes can bring reinforcing benefits.

Conclusions

This paper tried to explain how Taiwan's rapid economic growth was possible when the financial sector was so backward. In other words, the financial sector was highly regulated and oppressed. How could this help Taiwan's growth performance? Our empirical evidence shows that in loan decision-making, banks were conservative, and the efficiency of credit allocation was inefficient. The regression results show that both the collateral and the past relationship between the banks and firms, rather than the borrowers' profitability performance and the industry's business cycle, were important factors in rationing credit. In our theoretical model, we argue that if the informal sector can supplement the inefficient formal financial sector, then the economy can grow strongly. The reason is, on the one hand, the competitive export-oriented industries with a lot of small firms can obtain little credit allocated by the formal financial sector. But, fortunately, this active sector can develop very well by means of funds from the informal financial sector. On the other hand, the monopolistic, domestic-oriented industries with a few large firms received major loans from the formal sector. As a result, DMS and the dual financial system are a twin system which facilitated Taiwan's economic development. However, this twin system seems to have changed since the transition stage after 1986. Both the dichotomy of the market structure and the dualism in the financial sector would be gradually terminated, and a more mature economy, market structure and financial system, could be optimistically expected.

Notes

1. The phenomenon of the over-industrialization occurred in Taiwan's industrial structure, particularly shown by the share of industrial, or manufacturing sector in GNP. The share of manufacturing value-added reached 42 per cent. However, significant structural changes have happened since 1986, the share of the service sector has risen two percentage points each year for the past three years. Since then Taiwan has entered the "post-industrialization" stage (Chou and Wu 1990).
2. The interest ceiling regulation was cancelled in the revision of Bank Law in 1989. However, it still has an interest ceiling in the present Central Bank Act. Because this ceiling is too high to effectively restrict the market interest rate, there is no regulation on interest in legal terms.
3. Concerning financial repression, please see McKinnon (1973) and Fry (1988). In many developing countries, financial repression is due to interest regulation. However, whether interest liberalization could solve the problem of financial repression is still challenged by new structuralists. Concerning these arguments, see Buffie (1984), Cho (1985, 1990), Collier and Colin (1989), Hamilton (1989).
4. The definition of an organized financial system is confined to the institutions receiving the licence from the Ministry of Finance (Liu 1984: 316). In this paper, informal sector, kerb market and unorganized financial system are exchangeably used. Concerning the dual financial system in Taiwan, see Shea (1983), Shea and Kuo (1984), Shea *et al.* (1985), Shea and Yang (1989).
5. Since 1982 the deposits of postal saving branches have been re-deposited in the Central Bank, then the Central Bank has allocated these deposits to four specialized banks (Communication Bank, China Farmer Bank, Central Trust Bank, and Taiwan SME Bank). Hence, the postal saving system has an indirect intermediation function.

6. This is because of the increase in non-banks. e.g. postal saving branches, trust and investment companies, and because of the freezing of bank licences.
7. For measurement of concentration in Taiwan's banking industry see Chou et al. (1990) and Chou (1991).
8. The phenomenon of dramatic fluctuation of Taiwan's stock market can be seen from Table 3.6.
9. At the end of 1989, the trading value of Taiwan's stock market reached US$970 billion, the Tokyo stock market was US$2,431 billion and the New York market was US$1,542 billion.
10. In the case of very efficient credit allocation, the welfare loss is ΔABE, otherwise the welfare loss should be larger than ΔABE. Concerning the relationship between social welfare and efficiency of credit allocation, see Shea and Kuo (1984) and Liu (1984).
11. Concerning the argument of substitution and complementarity between formal and informal financial sectors, see Yu (1991), Liu (1984), Lin and Chu (1989).
12. The profit-sales ratio, on the average in 1977–88 was 7.88 per cent for public-owned specialized banks, 14.55 per cent for public-owned commercial banks, 15.86 per cent for private commercial banks, and 13.44 per cent for foreign banks (Yang 1990:36, Table 7).
13. Here the expected failure ratio is a behaviour of rational expectation.
14. The non-performing loan ratio in 1977–88, on average, was 8.81 per cent for foreign banks, 4.41 per cent for public-owned commercial banks, 4.65 per cent for public-owned specialized banks, and 4.81 per cent for private commercial banks (Yang 1990, Table 9–12).
15. This can be proven as follows: $(7) - (1) = D_{m1} - D_{m2} = 1/\pi[(1-\pi)\delta Q - iQ - \overline{PR}] = 0$, because the first term in $[\cdot]$ is expected revenue, the second term is expected bad loan loss; and the difference between these two terms should be required profit $(\overline{PR})$.

16. In the process of empirical exercises, many other independent variables and alternative proxy variables are tried. Even the variables in time-lag are also used. However, only the best result is presented here.

17. It is not easy to explain why the sign of SA is significantly negative, because this is invalid from the theoretical point of view. However, this again highlights that performance-oriented variables could not be good factors to be considered in lending decisions.

18. Concerning the hypothesis of the dichotomous market structure, see Chou (1986, 1988a). Recently, Chen (1991) also supported this hypothesis by studying the dynamic process of industrial concentration.

19. The operation of the informal sector in Taiwan's financial system is an interesting and important issue, but the discussion of this topic in detail would exceed the context of this paper. However, some information can be found in Figure 3.1.

References

Buffie, E.F. (1984), "Financial Repression, the New Structuralists, and Stabilization Policy in Semi-industrialized Economies," *Journal of Development Economics*, 14, pp.305-22.

Chen, G.L. (1991), "Dynamic Adjustment of Market Concentration - the Impact of Industry Policy," *Conference on the Political Economics*, Chinese Economic Association, Taipei (in Chinese).

Cheng, T.J. (1991), "Guarding the Commanding Heights: the State as Banker in Taiwan." Paper presented at *Government, Financial System and Economic Development: A Comparative Study of Selected Asian and Latin American Countries*, at the East-West Center, Hawaii.

Cho, Y.J. (1986), "Inefficiencies from Financial Liberalization in the Absence of Well Functioning Equities Markets," *Journal of Money, Credit and Banking*. 18 (2), pp.191–99.

——— (1990), "McKinnon-Shaw versus the Neostructuralists on Financial Liberalization: A Conceptual Note," *World Development*, 18 (3), pp.477–80.

Chou, T.C. (1986), "Concentration, Profitability and Trade in a Simultaneous Equation Analysis: the Case of Taiwan," *Journal of Industrial Economics*, 34 (3), pp.429–41, also the chapter 5 of this book.

——— (1988a), "Concentration and Profitability in a Dichotomous Economy: the Case of Taiwan," *International Journal of Industrial*

Organization, 6 (4), pp.409–28, also the chapter 6 of this book.

―――― (1988b), "Loans to SMEs and Economic Development in Taiwan," *Taiwan Community Financial Journal*, 17, pp.17–41 (in Chinese).

―――― (1991), "A Measurement on the Concentration of the Banking Industry in Taiwan," *Bank of Taiwan Quarterly*, 42 (2), pp.40–56 (in Chinese).

―――― Hwang, P.I. and C.L. Wang (1990), "Concentration Ratios of Taiwan's Banking Industry at Branch Level," *Taiwan Community Financial Journal*, 21, pp.61–73 (in Chinese).

―――― and H.L. Wu (1990), "Industrial Structural Changes and Deindustrialization," *Free Industry of China*, 74 (4), pp.11–25 (in Chinese).

Collier, P. and C. Mayer (1989), "The Assessment: Financial Liberalization, Financial Systems, and Economic Growth," *Oxford Review of Economic Policy*, 5 (4), pp.1–12.

Fry, M.J. (1988), *Money, Interest, and Banking in Economic Development*, Johns Hopkins University Press, Baltimore.

Hamilton, C. (1989), "The Irrelevance of Economic Liberalization in Third World," *World Development*, 17 (10), pp.1523–30.

Lee, C. (1990), Government, Financial Systems and Economic Development (mimeo).

Lin, C.C. and Y.P. Chu (1989), "Interest Rates, Interactions between Dual Financial Markets," *Journal of Economic Development*, pp.107–15.

Liu, J.L. (1984), "The Intermediate Process under Dual Financial System," in *Proceedings of the Conference on Financial Development in Taiwan*, Institute of Economics, Academia Sinica, Taipei, pp.315–34 (in Chinese).

―――― (1988), "The Development and Prospects of Financial Institutions in Taiwan," in *Proceedings of the Conference on the Modernization of Services Industries in ROC*, Chinese Economic Association, Taipei (in Chinese).

McKinnon, R.I. (1973), *Money and Capital in Economic Development*, Brookings Institution, Washington, D.C.

Patrick, H.T. (1990), "The Financial Development of Taiwan, Korea, and Japan: A Framework for Consideration of Issues," Paper presented at the *Conference on Financial Development on Japan, Korea and Taiwan*, Institute of Economics, Academia Sinica, Taipei.

Shaw, E.S. (1973), *Financial Deepening in Economic Development*, Oxford University Press, New York.

Shea, E.S. (1983), "Financial Dualism and the Industrial Development in Taiwan," in *Proceedings of the Conference on Industrial Development in Taiwan*, Institute of Economics, Academia Sinica, Taipei (in Chinese).

──── and P.S. Kuo, (1984), "The Allocative Efficiency of Banks' Loanable Funds in Taiwan," in *Proceedings of the Conference on Financial Development in Taiwan*, Institute of Economics, Academia Sinica, Taipei (in Chinese).

──── Laing, M.Y., Y.H. Yang, S.H. Liu and K.M. Chen, (1985), "A Study of the Financial System in Taiwan," *Economic Papers*, No.65, Chung-Hua Institution for Economic Research, Taipei (in Chinese).

──── and Y.H. Yang, (1989), "Financial System and the Allocation of Investment Funds in Taiwan," Paper presented to the *Conference on State Policy and Economic Development in Taiwan*, Soochow University and University of California, Los Angeles.

──── and ──── (1990), "Financial Development in Taiwan: A Macro Analysis," *Conference on the Financial Development of Japan, Korea and Taiwan*, Institute of Economics, Academia Sinica, Taipei.

Tsiang, S.C. (1956), "Liquidity Preference and Loanable Fund Theories, multiplier and velocity analysis: a synthesis," *American Economic Review*, pp.539–64.

Yang, Y.H. (1990), "A Micro Analysis of the Financial System in Taiwan," *Conference on the Financial Development of Japan, Korea and Taiwan, Institute of Economics*, Academia Sinica, Taipei.

Yu, C.C. (1991), *The Effects of Interest Liberalization under the Dual Financial System*, unpublished M.A. thesis, National Chung-Hsing University.

Part II
Structure, Trade & Performance

4 The Evolution of Market Structure*

Introduction

This paper tries to investigate how economic developent influences market structure, and how the economy's mode of organization operates in the course of industrialization. In order to achieve exactness, we define economic development and market structure as follows.

Economic development is a process of relaxing growth constraints or bottlenecks in order to aim at a self-sustained growth. This is also called industrialization process for less developed countries (LDCs). The analysis of market structure implies the analysis of (1) ownership structure, scale of production and market orientation, (2) the structure of domestic and export distribution systems, and (3) the aggregate concentration and degree of monopoly.

Before observing the evolution of market structure in Taiwan's case, we need to interpret how market structure evolved in different phases of the industrialization process. Since trade patterns and trade policy are the most important factors to divide industrialization phases in Taiwan (Chou, 1985), both play an important role in influencing Taiwan's market structure. As a result, the economy's mode of market structure in the course of economic development can be determined.

---

*This paper was reproduced from *Rivista Internazionale di Scienze Economiche e Commerciali*, Vol. 35, No. 2, February 1988, pp.171–194, with permission of the publisher.

This paper is organized as follows: the first section briefly describes the characteristics of industrialization process and their effects on market structure. The evolution of ownership structure is induced theoretically. Then the structural change of ownership is studied empirically in section 2. There were differences in enterprise scale among different ownerships. Then market orientation of different ownerships is examined in section 3 to show their market power in the domestic and export markets. Inward-orientation of both public and big enterprises is impressive The domestic and export distribution systems are also studied in this section to show the existence of the dichotomy: the monopolistic domestic market contrasted to the competitive export market. Section 4 examines the evolution of aggregate concentration and degree of monopoly. However, there is no significant trend of aggregate concentration. Finally, concluding remarks are contained in the last section.

Industrialization phases and market structure

Chou (1985) divides Taiwan's industrialization process into three phases for the period 1953–80 as follows: S_2-primary IS (1953–61), S_3-primary ES (1961–75), and S_4-2nd IS cum ES (post 1975). This division is mainly based on the pattern and policy of trade. The characteristics of each phase and their effects on market structure are analyzed below.

After the evacuation of the Nationalist government to Taiwan, the main goal of economic policy was to recover plants and activities from the damages and disturbances of the Pacific War. After the end of the colonial economy's mode of operation, shortage of foreign exchange and lack of entrepreneurship were very serious. Facing the constraint of these scarctites, the government played an important role. On the one hand, the government took over Japanese private enterprises: hence public enterprises gained a high record in economic activities. On the other hand, the by-product of foreign exchange shortage, protective import substitution measures, were introduced by the government. The primary IS (S_2) phase started in 1953–61.

In that phase, there were two effects on the economy's mode of market structure. (1) Institutional barriers were raised by import licensing, i.e. who had the privilege of import permission and exchange settlement certificates could import the needed materials and intermediate goods. This created barriers to entry against potential entrants who had no such privilege. (2) Barriers to foreign entry were high to prevent import competition. Barriers at both the production and importation stages[1] sustained monopoly profits of the existing firms which had incentives to internalize excess profits on the basis of nepotistic practices by family groups. This probably created a special organizational type: the business groups for internalizing uncertainty, information, factor market flows, and excess profits.

Also, high tariffs on imported materials and equipment made exportation of processed manufactured goods difficult. This restrained the possibility of enlarging market size. Under the circumstances, inward direct investment which could share domestic monopoly profits was not welcome. Also, owing to the rise of nationalism after independence, foreign direct investment was less important in that phase.

Due to the adaptation to the repressive state in the colonial period, Taiwan's labor unions were restrained to raise wages. The factor price distortions did not seem serious. Therefore, labor-intensive production process enjoyed a comparative advantage, and import substitution was developed to nondurable consumer goods industries. This avoided the further need to increase barriers to entry.

Unfortunately, the small domestic market size constrained the economy and induced some syndrom to occur in the late 1950s. The shift of development strategy from import substitution to export substitution was the emergence of an offsetting policy package. The degree of protection in terms of import licensing and tariffs was reduced, but protective functions were sustained, and still are. Under these circumstances, exportation could not develop even with low wage rate. To export successfully a country needs to remove high tariffs on imported materials and equipment. Therefore, a tax rebate system for exportation was necessary. As shown in Chou (1985), an offsetting policy package-export incentives policies designed to neutralize the biases of import protection measures-was constructed to reach both protection and exportation simultaneously. This shift started the primary ES (S_3) phase in the early 60s in Taiwan.

In the S_3 phase, labor-intensive export industries released the constraints on market size, continued to evade relative factor price distortions, and also solved the problem of foreign exchange shortage. This induced the government to lower barriers to entry at the production stage but barriers to entry at importation stage were still high. Due to exports of standardized and taste-taker goods, and also due to no selling efforts at the export market, domestic firms faced a very comprtitive export market. This was the main cause of and reinforced a dichotomous market structure: the monopolistic domestic market was accompanied by the competitive export market.

Because private enterprises were prosperous due to low risks of export activities in that phase, the share of public enterprises, which concentrated on non-exporting industries, e.g. tobacco and wine, fertilizer, and paper making, was reduced. The foreign direct investment being high export oriented was welcome to replace U.S. aid to partly solve the problem of foreign exchange shortage. Therefore, the value of foreign direct investment (FDI) surged in phase S_3.

After the mid-1970s, industrialization was developed toward the secondary IS industries and entered the S_4 phase. In this phase, high risks accompanied by relative high technological barriers could increase barriers to entry again. Also, excess demand for entrepreneurship occurred due to high risks of these investments. As Leff (1979a) shows, this led to increasing the importance of public enterprises and business groups. Since 1974, the government increased investment in basic and heavy industries (e.g. nuclear energy plant, communication infrastructure, steelworks, shipbuilding, heavy cars plant, and the upstreams of petrochemistry). Besides, the purpose and the criteria of inward direct investment changed in this phase. Domestic market oriented FDI probably increased. All these induced the structural change of ownership.

The effects of trade on market structure depend upon the degree of easiness of these secondary IS industries to develop their secondary export substitution. If they can export successfully, it prevents barriers to entry from increasing further. Furthermore, whether more serious protective policies play government's complementary role or not was an arguable question (Chou, 1985) and also was a factor influencing ownership structure.

In sum, two significant aspects of organizational structural change can be found in Taiwan's industrialization process. The time-series aspect is the evolution of ownership structure: (1) the share of public ecterprises had a U trend at these three phases , i.e. high level in phase S_2, low level in phase S_3 and increased again in phase S_4; (2) the share of inward FDI had an inverted U trend during the S_2, S_3 and S_4 phases; and (3) the share of business groups was increasing. The cross-section aspect is that barriers to entry in the domestic market are higher than that in the export market, so that the dichotomy can emerge from the effects of market orientation and foreign/domestic distribution channel systems. Empirical evidence of the evolution of Taiwan's market structure is presented in the following sections.

The evolution of the ownership structure

In this section, we survey the changes in Taiwan's ownership structure. Some findings are interesting to note. Firstly, the trend of the relative poitions of public, foreign and the Group firms, as shown in Section 1, has a close relationship with industrialization phases.

Secondly, the relative average scale among different organizations has a distinctive pattern. Public enterprises have the largest scale, then the participants in the Group, the foreign firms, and the private firms in descending order.

Finally, the structure of Top enterprises is studied to indicate that public enterprises control important economic activities in Taiwan. The importance of state-owned banks should be noted in the analysis of Taiwan's market structure.

The structural change of ownership

The Chinese nationalist government took over Japanese private enterprises and was actually operating them in May 1946, after first consolidating those Japanese firms into 22 large public corporations (Lin, 1973, pp.27-29). During the colonial period, Taiwan's "minor" (enclaved) industrial sector was almost completely controlled by the Japanese. Therefore, as Sheaham (1976, p.205) says, the main reason why public enterprises played a major role after independence was due to a "historical accident". In Taiwan's case, it was the government taking over enterprises from the Japanese. The share of production of public firms was about two-thirds of total production in 1949.[2] This historical background gives us a fundamental reason why public enterprises had a high percentage share in the whole economy in the 50s and 60s.[3]

Table 4.1 indicates the evolution of ownership structure during 1951-81. The most meaningful phenomenon is that the percentage share of public enterprises in terms of three indices (capital formation, employee's compensation and production value) had a U trend during the whole industrialization process. That is, public enterprises held a high share during phase S_2 (1952-61), then decreased to a low record during phase S_3 (1962-75), and finally rose again after phase S_4. Particularly, capital formation from public enterprises in phase S_4 was higher than in phase S_2. This indicates that investment activities since S_4 were turning to relative capital- and technology-intensive types. This shift bears much risk and uncertainty and then leads to excess demand for entrepreneurship. The excess demand is alleviated by the 'substitutive role' of public enterprises. The U trend of percentage share of public

Table 4.1

The structural change of ownership, 1951–1981 (percentage)

Average	Public enterprises		Foreign firms		The Group[1]	
	Capital formation	Employee's compensation	Production value	Capital formation	Employees	Turnover
1951–61	43.4	20.6	20.8	1.9	—	—
1962–75	34.9	14.5	16.5	5.5	16.0	27.3
1976–81	46.4	14.6	17.1	3.0	16.5	30.2

Sources: 1. Directorate-General of Budget, Accounting & Statistics (DGBAS), Executive Yuan, *National Income of the Republic of China*, 1981, Tables 6, 7 and 17, pp.137, 140–45 and 182–89.
2. Foreign Investment Commission, Ministry of Economic Affairs, *Statistics in Overseas Chinese & Foreign Investment, Technical Cooperation, Outward Investment*, R.O.C., 1981.
3. China Credit Information Services, *Studies on Group Enterprises in Taiwan*, 1982, pp.24–35.

[1] The average data for the concerned period come from: 1972 and 1974 for the period 1962–75; 1976, 1978 and 1980 for the period 1976–81.

enterprises during the industrialization process verifies the deduction of Section 1.

Foreign direct investment was not welcome when Taiwan was newly independent, due to the rise of nationalism and the excess profits due to protection. Then, in order to replace U.S. aid to solve the problem of foreign exchange shortage, the government changed his attitude and welcomed FDI since the 60s (Wu et al., 1980, pp.15–32). Also, in order to protect domestic firms from the competition of multinationals at home, export-oriented FDI were more welcome than domestic market-oriented FDI. This led to the surge of FDI during phase S_3. Table 4.1 confirms this expectation, i.e. the contribution ratio of FDI to domestic capital formation was 1.9%, 5.5%, and 3% during phases S_2, S_3, S_4 respectively.

In the whole period, there was a minor record of outward foreign investment from Taiwan: no record in 1951–61, less than US$ 2 million of annual average amount in 1962–75, and US$ 14 million in 1976–81. The total amount of outward foreign investment was only 3.6% of inward foreign investment during the last three decades. According to Dunning's (1981) eclectic theory, net outward investment of developing countries corresponds to their different development stages. In Taiwan's case outward foreign investment is still less important and can therefore be neglected.[4]

The data of Taiwan's business groups dated from 1972.[5] There were no data on the situation of business groups in phase S_2. However, a significantly increasing trend of the "Group" was found in phases S_3 and S_4. This seems to confirm the expectation that the Group is a special organizational type solving partly the problem of "basic scarcity".[6] That is, business groups are also a supplementary way to fill up the shortage of entrepreneurship.

Characteristics and incentives to organize the Group in Taiwan are similar to that of other LDCs. That is, "participants (of the Group) are people linked by relations of interpersonal trust" (Leff, 1978, p.663). In Taiwan's case, the interdependence among participants of the Group is on the basis of nepotistic practices or family groups.[7] In this case, it seems plausible to expect that "industrial groups increase the concentration of sales in markets" as shown by Encaoua and Jacquemin (1982, p.48).

Liu et al. (1981, pp.12–13) made a survey in Taiwan to see the incentives to organize business groups and found that (1) entering new industries (100%),[8] (2) training successors (80%), (3) receiving tax benefits (80%), are the most important factors. Among them, reason (3) is a result of Taiwan's tax system which permits five year tax holidays for new enterprises. Reasons (1) and (2) verify the conclusion of Leff (1978, p.671), that is, "reinforce(ing) a group's propensity for entrepreneurial expansionism" is an important incentive to organize business groups.

Comparative analysis of scale among ownerships

Studies of the influence of ownership structure on market power should consider scale. Table 4.2 compares enterprise scale of the 1976 manufacturing sector among all firms, public firms, foreign firms and firms in the Group. It is very clear that the average scale of public enterprises is the largest in terms of operating assets, persons engaged and turnover. Also, we can measure the K/L ratio and find that public enterprises are 4 times above average.

The average scale of the individual participants of the Group was larger than that of foreign firms and the whole manufacturing, but smaller than the average scale of public enterprises. It is interesting to find that the scale of foreign firms is not so large. Particularly, the low K/L of foreign firms should be mentioned. This is partly because of the different base of data (fixed assets being used to replace assets). However, this probably reveals the aim of foreign firms coming to Taiwan was the domestic low cost advantage at that time. This point will be confirmed later.

Lin (1981, Table 4.2) in addition shows that there was a significant distinction of scales among the members of the Group. The *Formosa Plastics Corporation* group maintained its leading position throughout the period from 1972 to 1980. The turnover of the *Formosa Plastics* group in 1980 was NT$ 59,479 million, contributing 4.1% to GNP. There were eight groups whose individual turnover was over 1% of GNP in 1980 and their total turnover reached 15.32% of GNP and a half of all Group's turnover. More than 90 other groups shared another half of total Group's turnover.

Structure of top enterprises

In the case of most LDCs, public enterprises do not exist only in the manufacturing or industrial sectors. Public enterprises also play an important role in the service sector, e.g. in banking, transportation and communication. Table 4.3 reveals the numbers of public enterprises in

Table 4.2
Number of firms and their characteristics on manufacturing industries,[1] 1976

	Total manufacturing	Public enterprises	Foreign enterprises	Group's enterprises
Numer of firms	69,517	89	988	673
Average size in terms of				
– Assets in operation (NT$ million)	15.1	3,474	119.3[2]	375.5
– Employees (persons)	27	1,493	266	446
– Turnover (NT$ million)	11.3	1,445.1	137.9	289.6
K/L ratios[3] (NT$ thousand persons)	599	2,327	449	842

Sources: 1. DGBAS, Executive Yuan, *National Income of the Republic of China*, 1981, Tables 6, 7 and 17, pp.137, 140–45 and 182–89.

2. China Credit Information Services, *Studies on Group Enterprises in Taiwan*, 1982, pp.24–35.

3. The Committee on Industrial and Commercial Censuses of Taiwan-Fukien District of the Republic of China (ICCT), Executive Yuan, *The Report of 1976 Industrial and Commercial Censuses*, 1976, Vol. 3, Bood 1, Table 1, pp.1–2.

1. Business groups include the non-manufacturing sector.

2. This is estimated from the ratio of foreign firms to total manufacturing firms in terms of fixed assets.

3. The ratios of assets of operation to employee.

the leading 100 (and also 500) industrial and service enterprises for the year 1982. Due to the large scale characteristic of public enterprises, they formed a major part of the top enterprises in terms of turnover: 58% of the top industrial firms, 66% of the top service enterprises.

It should be noted that the influence of public enterprises on the economy goes beyond these figures, because public enterprises control domestic financial intermedia, including banks and non-banking institutions. There are 48 banks and insurance corporations ranked in the Top 100 service firms. Among them, 20 banks are state-owned. The turnover of stateowned banks has a record of about 89% of the Top banks. The percentage share of the turnover of state-owned non-banking institutions is 49% of the Top non-banking institutions. Therefore, as the case of Pakistan in which a few large families control financial institutions (White, 1974), public enterprises have a stronger economic power than the surface shows through the allocative function of scarce capital.

The characteristics of no gigantic scale in foreign firms can be also verified in Table 4.3. There were only 18 foreign firms, whose turnover only amounted to 7%, ranked among the leading 100 industrial enterprises in 1982. Again, this reveals that foreign firms were not the biggest ones in Taiwan. However, the importance of foreign firms is still not forgotten. There were 49 foreign firms ranked among the leading 500 industrial enterprises and they yielded about 50% of total Top 500 firms' turnover. Table 4.3 also indicates the importance of foreign banks in Taiwan, i.e. their turnover is equivalent to that of domestic private banks. Therefore, it is necessary to pay much attention to the impact of foreign banks on capital allocation in the future.

One thing should be also noted that in the structure of business groups more and more banks and insurance corporations participated in the Group. There were 6 banks and insurance corporations participating in the Group in 1980, then the number increased to 36 in 1983. Enterprises associating with financial institutions can increase their economic power.

Table 4.3
The structure of top industrial & service enterprises[1]
in 1982 (NT$ million)

	Total		Public enterprises		Foreign enterprises	
	Number of firms	Turnover	Number of firms	Turnover	Number of firms	Turnover
Industries, Top 100	100	905,941	15 (15.0)	523,776 (57.8)	18 (18.0)	62,656 (6.9)
Industries, Top 500	500	1,247,629	20 (4.0)	528,380 (42.3)	49 (9.8)	576,068 (46.2)
Services, Top 100	100	459,715	30 (30.0)	305,187 (66.4)	15 (15.0)	13,889 (3.0)
– Finance & insurance	48	303,814	20 (41.7)	217,013 (71.4)	6 (12.5)	8,723 (2.9)
– Banks	25	170,754	14 (56.0)	151,684 (88.8)	6 (24.0)	8,723 (5.1)
– Non-banks	23	133,060	6 (26.1)	65,329 (49.1)	0 (0.0)	0 (0.0)
– Transportation & communication	12	96,346	7 (58.3)	68,822 (71.4)	1 (8.3)	2,192 (2.3)
– Commerce	33	53,735	2 (6.1)	14,643 (27.3)	2 (6.1)	2,984 (5.6)
– Others	7	5,820	1 (14.3)	4,709 (80.9)	0 (0.0)	0 (0.0)

Sources: 1. Commonwealth, Top 500 Enterprises in the Republic of China, *Commonwealth: A Business Monthly*, 1983, 28, pp.68–83.

2. Commonwealth, Top 100 Services Enterprises in the Republic of China, *Commonwealth: A Business Monthly*, 1983, 29, pp.78–83.

1. Brackets denote the percentage share of the total.

The evidence of dichotomous market structure

The data of concentration and monopoly power cannot be distinguished between the domestic and foreign market; some indirect data should therefore be collected to verify the existence of dichotomous market structure. Also, the export data of individual firms, and the domestic and export distribution channels are not directly observed empirically. We can only observe the relative scale and the number of manufacturers and distributors at home and abroad respectively. This reveals a different market power in these two dichotomous markets. Large-scale public enterprises, top enterprises and participants in the business groups were significantly inward-oriented, i.e. relying heavily on domestic sales. Furthermore, numerous small-scale distributors in the domestic market weaken the bargaining power of distributors and strengthen the monopoly power of large-scale manufacturers. This leads to monopolizing the domestic markets which can evade high import competition. Contrarily, due to the low outward orientation of large-scale firms and numerous small-scale trading companies, market power is almost controlled by foreign buyers in the export market. This creates a very competitive export market for domestic manufactures. That is to say, Taiwan's market structure is dichotomous.

Market orientation according to ownership

Though there is no series of data to show the export propensity of public firms, the estimation of Li (1973, p.12) shows that the export shares of public institutions decreased from 77.7% in 1852 to 6.7% in 1972.[9] Excluding rice and sugar, public enterprises only make a very minor contribution to Taiwan's exports. In 1981 their percentage share of exports was only 3.2% (including 0.6% of exports of sugar and 0.1% of rice).

It is very clear that public enterprises were inward oriented. This orientation is partly because of the choice of industry — toward domestic monopolized industries or backward linkaged industries; and partly

Table 4.4

Export intensity and export share of the top 500
enterprises and foreign firms, 1975–81 (%)

	Export intensity Top 500 enterprises	Foreign firms	Grand total exports (NT$ billion)	Foreign firms	Exoprt share Top 500 enterprises	Top 500 exporters
1975	—	56	201.5	29.4	—	—
1976[1]	39.1	61	309.9	28.6	25.0	11.7
1977	35.4	61	355.2	29.0	25.9	11.9
1978	36.4	60	468.9	29.1	28.0	13.1
1979	43.0	54	579.3	28.4	25.8	12.4
1980	27.9	53	712.2	26.3	24.0	12.9
1981	35.5	54	829.8	25.6	32.4	—

Sources: 1. Foreign Investment Commission, Ministry of Economic Affairs, *An Analysis of the Operations and Economic Effects of Foreign Enterprises in Taiwan*, 1982, Table 4, 61–63.

2. China Credit Information Services (various year), *Top Private Enterprises*.

3. Yao, 1982, pp.89–93.

[1] Only Top 400 enterprises in 1976.

because of the important role of public enterprises in the non-traded service sector. This inward orientation also provides public enterprises opportunities to evade international competition, to operate inefficiently, and to use relatively capital intensive methods. This intensity and pattern of production may have a further disadvantage for exports, and thus restrain export propensities and position again.

Table 4.4 shows that FDI was significantly more highly export oriented than top enterprises. More than one half of foreign firms' production were for exportation, only about one-third of Top 500 (or 400) firms' production was for exportation. However, the differences of percentage export shares (contributions to total exports) between foreign and top enterprises were not significant, only around 1%–3% in 1975–80. The high export propensity of FDI can be explained by the fact that foreign firms come to Taiwan mainly for using local low cost advantages but not aiming at the local market.[10] But the decreasing trend of foreign firms' export share and propensity seems to suggest that the purpose of inward oriented FDI have gradually shifted from export orientation to import substitution. Domestic market oriented FDI should be approved by the government in a stricter and more selective way. This is perhaps the reason why the percentage share of FDI to gross domestic capital formation decreased during phase S_4 as shown in Table 4.1.

Finally we compare the export propensity of the Group. The data collected by Lin (1981, Table 2) show that in 1980 the percentage share of turnover from the ten leading groups to GNP was 16%, while their percentage of exports was 11%. Further comparing these two percentages, we find that only the *Formosa Plastics Corporation* group had a higher ratio in exports (5.4%) than that in production (4.1%) and other groups had a significant lower export ratio in 1980. In these ten groups, 60% of the exports concentrated in two groups only (*Formosa Plastics Corporation* and *Fareast Corporation*), other groups making very minor contributions to exports. This implies that big and grouping enterprises are significantly inward oriented.

The export structure of different organizations in 1981 reveals that the 100 leading exporting firms had 20% of total exports (Yao, 1982). Among them, foreign exporting firms had the highest record: 42% of the exportation of the 100 leading exporting firms, or 8.5% of total exports. Firms in *Export Processing Zones* contributed 17.6% of the exportation of the 100 leading.exporting firms, or 3.6% of total exports. Only 6.8% of the exportation of leading exporting firms were of trading companies whose exports were only 1.4% of total exports. This shows that big general trading companies were of little importance. The low percentage share of total exports by public enterprises (3.2%) and firms whose exports were above US$ 100 million (4.4%) support our statement: large firms are little export oriented.

Numerous small distributors at home

Holton (1962, p.267) distinguishes three levels of competition in distribution systems, i.e. at the retail level, at the wholesale level, and at the manufacturing level. His study emphasizes the role of competition and monopoly at the distribution stage. Porter (1974) also studies the bargaining between retailers and producers. Different types of goods (e.g. producer/consumer goods, convenience/nonconvenience goods) and different patterns of wholesalers and retailers (e.g. chain stores, department stores and supermarkets) may determine a different market power for distributors relative to producers. However, the structure of distributors (the number and the scale of retailers and wholesalers) is a determinant of market power.

Table 4.5 shows this structure of Taiwan in 1976. It is impressive that there was an enormous number of small-scale distributors in Taiwan, i.e. 209,028 retailers and 23,913 wholesalers existed in 1976 to serve a population of about 16.6 million. This represents about 12 retailers and 1.4 wholesalers for every one thousand persons; or one retalier for every 79 persons and one wholesaler for every 714 persons. It is interesting to note that Japan's retail sector had a similar ratio of employees to persons to serve in 1972.[11] In terms of the number of employees, every retailer had only two persons, and every wholesaler had fewer than six persons. The large number of small distributors is similar to Japan's distribution structure for that period. Modern and large scale retailers, department stores and supermarkets, were relatively less important in both Taiwan and Japan during the periods concerned.

Another structural characteristic of Taiwan's distribution system is the length of the distribution channel. Table 4.5 also shows that one wholesaler serves fewer than nine retailers. The distribution channel in Taiwan, though, is shorter than that in Japan (one wholesaler serves for fewer than four retailers). This seems possibly caused by the large territory of Japan. However, it is still significant that Taiwan has lengthy, multilevel distribution channels with a lot of small distributors in its distribution system. As in Japan's case, the structural characteristics of Taiwan's domestic marketing could protect the domestic market from import competition by constituting invisible barriers to foreign products on the one hand. On the other hand, this system can encourage some manufacturers to export because of simpler export distribution channels (Shimaguchi, 1980, pp.5–6). These two effects can be reinforced by the same behavioral characteristics as in Japan.[12] As a result, there are relatively large-scale manufacturers with small-scale distributors existing in a protective domestic market, therefore high barriers to entry and monopoly power in the domestic market can be expected.

Export distribution channels and their scale

In terms of national economy, besides product differentiation the market power in export markets is determined by the structure of exporting firms and trading companies, i.e. their numbers and scale. Porter (1974) indicates that the larger the scale and the fewer the number of firms and trading companies in one export market, *ceteris paribus*, the higher the bargaining power and the market power. Therefore, export distribution channels and its scales are the topic here.

There are few systematic studies on export distribution channels in Taiwan. However, Hwa and Lee (1973) and Chen (1974) are two of them. The former study large exporting firms and the latter investigates small exporting businesses respectively. Around 47% of small exporting firms export directly and 53% of them export indirectly. Among them, 35.3% go through domestic trading companies, 9.6% through foreign companies, 5.5% through cooperative exportations, and 3.2% go through government institutions (Chen, 1974, pp.17 and 23). There were 76% of firms who receive exportation opportunity information from foreign customers, 33% from representatives abroad and 28% from foreign partners (Hwa and Lee, Table 8). This shows that Taiwan's exports depend highly upon foreign information. This is the reason why domestic firms have no market power abroad.

Table 4.5

Characteristics and size of domestic distributors in 1976 (NT$ million)

	Number of firms	Persons engaged (persons)	Net sales	Inventory at end of the year	Net value-added	Average size of distributors			
						Persons engaged	Net sales	Inventory	Value-added
							(NT$ thousand)		
Wholesale	23,913 (1.4)[1]	137,004 (8.3)	99,204 (5.98)	27,112	10,203	5.7	4,149	1,134	427
Retail	209,028 (12.6)	455,874 (27.3)	151,533 (9.14)	17,226	34,715	2.2	725	83	166
Department stores and supermarkets	765 (0.1)	15,049 (0.9)	16,595 (1.00)	1,262	8,077	19.7	21,693	1,649	10,558

Sources: ICCT, Executive Yuan, *The Report of 1976 Industrial and Commercial Censuses*, 1976, Vol. 6, Table 1, pp.2–4.

[1] Brackets denote the ratios of distributors per thousand persons; the population of the year was 16,576,190 persons.

This point can be confirmed by observing the scale of trading companies. Table 4.6 indicates that there were 13,883 trading companies in Taiwan in 1976. Among them, the number of specialized export trading companies, specialized import trading companies, and export-cum-import trading companies were 6,632, 1,495 and 5,756 respectively. The average size of trading companies was small in terms of employees (8.6 persons), net sales (NT$ 8.6 million), inventory (NT$ 1.3 million) and net value added (NT$ 0.8 million). Particularly, the specialized export trading companies were of the smallest size, i.e. the average export trading company had little more than NT$ 5 million (only US$ 0.14 million) net sales in 1976. It is reasonable to say that export trading companies in Taiwan rely only passively on information provided by foreign buyers: they cannot actively control marketing information by themselves.

In contrast to the domestic highly monopolized market, the export market is competitive with relatively small-scale manufactures and small scale export trading companies, i.e. there is no monopoly and bargaining power in the export market in which domestic manufacturers are taste-takers and price-takers. This is called "dichotomy" by which we mean that a competitive export market and a monopolistic domestic market exist simultaneously.

The evolution of aggregate concentration and market power

This section tries to investigate the "time-series" evolution of aggregate concentration ratios and degree of monopoly. This is because both are important measures of monopoly power. If the positive relationship among barriers to entry, concentration ratios and degree of monopoly holds at the aggregate level,[13] a U trend of aggregate concentration ratios and degree of monopoly in S_2, S_3 and S_4 phases is expected according to the above discussions.

However, in the case of Taiwan, there was no significant trend of aggregate concentration ratios during 1970–80. But there was a rough

Table 4.6

Characteristics and size of import and export trading companies in 1976 (NT$ million)

	Number of companies	Persons engaged (persons)	Net sales	Inventory at end of the year	Net value-added	Average size of trading companies			
						Persons engaged	Net sales	Inventory	Value-added
							(NT$ thousand)		
Import reading companies	1,495	17,364	30,039	8,142	3,127	11.6	20,093	5,446	2,092
Export trading companies	6,632	49,202	35,322	1,632	2,815	7.4	5,326	246	424
Import and export trading companies	5,756	52,762	53,472	8,248	4,726	9.2	9,290	1,433	821
Total	13,883	119,328	118,833	18,021	10,668	8.6	8,560	1,298	769

Sources: ICCT, Executive Yuan, *The Report of 1976 Industrial and Commercial Censuses*, 1976, Vol. 6, table 1.10, pp.74–76.

trend of aggregate degree of monopoly related to the industrialization process. Data limitations restrict us to take one step ahead here. Anyway, the relationship between barriers to entry, concentration ratios, measurement of market power, and other market structures at this aggergate level will be further treated.

Changes in aggregate concentration

White (1981a, p.223) indicates that aggregate concentration is "the percentage of some national economic measure controlled by the leading companies in the nation". He shows that the shares of value-added controlled by the largest 50, 100, or 200 manufacturing firms (CR50, CR100, CR200 respectively) are useful indices of aggregate concentration. Similarly, aggregate concentration in the entire private sector can be indicated by the shares of non-agricultural private sector employment or corporate after-tax income of the largest 100, 200, or 300 firms.[14]

Owing to the lack of data, we can measure aggregate concentration only in the manufacturing sector from 1970–1981. Only the data of turnover, employment and assets are available. Because public enterprises are not listed in the leading firms, we can only measure the relative size of private top enterprises (leading 50, 100, or 200 firms) to whole manufacturing and to private manufacturing respectively. The former is presented in the upper part of Table 4.7, and the latter in the lower part of that table.

There are no clear trends in aggregate concentration ratios. The CR100 and CR200 peaked in 1974 and 1979, then dropped in 1977 and 1980 respectively. There is also no clear picture to show a U trend of aggregate conecntration ratios as expected. There are some causes of this result: (1) the positive relationship of barriers to entry and monopoly power is too oversimplified to yield some potential meaning; (2) there are other factors to determine the changes in aggregate concentration ratios, e.g. the initial level of concentration, economies of scale and etc. (Curry and George, 1983); (3) the used data are not suitable. However,

Table 4.7

Aggregate concentration ratios in the manufacturing industry, 1970–1980

	1970	1971	1972	1973	1974	1975	1976	1977	1978	1979	1980
A. Percentage of manufacturing
% share of turnover											
Largest 50	—	16.2	—	17.2	16.9	15.8	15.1	15.2	17.3	16.1	16.4
Largest 100	21.0	23.2	22.7	25.2	23.4	21.7	20.7	22.4	23.2	21.7	21.9
Largest 200	—	—	—	33.2	31.2	28.7	27.0	28.9	30.3	28.0	28.2
% share of employment											
Largest 50	—	7.6	—	7.6	6.8	7.2	6.8	7.3	7.4	8.3	7.8
Largest 100	11.1	11.1	11.1	10.9	9.1	10.8	10.1	10.6	10.4	11.2	10.6
Largest 200	—	—	—	16.0	14.5	15.8	14.6	14.9	14.9	15.7	14.8
% share of assets											
Largest 50	—	19.0	—	18.2	16.4	18.2	18.2	19.5	21.5	23.3	19.3
Largest 100	21.6	26.3	22.9	26.8	32.3	26.8	26.1	25.6	28.7	30.8	25.9
Largest 200	—	—	—	35.0	42.8	35.6	36.0	32.9	37.3	39.7	32.9
B. Percentage of total private sector manufacturing
% share of turnover											
Largest 50	—	20.8	—	19.7	20.3	19.3	17.8	18.1	20.7	19.0	20.4
Largest 100	—	29.7	26.4	28.7	28.1	26.4	24.4	26.8	27.8	25.6	27.4
Largest 200	—	—	—	37.8	37.5	34.9	32.4	34.5	35.9	33.0	35.3
% share of assets											
Largest 50	—	24.7	—	22.6	20.9	24.9	25.9	27.0	32.0	33.6	26.3
Largest 100	39.2	34.1	29.2	33.3	40.8	36.7	37.2	35.4	42.6	44.4	35.4
Largest 200	—	—	—	43.5	54.3	48.7	51.4	45.5	55.4	57.2	44.8

Sources: 1. China Credit Information Services (various year), *Top Private Enterprises.*
2. Department of Statistics, Ministry of Economic Affairs (various years), *Report on Industrial and Commercial Survey.*
3. DGBAS, Executive Yuan (various years), *Yearbook of Labor Statistics, R.O.C.*

here, we cannot judge and examine which one is right. Since this is the first study on aggregate concentration in Taiwan, further efforts are needed.

Changes in aggregate degree of monopoly

In the conventional structrue-performance paradigm in industrial economics, price-cost margins (PCM, also Lerner index) are frequently used as a performance measure to indicate the degree of monopoly. There are many determinants to influence the degree of monopoly, e.g. concentration ratio, degree of collusion, barriers to ectry, and elasticity of demand. The evolution of the degree of monopoly can be indicated as a synthetic effect of many market structural elements.

It is difficult to estimate economic profits for measuring PCM, empirically, therefore PCM is measured by the ratio of value-added minu labor and rent costs from production value. This is called "gross" PCM by Feinberg (1980), because the 'true' Lerner index should subtract a normal return (opportunity cost) from accounting profits. But, it is difficult to compute "opportunity cost of capital" empirically. The "gross" PCM is measured by proxy in manufacturing during 1961 to 1981. Figure 4.1 shows this aggregate measurement of market power.

If the data are reliable, the former part of the U trend does appear in 1961–76; more data, after 1976, are required to determine whether the latter part of the U trend occurs or not. It is reasonable to say that the aggregate degree of monopoly in the manufacturing decreased significantly during the phase of export expansion. This seems plausible to partly support our above expectation.

Concluding remarks

The ownership structure, aggregate concentration ratios, and degree of monopoly are examined in this study. Under the time-series aspect,

```
  %
  │
  │
  │  •0.43
  │      \
  │       \
  │        •0.18         0.12
  │            \        •    •0.11
  │             \      /
  │              •0.06
  └──┬─────┬─────┬─────┬─────┬──
   1961  1966  1971  1976  1981
```

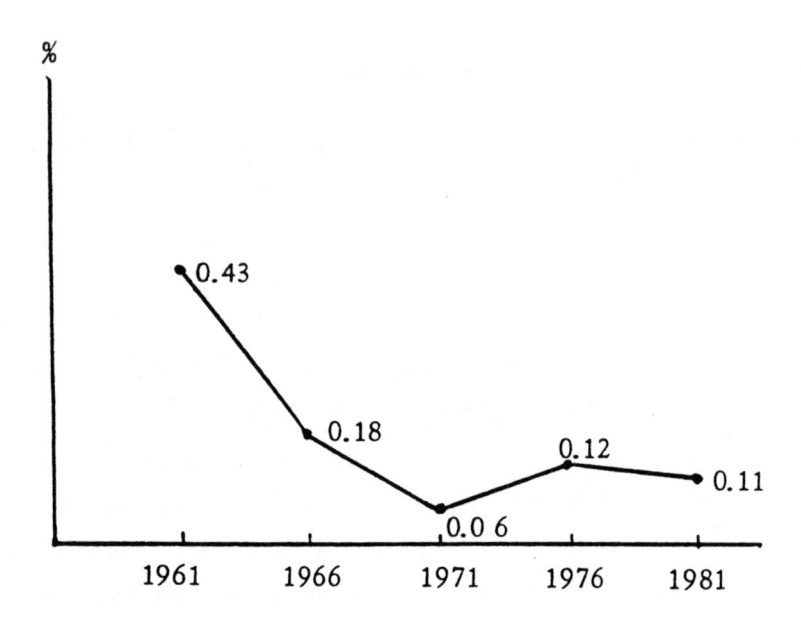

¹ Price-cost margins$= (VA - W)/Y$, where VA denotes net value-added at market price, W is salaries and wages, Y is production value.

Sources: 1. ICCT, Executive Yuan (various year), *The Report of Industrial and Commercial Censuses*.
2. Department of Statistics, Ministry of Economic Affairs, *Report on Industrial & Commercial Survey*, 1981, Tables 8 and 12, pp.150 and 220–221.

Figure 4.1 Aggregate price-cost margins[1] in the manufacturing, 1961–1981

ownership structure does appear as predicted theoretically, i.e. the relative share of public enterprises was high during the import substitution phase and low during the export expansion phase. Also, an inverted U trend of the contribution of foreign firms to gross domestic capital formation was found in Taiwan's industrialization process. But aggregate concentration ratios and the degree of monopoly give only vague answers.

On the cross-section aspect, we present market orientations among different ownerships and organizations. We find that large-scale public enterprises and member firms in the Group are inward oriented. These relatively large-scale manufacturers facing numerous small-scale distributors, under a protective offsetting policy package, can increase market power in the domestic market. On the contrary, the relative small-scale private enterprises are export oriented. Besides, enormous numbers of small trading companies and the characteristics of export goods (standardized and taste-taker) further eliminate market power in the export market. As a result, the domestic market and the export market are dichotomous: the latter is competitive and the former is monopolistic.

Notes

1. To distinguish barriers to entry between these two stages, see White (1974, Ch. 2).
2. See Tables 6 and 28 of Chiang (1951, pp.177–78 and 207).
3. Aharoni (1977, pp.54–55) makes a comparison of the ratio of public investment to total investment and GNP among LDCs, then he finds that Taiwan had a higher ratio of public investment than other LDCs during 1961–66.
4. For a case study of Taiwan's outward direct investment see Ting and Schive (1981) and Chung (1976). The issues regarding multinationals coming from LDCs have been discussed in Kumar and Mcleod (1981) and Agmon and Kindleberger (1977).

5. From 1972 on, the Group's data were published every two years (see note 7) and the number of the Group was kept around 100 including 650 to 800 firms.
6. For the problem of entrepreneurship, see a series of studies of Leff (1978, 1979a and 1979b).
7. According to *Studies on Group Enterprises in Taiwan* published by China Credit Information Service, Taiwan's business groups are classified into "Sister" type, "Mother-Son" type, and "Married" type in terms of the relationship among participants of the groups. One common basis among these types is the family. This specific organizational form is perhaps different from that in European, Canadian and Japanese industrial groups (see Encaoua and Jacquemin, 1982).
8. The figure in brackets denotes the precentage of investigated managers who recognize that this is at least a considerable factor to organize the Group.
9. It should be noted that most exports of public institutions were rice and sugar in 1952 (sugar exports amounted to 77% of total exports). The significant drop of contributions to exports was also caused by the declining exportation of rice and sugar. The export percentage of sugar and rice to total exports was only 2.8% and 0.1% respectively in 1972.
10. The low K/L ratio of foreign firms shown in Table 4.2 supports this point.
11. Shimaguchi (1980, p.4) notes that approximately 1,495.000 retailers and 260,000 wholesalers existed in 1972 to serve a population of a little more than 100 million, i.e. one retailer for every 72 persons, and one wholesaler for every 415 persons.
12. For instance, the rebate system, promissory rates, return privileges, frequent delivery, and dealer aids, see Shimagughi (1980, pp.12–21).

13. For the relation between concentration ratios and market power at the inter-industry or intra-industry level, see Encaoua and Jacquemin (1980). However, as far as we know the relationship among those factors at the more aggregate level is not discussed yet.

14. Feinberg (1981, p.217) criticizes these measures as inappropriate to provide information on changes in the distribution of value-added. White (1981b) replied to this critique with the argument about an inequality measure and confirmed that his measure is more useful and appropriate to show the political and social consequences of the size of giant enterprises.

References

Agmon, T. and Cp. Kindleberger (1977), eds., *Multinationals from Small Countries*, Cambridge, The MIT Press, Mass.

Aharoni, Y. (1977), *Markets, Planning and Development: The Private and Public Sectors in Economic Development*, Ballinger Publishing Co., Cambridge.

Chen, M.C. (1974), "Promotion for Exporting Small Business," *Industry of Free China*, 6, 42, pp.11–29 (in Chinese).

Chiang, W.Y. (1951), "Taiwan's Private Enterprises," *Bank of Taiwan Quarterly*, 3, 27, pp.59–78 (in Chinese).

Chou, T.C. (1985), "The Pattern and Strategy of Industrialization in Taiwan: Specialization and Offsetting Policy," *The Developing Economies*, 23 (2), pp.138–57, also the Chapter 1 of this book.

Chung, E.N. (1976), "Foreing Investment from Taiwan's Private Enterprises," *Bank of Taiwan Quarterly*, 27 (1), pp.21–57 (in Chinese).

Curry, B. and K.D. George (1983), "Industrial Concentration: Survey," *Journal of Industrial Economics*, 31 (3), pp.203–56.

Dunning, J.H. (1981), "Explaining Outward Investment of Developing Countries: In Support of the Eclectic Theory of International Production," in K. Kumar and M.G. McLeod, eds., pp.1–22.

Encaoua, D. and A. Jacquemin (1980), "Degree of Monopoly, Indices of Concentration and Threat of Entry," *International Economic Review*, 21 (1), pp.87–105.

_____ and _____ (1982), "Organizational Efficiency and Monopoly Power: The Case of French Industrial Groups," *European Economic Review*, 19 (1-2), pp.25-52.

Feinberg, R.M. (1980), "The Lerner Index, Concentration and the Measurement of Market Power," *Southern Economic Journal*, 4, pp.1180-86.

_____ (1982), "On the Measurement of Aggregate Concentration," *Journal of Industrial Economics*, 31 (2), pp.217-22.

Holton, R.H. (1962), "The Role of Competition and Monopoly in Distribution: The Experience in the United States," in J.P. Miller, ed., pp.263-307.

Hwa, Y. and Y.S. Lee (1973), "Survey of the Manufacturing Firms in Taiwan," *Economic Essays*, 4, pp.223-48.

Kumar, K. and M.G. McLeod (1981), eds., *Multinationals from Developing Countries*, D.C. Heath and Company, Lexington.

Leff, N.H. (1978), "Industrial Organization and Entrepreneurship in the Developing Countries: The Economic Groups," *Economic Development and Cultural Change*, 4, pp.661-75.

_____ (1979a), "Entrepreneurship and Economic Development: The Problem Revisited," *Journal of Economic Literature*, 17, pp.46-64.

_____ (1979b), "Monopoly Capitalism' and Public Policy in Developing Countries," *Kyklos*, 32 (4), pp.718-38.

Li, K.T. (1973), "The Role of Private Enterprise in the Economic Development of the Republic of China," *Industry of Free China*, 39 (6), pp.2-13.

Lin, C.S. (1981), "Analysis of 10 Leading Groups," *Commonwealth: A Business Monthly*, 6, pp.42-48 (in Chinese).

Lin, C.Y. (1973), *Industrialization in Taiwan, 1946-72*, Praeger, New York.

Liu, S.S., K.M. Kuo, C.E. Huang and T.S. Szutu (1981), "Causes, Operations and Effects of Corporate Groups in Taiwan," *Medium*

Business Bank of Taiwan Quarterly, 4 (3–4), pp.5–19 and 5–23 (in Chinese).

Miller, J.P. (1962), ed., *Competition, Cartels and Their Regulation,* North-Holland, Amsterdam.

Porter, M.E. (1974), "Consumer Behavior, Retailer Power and Market Performance in Consumer Goods Industries," *Review of Economics and Statistics,* 56 (4), pp.419–36.

Sheaham, J.B. (1976), "Public Enterprise in Developing Countries," in W.G. Shepherd, ed., *Public Enterprise: Economic Analysis of Theory and Practice,* D.C. Heath and Co, Lexington.

Shimagughi, M. (1980), *Japanese Distribution Channels: Traditions, Customs, and Evolution,* Université Catholique de Louvain: Japan-Europe Economic Research Center.

Ting, W.L. and C. Schive (1981), "Direct Investment and Technology Transfer from Taiwan," in K. Kuman and M.G. McLeod, eds., pp.101–14.

White, L.J. (1974), *Industrial Concentration and Economic Power in Pakistan,* Princeton University Press, Princeton.

———— (1981a), "What Has Been Happening to Aggregate Concentration in the United States," *Journal of Industrial Economics,* 29 (3), pp.223–30.

———— (1981b), "On Measuring Aggregate Concentration: A Reply," *Journal of Industrial Economics,* 30 (2), pp.22–24.

Wu, R.I., C.F. Wanglian, T.C. Chou and C.K. Li (1980), *Economic Effects of American Firms' Investment in Taiwan,* Institute of American Culture, Academia Sinica, Taipei. (in Chinese)

Yao, M.C. (1982), "The Leading 100 Exporting Firms," *Commonwealth: A Business Monthly,* 18, pp.89–93 (in Chinese).

5 Concentration, Profitability and Trade in a Simultaneous Equation Analysis *

Introduction

Many studies[1] have argued that a joint determination rather than a causal relation exists between concentration and profitability. That is because the price-cost margins (PCM) equation is derived from an equilibrium condition for profit maximization. Clarke and Davies (1982) pressent the simultaneity of profitability and concentration. Many efforts have also been made to treat the simultaneity of concentration, advertising intensity, and profitability.[2]

Recently, more and more studies have integrated trade into such a simultaneous framework in parallel with an analysis of the role of foreign trade in the study of structure-performance.[3] Jacquemin et al. (1980) show the effects of trade in a recursive two-equation model to describe the determinants of PCM and concentration. Pugel (1978) specifies the import and export share equations (as well as equations for concentration, profitability, foreign direct investment and advertising intensity) in a simultaneous equation system. De Ghellinck et al. (1984) confirm that there is a feedback of trade on industry performance. The results of Geroski (1982a) suggest that trade rather than advertising intensity is suitable as an endogenous variable in a simultaneous system.

---

*This paper was reproduced from *The Journal of Industrial Economics*, Vol. 34, No. 4, June 1986, pp.429–443, with permission of the publisher.

This paper uses a simultaneous equation system to study, in the case of Taiwan, the interaction of trade (exports and imports), concentration and profitability. Variables measuring barriers to entry, economies of scale, and relative factor intensity are included with other exogenous variables to explain four endogenous variables: concentration (Hd), PCM, export (Tx) and import intensity (Tm). Beside traditional elements, the impact of public enterprises on structure and performance is emphasized in the study. The results reveal some features of Taiwan's economy, in particular, the role of public ownership and the impact of international linkages on concentration and performance.

In section I, the formulation and specification of the models are discussed. In section II, the empirical implementation of our model and the data are presented. Then the empirical results are given in section III. Section IV contains concluding remarks and policy implications.

The models: formulation and specialization

In "import discipline" models, we can obtain a general PCM equation which comes from the first order condition of profit maximization. In the equation, PCM is determined by the degree of domestic producers' competition (based on the firm's market share or its related measures) and demand (being represented by the relevant elasticity). Both variables include import share and export share in an open economy. Due to the simultaneity of equilibrium condition and considering the important role of comparative advantage in trade we can write a simultaneous four-equation system as:

$$Hd = f_1(MA, Tx, Tm) \quad \text{the concentration equation,} \qquad (1)$$

$$PCM = f_2(Hd, MA, Tx, Tm) \quad \text{the profit equation,} \qquad (2)$$

$$T_x = f_3(Hd, PCM, MA, CA) \quad \text{the export intensity equation,} (3)$$

$$T_m = f_4(Hd, PCM, MA, CA) \quad \text{the import intensity equation,} (4)$$

where MA and CA represent the variables of market stucture and the state of comparative advantage respectively, and both are exogenous. Formulation and specification for each equation could be advanced in turn.

The concentration equation

It is generally hypothesized in conventional industrial economics that inter-industry variation in concentration can be explained by a combination of explanatory variables such as barriers to entry, scale economies, and the size of the market.[4] Therefore, three variables—the market size (MS), minimum efficient plant size (MES), and capital requirement (KR)—are included in the concentration equation. The expectation is that the larger the capital requirement and the higher the minimum efficient size, the higher would be the level of concentration. Also an inverse relationship is expected between market size and concentration.

Besides, an indicator of public ownership in Taiwan's economy should be introduced as a determinant of market structure (and performance). The role of Taiwan's public firms in economic activities, even in manufacturing, are very evident (Chou, 1985; Ch. 3). On average in the 1970s, 26% of manufacturing assets were controlled by the public sector which contributed 17% of turnover in the manufacturing. Furthermore, large-scale and domestic-orientation (very low export intensity) of public enterprises are noticeable features in Taiwan. Hence it would be expected to have a significant and positive impact on concentration. A dummy variable (PE) representing the position of public ownership is introduced in the concentration equation with positive expectation.

Three international linkages are included to complete the concentration equation in an open economy. The first one is Tm, measured as imports divided by total sales, that is, the fraction of industry sales provided by foreign suppliers. A positive impact would be observed if threat from imports induces mergers among domestic firms,[5] or if import penetrations force out inefficient producers.[6]

The second external variable is Tx, measured as exports divided by total sales, that is, the fraction of domestic production that is exported. To the extent that export intensity acts as a deconcentration force via enlarging of the market size, it would be expected to be inversely related to industry concentration. This negative relationship may be reinforced either if the fixed costs associated with exporting activities are not high, or if economies of scale in production or distribution are not important because a larger market size resulting from export opportunities can support a greater number of producers. Otherwise, the importance of scale economies and high fixed costs of exporting business would alter the sign to be a positive one (de Melo and Urata, 1984). Taiwan's exports concentrating on simple processed and light industrial products suggest a negative influence.

The third external variable is foreign direct investment (FDI). Caves (1980) shows that the general presumption for FDI causing concentration is not automatically supported in the LDCs. It seems to depend on the category of goods (consumers goods industries or producer goods industries) and their market orientations. For instance, export-oriented foreign subsidiaries may have been able to surmount domestic barriers and so reduce concentration.

The resulting concentration equation, with the expected sign indicated below each independent variable, is thus:

$$Hd = f_1(\underset{-}{MS}, \underset{+}{MES}, \underset{+}{KR}, \underset{+}{PE}, \underset{+}{Tm}, \underset{-}{Tx}, \underset{-}{FDI}) \tag{5}$$

The profit equation

PCM (which is the industry profit-sales ratio) is jointly determined by the degree of domestic producers' competition and the condition of market demand. Pugel (1980, p.122) indicates that domestic producer concentration and barriers to entry are interactive in representing the degree of competitiveness in domestic production. The Herfindahl index of concentration is an appropriate candidate for measuring producer concentration.[7] Two entry variables, MES and MS, can be rearranged into one, $MESMS$, measured as MES divided by MS (total sales minus exports plus imports), that is, the fraction of domestic market size necessary to achieve the minimum efficient size. The annual growth rate of industry production value (GRS), representing the condition of market demand, is included in the profit equation. It would be expected with familiar reasons that the above variables have positive influences on the PCM.

It is interesting to examine the effect of public enterprises on profits. Therefore, a dummy variable, PE, is included in the profit equation. The sign of this variable depends upon its efficiency and pricing policy. If the government is likely to take over inefficient firms or public enterprises adopt low prices rather than a profit maximization policy, as in the case of Spain (Donsimoni and Leoz-Arguelles, 1981), it is expected to have a negative impact on profits. On the contrary, if state owned enterprises operate efficiently (Aharoni, 1980) or adopt high protected prices, a positive effect is expected. However, for Taiwan's case, the author (1985, Ch. 3) shows high prices are adopted by public enterprises and protected by the government for fiscal purpose, hence the expectation of a positive effect.

Previous studies indicate that a negative relation would hold between import intensity and profitability, because foreign competition, as a fringe, would restrain the exercise of market power in the domestic market. However, the relationship becomes ambiguous as soon as one leaves the simple dominant firm case,[8] and may be positive if the implicit collusion between domestic firms is lower than that between domestic and foreign firms (de Melo and Urata, 1984), or if an oligopolistic firm is engaged in both producing and importing simultaneously. Due to strict import controls in Taiwan, it seems reasonable to treat imports as a competitive fringe. If so, a negative sign is expected.

The impact of export intensity on profits is complex. It depends upon the degree of competitiveness of industry at home (for example competitive sectors vs. monopolized sectors) and upon whether or not the exporting firms can dump abroad and prevent re-imports (Jacquemin *et al.* 1980) Moreover, Huveneers (1981) indicates that, even in the case of price discrimination and homogeneous goods, the effect of export intensity depends on cost conditions.[9] On the other hand, in the differentiated goods case, he shows that the influence of exports on profits depends on whether the profits abroad exceeds or is less than that at home. If PCM abroad is less than PCM at home, a negative impact is expected. It seems acceptable to assume (1) that goods made in Taiwan are differentiated from those made in MDCs (for example the largest export market of Taiwan, the US), and (2) that Taiwan's producers have smaller market position in export markets than at home, that is, PCM at home being large than PCM abroad (this is also verified by the author, 1985, Ch.4). Thus a negative sign is expected.

Some studies have explained the effect of FDI on performance, but almost all of them emphasize "outward" rather than "inward" direct investment. The study of Caves (1980) is an exception. Like many other LDCs, Taiwan only has a minor record of outward investment, and thus FDI is not endogenized, as in Pugel (1978). As Caves (1980) shows, whether the relation between FDI and profits is positive or negative is still an open question. However, if the manipulation of transfer prices is adopted by the export-oriented multinational enterprises because of a high level of tax in Taiwan, a negative relation would be expected. Or, if foreign subsidiaries being as a fringe, like imports, play a competitive role to restrict the market power of domestic firms, a negative sign is also expected.

Therefore, the resulting profit equation and the expected signs are:

$$PCM = f_2(\underset{+}{Hd}, \underset{+}{MESMS}, \underset{+}{GRS}, \underset{+}{PE}, \underset{-}{Tm}, \underset{-}{Tx}, \underset{-}{FDI}) \qquad (6)$$

The trade equations

Few theoretical specifications of trade equations with embodiment of imperfect competition can be found, two exceptions being Lyons (1981) and Pugel (1978). Lyons derives an import share equation from a generalized Cournot model. Pugel explores the determinants of export intensity and import intensity separately, both to extend the analysis of comparative advantage and to test other hypotheses developed in industrial organization. This is similar to equations (3) and (4). They should be further specified in detail.

First, there do not exist many studies to discuss the impact of concentration on export and import intensity. However, the study of Glejser *et al.* (1980) shows that the firms in concentrated sectors would be encouraged to export. On the other hand, foreign producers may not enjoy a very competitive domestic market; therefore the higher concentration, the more important penetration is expected. Therefore, concentration influences both export and import intensity with positive expectations.

Second, PCM could affect the incentives both to export and to import. Incentives depend on the differences between price and costs. If the domestic price is elevated above the domestic producer costs, foreign producers perceive an incentive to export. Therefore, the higher the PCM, the higher the import penetration which is expected. However, this "signal" effect could be restrained or distorted by import control measures. By contrast to this, domestic producers who enjoy market power at home will avoid exporting in order not to attract foreign producers' attention. Therefore, PCM is expected to influence exports in a negative direction.

Third, export and import intensity would be respectively affected by other market structures. Because export-oriented foreign investment is more welcome and easily approved by the government than the domestic-oriented one, FDI is included in export intensity with positive expectation. On the other hand, import intensity is influenced by government's import policy. There is a complex import control policy package in Taiwan (Chou, 1985; Ch.2). Generally, imports of consumer goods are strictly controlled by non-tariff measures for purposes of saving foreign exchange. Imports of backward linkaged goods are restricted by high tariff for protection. The level of protection is positively related to the level of scale economies. To catch both considerations, a dummy variable (DPC) to distinguish the producer goods industries from the consumer goods industries, and $MESMS$ are included in the import intensity equation. Accordingly, the impacts of DPC and $MESMS$ on import intensity are expected with positive and negative signs respectively.

Finally, two variables representing conventional international trade theories (factor intensity argument) are included in export and import equations: the capital-labor ratio (KL), the skilled labor ratio (SK). Conventional influences on the signs of terms in export and import equations are expected. The variables presented above indicate the determinants of either intra-industry (for example, Hd, PCM and $MESMS$) or inter-industry trade patterns (for example, KL and SK). However, additional variables which explain both kinds of trade pattern are not explored, for example, product differentiation and technology intensity (or the ratio of R & D to sales). Also, trade policy (beside DPC), one of the most important elements of trade patterns, and grographical distance are not included. Therefore, one index, which implicitly contains the determinants of both intra- and inter-industry trade, is included in both export and import intensity, that is, the variable IN, measured as the ratio of imports ($\times 2$) to total trade.[10] It would be expected that the impact of IN on export intensity is negative and the impact on import intensity is positive.

The resulting export intensity and import intensity equations and the expected signs are:

$$Tx = f_3(\underset{+}{Hd}, \underset{-}{PCM}, \underset{+}{FDI}, \underset{-}{KL}, \underset{-}{SK}, \underset{-}{IN}) \qquad (7)$$

$$Tm = f_4(\underset{+}{Hd}, \underset{+}{PCM}, \underset{+}{DPC}, \underset{-}{MESMS}, \underset{+}{KL}, \underset{+}{SK}, \underset{+}{IN}) \qquad (8)$$

Estimation and data

The structure and estimation of the model

In our four structural equations, (1) both export and import intensity appear in both the profit margins and concentration equations; (2) concentration appears in the profit, export and import equations; and (3) the profit margins appear in both export and import equations. Thus it is necessary to treat all four variables as endogenous. Their values are jointly determined in the simultaneous equation system consisting of equations (5) to (8).

There are 12 exogenous variables (constant, D, MS, MES, KR, GRS, FDI, $MESMS, DPC, KL, SK, IN$). No equation has more than 13 coefficients to be estimated so all equations satisfy the necessary (or order) condition for identification and each equation in the system is overidentified.[11] Since MS, MES and KR appear only in (5), GRS appears only in (6), and DPC appears in (8) only, all equations satisfy the sufficient (or rank) condition for identification as well (Martin, 1979; p.643). Our four-equation system is linear. Two-stage least squares (2SLS) estimation may yield consistent and unbiased estimates.[12]

The data

Most of the variables used in these equations are derived from the 1976 Census of manufacturing (*Industry and Commerce Census of Taiwan*),[13] except for imports, DPC, and GRS. Values for imports are taken from the 1976 Customs statistics. The industry production value in 1971 and 1976, used to measure the variable GRS, are taken from the Taiwan Industrial Production Statistics. In addition, the dummy variable for consumer and producer goods was assigned on the basis of judgment.

Industries are defined at the four-digit Standard Industry Classification (SIC) level. This follows the assertion of Pugel (1980). He says: "This level, rather than the more aggregate three digit level is often thought more nearly to approximate the appropriate level in defining economic industries, but no previous research on the effects of foreign trade is conducted at this level"[14] (p.125). Customs statistics of import data, based on the Standard International Trade Classification (SITC), are assigned to correspond to SIC four-digit industries with some arbitrary judgment. Concordance problems among the three main sources of data reduce the number of industries in the sample to 124.[15] The smaller data set still yields large degree of freedom, but some defects, owing to either the different basis between Census and reclassification of trade data, should be kept in mind when considering the applicability of the results. Brief variable definitions and sources are given in Table 5.1.

Empirical results

Ordinary least squares results

Table 5.2 shows ordinary least squares estimates of our four structural equations (5) to (8). Most of the coefficients of conventional variables bear the expected signs and are significantly different from zero. Profit rises with concentration and scale economies as conventionally expected. Concentration is influenced by entry barriers of relative market size (MS and MES) and capital requirement (KR). As expected, the variable IN determines export and import intensity in positive and negative directions respectively. Beside the conventional wisdom presented, other results are as follows.

First, public enterprises have a powerful impact on market structure and performance in a positive direction. The industries dominated by public ownership, for example, wine and tobacco, petroleum refinery, chemical materials, steel and heavy cars, tend to adopt high protected prices. Hence, a significant and positive impact of public ownership on concentration and performance is observed.

Second, international linkages (except imports) do affect concentration and performance. Import competition does not influence concentration and performance, probably because of the government's strict

Table 5.1

Sources and definitions of variable

Variable[1]	Source[2]	Defintion
PCM (10.52, 15.74)	(1)	"Production value minus intermediate expenses minus wages" divided by sales (%)
HD (0.12, 0.18)	(1)	Herfindahl index of concentration in terms of sales
Tx (29.18, 28.33)	(1)	Exports divided by sales (%)
Tm (65.57, 141.00)	(1) & (2)	Imports divided by sales (%)
FDI (2.35, 5.18)	(1)	The ratio of the number of foreign enterprise units to the total number of enterprise units (%)
PE (0.11, 0.32)	(1)	A dummy having the value of one if the percentage of sales from public enterprise is above the average level of 3-digit industry
MS (5.37, 10.02)	(1) & (2)	Sales plus imports minus exports (NT$ M.)
MES (0.18, 0.09)	(1)	The average size of the largest plants accounting for for 50% of industry sales (NT$ M.)
$MESMS$ (0.34, 0.52)	(1)	MES divided by MS (%)
KR (28.00, 128.46)	(1)	MES times "assets divided by sales"
GRS (21.12, 36.16)	(3)	The average growth rate of industry production value between 1971 and 1976, at 1976 prices (%)
KL (684.5, 986.6)	(1)	Assets divided by employment. (NT$ thousand per person)
SK (0.35, 0.16)	(1)	The skilled workers divided by total workers
DPC (0.42, 0.50)	(4)	A dummy having the value of one for producer goods industry
IN (0.87, 0.80)	(1) & (2)	The ratio of imports (×2) to total trade

[1] Mean and standard deviation shown in parentheses.

[2] Data sources are:

(1) *General Report of Industry & Commerce Census of Taiwan* (1976), The Committee on Industrial and Commercial Censuses of Taiwan, R.O.C.

(2) *The Trade of China, Taiwan District* (1976), Statistical Department, Inspectorate General of Customs.

(3) *Taiwan Industrial Production Statistics Monthly, Republic of China* (1982), Department of Statistics, Ministry of Economic Affairs.

(4) On the basis of the author's judgment.

Table 5.2

Ordinary least squares estimates of our models

	Hd	PCM	Tx	Tm
Intercept	0.12^a (5.74)	10.38^a (7.56)	59.66^a (10.05)	−33.96 (−1.15)
MS	−0.004^c (−1.55)			
MES	0.06^c (1.63)			
KR	0.92^a (3.41)			
GRS		0.003 (0.75)		
PE	0.11^a (2.54)	7.18^a (2.59)		
MESMS		476.21^a (2.86)		−1,793.15^a (−3.24)
Hd		14.34^a (2.64)	11.41 (0.71)	0.58 (0.75)
PCM			−0.63^a (−2.65)	0.64 (0.55)
KL			−0.004^c (−1.31)	−0.03^b (−1.92)
SK			−27.34^b (−1.78)	46.13 (0.62)
IN			−16.10^a (−5.72)	79.97^a (5.58)
DPC				74.13^a (3.24)
Tm	0.0001 (1.00)	−0.0001 (−0.03)		
Tx	−0.0006^c (−1.42)	−0.08^a (−2.62)		
FDI	−0.01^b (−1.89)	−0.35^b (−2.09)	0.84^b (1.70)	
R^2	0.50	0.30	0.33	0.35
F	16.51	7.03	9.49	9.04

Dependent variable shown across header.

t-statistics (one-tail test) are given in parentheses. Significance levels of coefficients are $a = 1\%, b = 5\%$ and $c = 10\%$.

import controls. Exports play a deconcentration role and foreign subsidiaries have the same impact due to their high export orientation (as confirmed by a positive and significant coefficient of FDI in the export intensity equation). Moreover, negative and significant impacts of both exports and FDI on performance are also observed.

Third, concentration does not significantly influence either export or import intensity. In the export intensity equation, performance as expected has a significant and negative impact. Besides, factor intensity evidently influences export intensity, that is, exports concentrating on low-skilled and labor-intensive goods. Also, foreign subsidiaries in Taiwan seem to exploit such advantages of low labor costs and tend to be export-oriented.

Consider now estimated coefficients in the import intensity equation. $MESMS, IN$ and DPC are remarkably significant with the expected sign. As mentioned, a significant and positive impact of DPC indicates that imports of consumer goods are strictly controlled. Even in the producer goods industries, a significant and negative impact of $MESMS$ shows that those industries which could exploit much advantage of scale economies are protected and prevent import competition. This protection should lower the capital-labor ratio of imports. Moreover, a high percentage of total imports comes from manufactured materials (65%, on average in 1974–78) and could further lower import's capital intensity because materials do not have a high capital intensity. As a result, a significant and negative impact of KL on import intensity, which contrasts with expectation, is observed. This could result from import control measures that distort the effect of factor intensity on import intensity and also restain the "signal" effect of industry concentration and performance on imports intensity. It also suggests elements contained in variable IN should be further explored in the future to clarify the determinants of imports.

Two-stage least squares

The results in Table 5.2 may be biased because of the simultaneous nature of the model. Two-stage least squares estimates which avoid this bias appear in Table 5.3. Most of the results (in terms of signs and statistical significance) found in the OLS estimates remain in the 2SLS estimates. However, two modifications are to be noted.

First, minor changes in significance level occur between OLS estimates and 2SLS estimates, but MS in the concentration equation improve in significance. On the other hand, $MESMS$ and Hd in the profit equation, SK in the export intensity equation, and KL in import intensity equation decrease in significance but still maintain a 10% of significance level.

Second, evident changes in significance level are to be observed and lead some significant impacts to lose their influences. For instance, the significance levels of FDI in concentration, Tx in performance, PCM in export intensity, and $MESMS$ in import intensity drastically decrease to insignificant levels. On the other hand, GRS and Tm improve their significance levels to influence performance significantly. As a result, the relations between international linkages and concentration as well as performance, although still observed, seem not so strong as in the case of the OLS estimates.

Conclusions

This study shows, firstly, that government interference plays a dominant role in Taiwan to influence both concentration and performance by public enterprises. Also, the conduct of government influences import intensity by import control measures (through the variable DPC), which offset potential impacts of imports on concentration and on performance, just as the case of Chile before her trade liberalization in 1976.

Table 5.3

Two-stage least squares estimates of our models

	\multicolumn{4}{c}{Dependent variable}			
	Hd	PCM	Tx	Tm
Intercept	0.16^a	11.04^a	50.71^a	-8.48
	(3.22)	(3.23)	(5.38)	(-0.21)
MS	-0.005^b			
	(-1.79)			
MES	0.05^c			
	(1.44)			
KR	0.95^a			
	(3.40)			
GRS		0.007^c		
		(1.32)		
PE	0.11^a	6.84^b		
	(2.45)	(2.05)		
$MESMS$		307.85^c		-801.47
		(1.42)		(-0.31)
Hd		19.33^c	3.16	47.02
		(1.58)	(0.07)	(0.27)
PCM			0.23	-2.15
			(0.33)	(-0.71)
KL			-0.006^c	-0.03^c
			(-1.57)	(-1.35)
SK			-26.42^c	44.52
			(-1.56)	(0.57)
IN			-15.62^a	79.33^a
			(-5.07)	(5.18)
DPC				68.98^a
				(2.88)
Tm	0.000002	-0.02^c		
	(0.01)	(-1.59)		
Tx	-0.002^c	-0.05		
	(-1.34)	(-0.64)		
FDI	-0.006	-0.38^b	1.10^b	
	(-1.06)	(-1.74)	(1.72)	

t-statistics (one-tail test) are given in parentheses. Significance levels of coefficients are $a = 1\%, b = 5\%$ and $c = 10\%$.

Secondly, both export and import intensities are mainly explained by comparative advantage, rather than market forces, which could be an engine of Taiwan's successful economic development in the last three decades (Chou, Ch. 2, 1985). Also, international linkage does not significantly influence performance and concentration. As in the case of a small open economy like Taiwan, this seems to suggest another way to demonstrate the effect of trade on market forces. This needs further studies.[16]

Notes

1. For instance, see Jacquemin et al. (1980), Geroski (1982a, 1982b), Clarke and Davies (1982) and Donsimoni et al. (1984).

2. See Greer (1971), Strickland and Weiss (1976), Martin (1979), and Pagoulatos and Sorensen (1981). For comments on the necessity for this simultaneity, see Sawyer (1982).

3. For dominant firms' models with trade, see Jacquemin (1982), Geroski and Jacquemin (1981) and Huveneers (1981).

4. At a space of one decade, two excellent surveys of the various theories of the determinants of concentration can be found in Ornstein et al. (1973) and Curry and George (1983).

5. Jacquemin et al. (1980, p.135) say: "Sectors characterized by a systematic high share of imports are expected to be also characterized by a high degree of defensive concentration of domestic producers, as long as imports are close substitutes for domestic product."

6. However, de Melo and Urata (1984) show that impact may be negative if inefficient producers improve their productive efficiency in response to an increase of imports. As a result of an increased number of efficient producers, the concentration ratio may decline.

7. The market shares of individual firms are used here as weights to sum over all firms' PCM to obtain the industry PCM (profit-sales ratio). This yields the Herfindahl index which is the appropriate proxy for performance in a Cournot behavior (Donsimoni et al. 1984).

8. For instance, in the contrary case where domestic firms are treated as the competitive fringe, the import intensity has no effect on profitability because domestic firms always act as a price-taker (Urata, 1984). In the mixed case where both domestic and foreign firms form a cartel, ther relation is ambiguous, see Geroski and Jacquemin (1981).

9. He shows that if the elasticity of the marginal cost is larger than the elasticity of average cost, the effect is positive.

10. On the one hand, de Ghellinck et al. (1984) use this variable to represent comparative advantage. On the other hand, this is also similar to the measure of intra-industry trade, that is the value of the ratio approaches one when intra-industry trade is maximized; otherwise, it approaches zero or two when no intra-industry trade occurs. Perhaps, someone may be worried about this variable which is very close to an identity with Tm and Tx. Further discussions and estimated results without the IN variable are presented in the Appendix.

11. See Johnston (1972, pp.356–65).

12. The implicit assumption here is that the disturbances in our structural equations are not contemporaneously correlated. Otherwise, three-stage least squares (3SLS) estimation should be used, see Johnston (1972, pp.380–98). Martin (1979) as well as Pagoulatos and Sorensen (1981) use 3SLS method to estimate a three-equation simultaneous system.

13. A census is held every five years in Taiwan since 1954 (i.e. 1954, 1961, 1966, 1971, 1976 and 1981). The 1976 Census data was

used because the 1981 Census has not yet been released. Its precision, four-digit classification, and its being the newest one are the reasons why the 1976 Census was chosen.

14. Also see the argument of Esposito and Esposito (1977) to discuss the influence of aggregation level on structure-profitability relationship.

15. There were 134 SIC four-digit industries in Taiwan. Of the ten industries deleted from the sample, one (3311) was because of defective data: negative value added, and three (3702, 3706 and 3909) were dropped for lack of concentration data. The six remaining industries (2011, 2521, 2529, 3501, 3708 and 3709) could not be used because of the somewhat aggregated presentation of foreign trade data.

16. However, the author (1985, ch. 6) shows that the significant effect of export orientation on concentration and performance exists by an implication of strategic group hypothesis.

Appendix

Appendix 5.1 Are IN and Tm (TX) close to an identity?

It is argued that the IN variable is much too close to an identity with the dependent variables: Tm and Tx respectively. We know, for instance, that if total trade is related to market sales by the relation $M+X = bS$, then $IN = 2M/(M+X) = 2M/bS$, therefore $Tm = M/S = (b/2)IN$. But, it is also clear that such a case is only based on the above condition. And we know, from this condition, that the sum of import intensity and export intensity is a constant, that is, $X + M = bS$, therefore $X/S+M/S = Tx+Tm = b$. This assumed relationship is too restrictive to discuss the determinants of Tx and Tm respectively as has been done in this paper. Therefore the IN variable is still included in our models. For comparison, the estimated results of the models without IN are also presented overleaf, and there is no significant variation between the results with and without the IN variable. However, the statistical results seem poor in the case without IN.

Table 5.4
OLS and 2SLS estimates of the models without IN

	\multicolumn{7}{c}{Dependent Variable}
	Tx	Tm	Hd	PCM	Tx	Tm
	(OLS)				(2SLS)	
Intercept	53.65^a (8.16)	8.53 (0.26)	0.13^b (2.32)	10.54^a (3.29)	53.26^a (5.09)	10.27 (0.23)
MS			−0.004 (−1.19)			
MES			0.06^c (1.58)			
KR			0.90^a (3.13)			
GRS				0.007^c (1.28)		
PE			0.11^a (2.52)	6.24^b (1.87)		
$MESMS$		−4,849.78^b (−1.99)		260.71 (1.25)		−4,466.08^b (−1.65)
Hd	2.02 (0.11)	75.83 (0.88)		23.28^b (2.15)	50.28 (0.99)	27.29 (0.14)
PCM	−0.59^b (−2.21)	0.56 (0.43)			−0.64 (−0.77)	0.41 (0.12)
KL	−0.01 (−0.25)	−0.04^b (−2.09)			−0.005 (−1.16)	−0.03^c (−1.37)
SK	−50.97^a (−3.08)	112.07^c (1.39)			−54.84^a (−3.02)	115.11^c (1.39)
DPC		100.11^a (3.99)				100.33^a (3.86)
Tm			−0.000004 (−0.02)	−0.02 (−1.25)		
Tx			−0.0007 (−0.46)	−0.04 (−0.50)		
FDI	0.32 (0.58)		−0.007^c (−1.53)	−0.43^b (−2.15)	0.05 (0.07)	
R^2	0.14	0.18				
F	3.73	4.18				

t-statistics (one-tail test) are given in parentheses. Significance levels of coefficients are $a = 1\%, b = 5\%$ and $c = 10\%$.

References

Aharoni, Y. (1980), "The State Owned Enterprise as a Competition in International Market," *The Columbia Journal of World Business*, 15 (1), pp.14–22.

Caves, R.E. (1980), *Multinational Enterprise and Economic Analysis* Cambridge University Press, Cambridge.

Chou, T.C. (1985), *Industrial Organization in The Process of Economic Development: The Case of Taiwan.* Ph. D. dissertation Université Catholique de Louvain, CIACO, Louvain-la-Neune.

Clarke, R. and S.W. Davies (1982), "Market Structure and Price-cost Margins," *Economica*, 49 (195), pp.277–87.

Curry, B. and K.D. George (1983), "Industrial Concentration: A Survey," *Journal of Industrial Economics*, 31 (3), pp.203–56.

De Ghellinck, E., P. Geroski and A. Jacquemin (1984), "Inter-industry and Intertemporal Variations in The Effect of Trade on Industry Performance," Institut des Sciences Economiques, Université Catholique de Louvain, *Working Paper*, 8401.

De Melo, J. and S. Urata (1984), "Market Structure and Performance: The Role of International Factors in Trade Liberalization," *The World Bank:* R-142 | JDD| d6.

Donsimoni, M.-P. and V. Leoz-Arquelles (1981), "Strategic Groups: An Application to Foreign and Domestic Firms in Spain," *in* P. Geroski and A. Jacquemin, eds., pp.291–306.

──── , P. Geroski and A. Jacquemin (1984), "Concentration Indices and Market Power: Two Views," *Journal of Industrial Economics*, 32 (4), pp.419–34.

Esposito, L. and F. F. Esposito (1977), "Aggregation and The Concentration-profitability Relationship," *Southern Economic Journal*, 44 (2), pp. 323–32.

Geroski, P. (1982a), "Simultaneous Equations Models of The Structure-performance Paradigm," *European Economic Review*, 19 (1), pp.145–58.

──── (1982b), "Interpreting a Correlation between Market Structure and Performance," *Journal of Industrial Economics*, 30 (3), pp.319–26.

──── and A. Jacquemin (1981), eds., "Symposium on Industrial Organization and International Competition," *Recherches Economiques de Louvain*, 47 (3-4), pp.197–355.

──── and ──── (1981), "Imports As a Competition Discipline," in P. Geroski and A. Jacquemin, eds., pp.197–208.

Glejser, H., A. Jacquemin and J. Petit (1980), "Exports in An Imperfect Competition Framework: An Analysis of 1446 Small Country Exporters," *Quarterly Journal of Economics*, 94 (3), pp.507–24.

Greer, D.F. (1971), "Advertising and Market Concentration," *Southern Economic Journd*, 38 (1), pp.18–32.

Huveneers, Ch. (1981), "Price Formation and The Scope for Oligopolistic Conduct in a Small Open Economy," *in* P. Geroski and A. Jacquemin, eds., pp.209–42.

Jacquemin, A. (1982), "Imperfect Market Structure and International Trade: Some Recent Research," *Kyklos*, 35 (1), pp.75–93.

──── E. de Ghellinck and Ch. Huveneers (1980), "Concentration and Profitability in a Small Open Economy," *Journal of Industrial Economics*, 29 (2), pp.131–43.

Johnston, J. (1972), *Econometric Methods*, McGraw-Hill Koga Kusha, Ltd, Tokyo. 2nd ed.

Lyons, B. (1981), "Industrial Behaviour, the Technology of Demand, and the Pattern of International Trade between Identical Countries, *in* P. Geroski and A. Jacquemin, eds., pp.243–58.

Martin, S. (1979), "Advertising, Concentration, and Profitability: The Simultaneity Problem," *Bell Journal of Economics*, 10, pp.639–47.

Ornstein, S.I., J.F. Weston, M.D. Intriligator and R.E. Shrieves (1973), "Determinants of Market Structure," *Southern Economic Journal*, 39 (4), pp.612–25.

Pagoulatos, E. and R. Sorensen (1981), "A Simultaneous Equation Analysis of Advertising, Concentration and Profitability," *Southern Economic Journal*, 47 (3), pp.728–41.

Pugel, T.A. (1978), *International Market Linkages and U.S. Manufacturing: Prices, Profits and Patterns*, Ballinger Publishing, Cambridge.

―――― (1980), "Foreign Trade and U.S. Market Performance," *Journal of Industrial Economics*, 29 (2), pp.119–29.

Sawyer, M.C. (1982), "On The Specification of Structure-Performance Relationships," *European Economic Review*, 18, pp.295–306.

Strickland, A.D. and L.W. Weiss (1976), "Advertising, Concentration, and Price-cost Margins," *Journal of Political Economy*, 84 (5), pp.1109–121.

Urata, S. (1984), "Price-cost Margins, and Imports in An Oligopolistic Market," *Economics Letters*, 15 (1-2), pp.139–44.

6 Concentration and Profitability in a Dichotomous Economy*

Introduction

How can the structure-performance paradigm apply to a newly industrializing country, for instance, Taiwan? Answers to this question form the subject matter of this study. To tackle this problem, Taiwan's market structure should first of all be characterized. A dichotomous market structure is hypothesized to exist in Taiwan, such that the distinctive characteristics, namely, the nature of the product, the technology (factor intensity), the firm size and the degree of monopoly exist in two dichotomous sectors: the domestic-oriented sector and the export-oriented sector. These characteristics are verified by two statistical tests, i.e. t-statistics and F-ratios. Some descriptive variables of market structure and performance are measured and compared between these two distinct sectors. The t-tests are first used to see whether the distinction that exists between those variables is significant in both sectors.

Secondly, F-ratios (Chow-tests) are calculated by a two-regime approach in both concentration and profit equations. That is, both equations are respectively estimated in two industrial groups. Also, due to the simultaneous determination of concentration and profitability, a recursive concentration-performance system is employed in this study.

---
*This paper was reproduced from *International Journal of Industrial Organization*, Vol. 6, No. 4, December 1988, pp.409–428, with permission of the publisher.

In the next section, the characteristics of Taiwan's dichotomous market structure are summarized and verified by using the t-test. In section 3, the formulation and specification of the structural model are discussed. In section 4, the empirical implication of the model and the test of the two-regimes hypothesis are described. The empirical results are then given in section 5 and the last section contains the concluding remarks.

Taiwan's dichotomous market structure: the t-test

The author (1988) has shown that Taiwan's market structure is influenced by export expansion strategies which consist of 'export incentives' and 'import protection'. There are two effects of this policy package, which are explained as follows:

First, exports with a comparative advantage due to their low labor costs concentrate primarily on labor-intensive industries, e.g. clothing, footwear, miscellaneous manufactures and electronic apparatus. Small firms using simple technology and which care little about brand names and after sales service prolong their existence on such an advantage. This is the reason why export-oriented industries tend to be more competitive. On the contrary, product differentiation (brand names), after sales service and sophisticated technology are important for the domestic-oriented industries which tend to be more monopolistic.

Second, under the export incentive measures, exporters can use cheaper imported materials and equipment nearly free of tariffs as will as enjoy low-interest export-promoting loans. They can also sell commodities at very competitive prices by taking advantage of both tax benefits and interest subsidies. Of course, these subsidies are covered by high tariff and tax revenues from the domestic-oriented industries. Thus, different situations occur in these two industrial groups as the result of the manipulation of the policy named 'domestic sales subsidize export sales'.

To distinguish these features, export-oriented industries and domestic-oriented industries are identified by export intensity (the share of exports to sales). Furthermore, 'export-oriented sector' is defined as comprising the industries whose export intensity is larger than the average of the whole of manufacturing industry; and the 'domestic-oriented sector' consists of the rest of them.

According to the definitions of these two dichotomous sectors, these sectors' distinct characteristics can be further examined. In the export-oriented sector, industry concentration, monopoly power, scale economies, and capital-and technology-intensity are low, but the growth of industry is high; however, in the domestic-oriented sector, the characteristics indicated above show an opposite pattern. In other words, the two sectors are quite distinct in terms of technology, firm size, and market structure. The export-oriented sector tends to have a low degree of monopoly while the domestic-oriented sector tends to have a high degree of monopoly.

The data of the 1976 Census are used here. Industries are at the four-digit Standard Industry Classification (SIC) level. Import data based on the Standard International Trade Classification ($SITC$) are assigned to correspond to SIC four-digit industrial data with some arbitrary adjustment. Concordance problems among different sources of data reduce the number of industries in the sample to 125.[1] The mean value of export intensity in all sampled industries is 30%. According to the definition, there are 48 industries in the export-oriented sector, while there are 77 industries in the domestic-oriented sector.

The following variables are presented to identify the characteristics of dichotomy. They are international linkage variables including export intensity (Tx), import intensity (Tm) and foreign direct investment (FDI), price-cost margins (PCM), industry concentration, scale economies, capital- and technology- intensity, and the growth of industry. The mean value and standard deviation of those variables from the two respective sectors are shown in table 6.1. These statistics could be used to calculate the t-ratios which are indicators to show if the difference in the mean value of these variables is significant between the two sectors. The results indicated that the dichotomy is generally existed. Brief definitions of the variables and sources of the data are also given in appendix 6.1.

As indicated in table 6.1, in the export-oriented sector 61% of goods produced are exported, while in the domestic-oriented sector less than 10% of the goods produced are exported. Although the share of the export-oriented sector in total exports is not found in the table, that is huge and amounts to 87.4%. Foreign investments are more often made in the export-oriented sector than in the domestic-oriented sector, but this difference is nonsignificant from the statistical point of view. Also, it should be indicated that import intensity is not significantly different because of the similar patterns of processing in the industries in both sectors. Obviously, it is impressive that the export-oriented sector has significantly lower technology-intensity, i.e. lower KL and SK. On the other hand, the large standard deviations of the scale variables show larger differences in the plant sizes and capital-intensity in the domestic-oriented sector. However, the differences in scale and the capital-output ratio between the two sectors is nonsignificant. This indicates that there is more homogeneity in terms of size and factor-intensity in the export-oriented sector. In other words, the domestic-oriented sector contains both large and small firms (plants).

Two indices of growth given in table 6.1 show opposite results. The average growth rate of industrial production ($GROWTH1$) between 1971 and 1976 at constant (1976) prices shows that the export-oriented sector has grown faster (almost twice as fast) than the domestic-oriented sector. On the contrary, the growth rate of value added at current prices ($GROWTH2$) moves in the opposite direction. If the ratio of value-added to production value does not change within that period, these opposite results indicate that prices increased in the domestic-oriented sector at a faster rate than those in the export-oriented sector.

Table 6.1

Characteristics of Taiwan's dichotomous market structure in 1976.[a]

		International linkage (%)			PCM (%)	Concentration indices			Scale economies		Capital-and technology-intensity			Growth rate (%)	
		T_x	T_m	FDI		Hd	C4	C8	MES (NT$ M.)	MESS (NT$ M.)	KY	KL	SK	GROWTH1	GROWTH2
Export-oriented sector $T_x > 30\%$ $N = 48$	mean	60.97	61.97	2.67	8.88	0.10	0.37	0.49	11.30	59.18	1.17	482.52	0.30	30.28[b]	88.88
	s.d.	18.35	162.42	3.70	5.20	0.19	0.24	0.24	23.61	126.53	0.89	697.32	0.16	53.17	60.43
Domesitic-oriented sector $T_x < 30\%$ $N = 77$	mean	9.36	67.86	2.15	11.55	0.13	0.47	0.59	22.20	220.17	1.35	810.34	0.39	15.53	105.21
	s.d.	8.03	126.93	5.93	19.65	0.18	0.24	0.24	107.90	1,154.90	1.29	1,116.10	0.16	17.94	95.92
t-ratio		18.42	0.21	0.60	2.14	0.88	2.27	2.27	0.85	1.21	0.92	2.02	3.06	1.86	1.17

[a] For definition and sources of variables see appendix 6.1.
[b] Excluding one industry due to no production in 1971.

Furthermore, this seems to suggest that the prices increased as a faster rate in a non-competitve market than in a competitive one.[2]

As far as we know, price-cost margins (PCM) of the industry may be used to measure the degree of monopoly.[3] The price-cost margins in the export-oriented sector is 8.88% which is lower than that in domestic-oriented sector (11.55%). This could also confirm that the export-oriented sector is relatively competitive.

Industrial concentration is another measure of monopoly power. Three indices of concentration are used here. Two of them, $C4$ and $C8$, consistently show that the export-oriented sector has a significantly lower industrial concentration. However, the variable Hd does not differ significantly between the two sectors. The statistical evidence shown above seem to reveal that the differences in market shares among leading firms is much more significant than those for all firms.

In short, the tests from the 1976 Census data indicate the statistically significant existence of a dichotomous market structure. The export-oriented sector is labor-intensive, low-skilled and grows rapidly, whereas the domestic-oriented sector is capital-intensive, high-skilled and grows slowly. Meanwhile, the domestic-oriented sector tends to have a higher degree of monopoly. This is also called a dichotomous economy. It should be noted here that these two sectors in this kind of economy still have some linkages related to policy issues.

A basic model

Curry and George (1983) indicate that industrial concentration as a measure of market power constitutes an important part of the structure of an industry, and thus it cannot be regarded as fundamental or exogenous. As suggested by Jacquemin et al. (1980), concentration ratios (CR) and performance (PCM) are jointly determined by two equations named the concentration equation and the profitability equation. In this two-equation system, concentration is not only determined by other elements of market structure, but is also a proxy for equilibrium performance[4] and thus as an explanatory variable in the PCM (observed profits) equation.[5] Therefore, by introducing the two-regimes approach in a dichotomous market structure, the basic recursive model can be constructed by means of the following two equations:

$$CR_i = \alpha_i + \theta_i D_i + K_i F_i + u_i, \qquad (1)$$

$$PCM_i = \beta_i + \tau_i CR_i + \delta_i D'_i + \phi_i F'_i + v_i, \qquad (2)$$

where $i = d, x$ denotes respectively domestic- and export-oriented sectors and indicates a two-regime approach, and the vectors of D, D', F and F' represent the variables of domestic market structure and international linkages. To estimate the regressions we should further specify vectors of variables D, D', F and F' in both equations. These variables have also been shown in table 6.1.

The concentration equation

To specify as completely as possible the relevant determinants of industrial concentration for a small open economy, we need to incorporate the usual explanatoy variables (D) besides the international variables (F) to explain the respective influences of the domestic market structure and international linkages. To start with, it is hypothesized that interindustry variations in concentration can be explained by a combination of explanatory variables such as scale economies, barriers to entry and the size of the market.[6] Public enterprise in Taiwan is an additional and important element of the domestic market structure (Chou 1986) and thus should be included in D. As a result, the vector of variables D includes four variables: a dummy variable of public enterprise (PE), absolute market size (MS) the minimum efficient scale ($MESS$), and capital requirement barriers (KR). In the vector of variables F, the import ratio ($Tm1$), export intensity (Tx) and foreign direct investment (FDI) are included.

The first explanatory variable (PE) reflects the importance of public enterprise in the domestic market. The very-large scale and high domestic-orientation of public enterprises demonstrated by Chou (1988) would lead us to expect that a positve effect of PE on CR in the domestic-oriented sector. However, in the export-oriented sector, this impact seems to be unimportant and indeterminate.

The $MESS$ and MS variables reflect economies of scale and the size of the domestic market respectively. A positive sign for $MESS$ and a negative sign for MS on CR can be expected in the domestic-oriented sector. However, the relationships of $MESS$ and MS on CR are ambiguous in the export-oriented sector, because the export-oriented sector is not restricted by the size of the domestic market.

The initial capital requirement (KR) which measures entry barriers is an explanatory variable in the concentration equations. The positive relationships are expected in both the domestic-oriented and export-oriented sectors because the larger the capital requirement is, the higher would be the level of concentration.

Now, let us turn to the causal effect of international linkages on CR. The import ratio ($Tm1$), measured as imports divided by domestic sales, is the fraction of industrial domestic sales provided by foreign suppliers. The marginal impacts of the $Tm1$ on CR depend upon the reactions of domestic producers with respect to imports. A positive impact would be observed if the threat from imports induced domestic firms to merge[7] or if import penetration forces inefficient producers to exit.[8] Both cases make CR to increase due to the decrease in the number of firms. In the export-oriented sector, imports as inputs of production which is proportional to the size of sales have also a positive effect on CR.[9]

The export intensity (Tx), measured as exports divided by sales, is the fraction of domestic production that is exported. To the extent that export intensity acts as a deconcentration force because it enlarges the market size, it would be expected to be inversely related to CR. The reasons of this negative relationship are: first, if economies of scale in production or distribution are not important, a larger market size resulting from better export opportunities can support a greater number of producers and reinforce this effect. Secondly, if the fixed cost associated with exporting activities is not high, the negative effect would easily be realized. However, if export expansion results in a reduction in average cost due to the occurrence of scale economies, it may result in a positive relation between Tx and CR. This effect seems unimportant in the domestic-oriented sector due to low export intensity.

The relationship between FDI and CR is ambiguous. Caves (1980a) shows the usual observation that FDI increases CR is not automatically supported in the LDCs. It seems to depend on the category of goods (consumer goods or production goods) and their market orientations. Foreign subsidiaries in Taiwan at their current small scale levels seem not to have a positive effect on CR in the export-oriented sector. In contrast, in the domestic-oriented sector, the effect of FDI or CR is similar to the effect of imports because FDI is a substitute of import penetration.

The profitability equation

The reasons of variables D' and F' being included in eq. (2) have been extensively discussed in the literature. Therefore they will only be briefly presented. On the other hand, the variable CR which is used as a conduct variable is a new concept introduced in this paper.

The basic hypothesis of our study is the claim that the conducts of export-and domestic-oriented industries belong to two different groups. In the group of domestic-oriented industries, a few large firms display oligopolistic behaviors due to the high protection measures in the domestic market. On the other hand, in the export-oriented industries, a lot of small firms behave as pure competitors in the world market. As a result, the performance of the domestic sector is significantly determined by the market structure variables, but the profitability of export sector is not.[10]

Donsimoni et al. (1984) demonstrate that different concentration indices could be emplored to capture distinctive solution concepts for oligopolistic conducts. Of course, a case by case study of each industry would permit us to attribute them with their respective solution concepts. Such an analysis goes beyond the scope of this study. To proceed, we simply assume that the industries within each sector display the same conduct but the industries across dichotomous sectors display different conducts. If the industry in the one sector behaves in the Cournot way, the Hd would be very significant in the profit equation. On the contrary, if the industry in the other sector behaves as a dominant firm, the $C4$ could be very significant. However, it is still an open question that which sector displays which kind of conduct. Therefore, two specifications of the variables CR, Hd and $C4$, are used at the same time with a two-regimes approach. The empirical results could reveal different conducts between two dichotomous sectors.

Two traditional vectors of variables D' and F' are included in the PCM equations for a small open economy. Variable D' denotes domestic market structure including entry barriers measured by scale economies ($MESMS$), the growth of industry ($GROWTH1$), capital-output intensity (KY), and PE. Variables F' is a vector of $Tm1$ and FDI. Some additional discussions could mow be put forward as follows.

Two variables MES and MS can be rearranged into one called $MESMS$, measured as minimum efficient scale divided by domestic market size. Theoretically, a significant and positive effect of $MESMS$ in the PCM equation of the domestic-oriented sector could be expected, but there would not be a significant effect in the export-oriented sector because exports offset the constraints of domestic market size.

In both the export- and domestic-oriented sectors, industries with high growth rates are traditionally associated with greater profitability since they allow greater exploitation of economies of scale (capacity utilization)as well as more frequent uses of new techniques of production. A positive effect of $GROWTH1$ on profits could also be expected if it reflects growth of demand.

Since profitability includes the net content of capital costs, variations in profits would partly reflect differences in inter-industry variations in capital intensity. To avoid this problem, KY is included in the regressions to control the different degree of capital intensity among industries. Usually, it is expected to have a positive impact of KY on profits. A negative effect will probably occur if an excessively capital-using technology is transformed from the capital abundant $MDCs$. To understand which (export- or domestic-) sector belongs to which situation is an empirical question. However, a competitve export-oriented sector seems unlikely to fall in the last category mentioned above. A relatively high capital intensity in the domestic-oriented sector would probably have a negative marginal impact on profits.

Additionally, a dummy variable (PE) is introduced to investigate the marginal impacts of public enterprise on profits. The impacts could be positive or negative. The negative effect is expected if industries with government control will have lower profitability either because public enterprises adopt low-price policy instead of a profit maximizing one or because they operate inefficienctly (Donsimoni and Leoz-Arguelles 1981). On the other hand, a positive effect is expected when either because public enterprises adopt monopolistic prices or because they operate more efficiently (Aharoni 1980). Again, empirical evidence is needed before it can be judged which is true.

Producers' ability to price above their minimum long run average cost could be reduced by import competition. Thus, profitablilty should be reduced when import ratio $(Tm1)$ increases in the domestic-oriented sector. Two more points should be discussed in this case. First, this negative relation is based on the assumption of imports as a fringe. Otherwise, the relation becomes ambiguous.[11] Secondly, domestic producers are not importers and cannot easily collude with foreign firms, otherwise a positive relation occurs.[12] So far as the export-oriented sector is concerned, great imports suggest high costs of materials and lower profits. Of course, all of the above impacts could be reduced by import controls.

Finally, FDI is introduced in the profit equations. In the domestic-oriented sector, the firms controlled by foreigners, like imports, play a competitive role to restrict the market power of domestic firms. Thus, a negative effect of FDI on profits is expected. Furthermore, this effect will increase when foreign subsidiaries operate more efficiently. In the export-oriented sector, the situation is more complex. Foreign subsidiaries could either be subcontractors of multinational enterprises or have international marketing networks. Their products can be more easily differentiated from domestic-made goods, resulting in a low degree of substitution of exports between domestic firms and foreign subsidiaries. In this case, the marginal impact of FDI in the profit equation of the export-oriented sector depends upon operational efficiency or pricing efficiency of foreign subsidiaries (Caves 1980a). High efficiency relative to the domestic-oriented sector may induce a positive impact on profits.

Testing two-regime hypothesis: the F-test

The data and estimation

As explained, the bulk of the variables originate from the 1976 Census conducted by the Committee on Industrial and Commercial Censuses. There are 134 industries at the four-digit level in the Census. Our final sample includes 125 industries: 48 industries belonging to the export-oriented sector and 77 industries belonging to the domestic-oriented one. The choice of four-digit ievel is advocated by Pugel (1980). He asserts that this is a better approximate of the appropriate level in defining economic industries.[13] Ordinary least squares estimation is used to estimate eqs. (1) and (2), because the model used in this study is recursive.

The F-test for two-regime hypothesis

The first test is to assess if the coefficients of two equations are statistically different in the two sectors. The mean value of $Tx(=30\%)$, as an

Table 6.2

Testing a two-regimes hypothesis in the concentration and profitability equation.[a]

Concentration indices	Concentration equation Hd	$C4$	Profitablilty equation (Hd)	$(C4)$
$SSRU$	1.326	4.142	9,769.9	10,225.9
$SSRR$	2.032	4.836	15,468.5	15,428.9
Chow test	7.25	2.28	7.95	6.93

[a] The partition is $Tx = 30\%$ in all equations. Two specifications of variables $CR(Hd$ and $C4)$ are used in equations (1) and (2) respectively.

arbitrary partition, is used to divide all sampled industries into two sectors. Furthermore, a Chow Test is applied here to select an appropriate partition.

The statistics associated with a Chow Test are provided in table 6.2. Two specifications of eqs. (1) and (2) have been respectively used, each corresponding to the two columns: the measured values of Hd and $C4$ in eq. (1) and the estimated value of Hd and $C4$ in eq. (2) In the first row, $SSRU$ is the sum of the squared residuals for the estimates of eqs. (1) and (2) respectively across the given partition ($Tx = 30\%$). The restricted $SSRR$ corresponding to the partition is indicated in the second row. By applying the Chow Test (shown in the third row) to determine whether or not the coefficients should be restricted to be equal across the two sectors, the results indicate that the null hypothesis (at 5% significant level in the $C4$ equation, at 1% significant level in others) is rejected. Thus, the statistics in table 6.2 show that industries can be allocated into two groups (in both two equations) and that these groups do not have the same functional form. In other words, a two-regime hypothesis is not rejected in this two-equation system.

Although the mean value of Tx as a criterion to allocate industries to respective sectors is clear from an economic point of view, the selected threshold has not been statistically determined. The 'optimal partition' could be obtained by minimizing the $SSRU$ over all possible partitions. The range of Tx from 10 to 50% in examined. The distribution of Chow Test over all partitions has a pair of peaks around two partitions (15% and 30%) in four equations. Using the value of $Tx = 15\%$ as a partition (except in the $C4$ equation) has a minimum $SSRU$.[14]

Using the value of $Tx = 30\%$ as a partition has a local (within Tx from 20 to 50%) minimum $SSRU$ (and the global minimum value in the $C4$ equation). This suggests that, first, the 15% seems to be too low to define the export-oriented sectors; and, secondly, only the partition of 30% for Tx obtains a significant Chow Test in the $C4$ equation to reject the null hypothesis. Therefore, mean value of Tx which is local (global) optimal partition in the $Hd(C4)$ equation and two profitability equations is still used.

Empirical results

The CR equation

The left part of table 6.3 provides the estimates of the regression coefficients associated with eq. (1). Two specifications (Hd and $C4$) are used and the partition is $Tx = 30\%$ in all equations.

The first result that emerges is that the estimated coefficients of domestic market structural elements have quite different signs between export- and domestic-oriented sectors, particularly in the Hd equation. The variables could now be investigated as follows. (1) Public enterprises strongly lead to concentration in the domestic-oriented sector but do not significantly influence market structure in the export-oriented sector. These meet our expectations.

(2) The relative market size, as expected, has a significant and negative impact in domestic-oriented concentration. By comparing the estimates of the two specifications (Hd and $C4$), it can be found that a negative impact comes from two sources of relative market size (MS

Table 6.3
Determinants of industry concentration in export-oriented and domestic-oriented sectors in 1976.[a]

Independent variables	Without adjustment of international linkages				With adjustment of international linkages			
	Hd as dependent variable		$C4$ as dependent variable		Hd as dependent variable		$C4$ as dependent variable	
	X-sector	D-sector	X-sector	D-sector	X-sector	D-sector	X-sector	D-sector
Intercept	0.10 (1.50)	0.12 (5.40)	0.43 (4.29)	0.50 (10.95)	0.02 (0.94)	0.11 (6.95)	0.27 (6.94)	0.46 (14.32)
PE	−0.03 (−0.33)	0.13 (2.93)	0.07 (0.58)	0.27 (3.09)	−0.01 (−0.15)	0.13 (3.24)	0.06 (0.52)	0.25 (3.12)
MS	0.01 (2.04)	−0.004 (−1.69)	0.001 (0.15)	−0.01 (−2.15)	0.01 (2.17)	−0.003 (−1.63)	0.01 (0.66)	−0.01 (−1.74)
$MESS$	−0.04 (−0.10)	0.20 (5.76)	0.13 (0.21)	0.10 (0.94)	−0.30 (−0.87)	0.20 (6.17)	0.40 (0.82)	0.10 (0.94)
KR	2.12 (3.26)	−0.52 (−1.53)	1.69 (1.74)	0.28 (0.40)	20 (4.41)	−10 (−2.14)	10 (1.63)	4 (0.74)
$Tm1$	0.00004 (1.11)	0.0001 (0.82)	0.0001 (2.20)	0.0002 (1.27)			0.0001 (2.17)	
Tx	−0.001 (−1.28)	−0.002 (−1.06)	−0.003 (−1.85)	−0.006 (−1.70)				
FDI	−0.01 (−0.73)	0.0002 (0.04)	0.01 (0.94)	0.007 (0.66)				
N	48	77	48	77	48	77	48	77
R^2	0.61	0.64	0.46	0.23	0.61	0.65	0.42	0.22
F	11.30	20.66	6.73	4.19	19.25	36.58	7.87	6.20
SSR	0.564	0.762	1.258	3.154	0.602	0.778	1.403	3.341

[a] t-statistics are given in parentheses.

and $MESS$) in the $C4$ equations respectively, that is, the largest firms (perhaps, the leaders) are more restricted by the domestic market size (MS is significant and negative in the $C4$ equation) than by the minimum efficient scale ($MESS$ is positive but insignificant), while all firms are more influenced by technological scale barriers ($MESS$ is significant and posifive in the Hd equation)[15] than by the domestic market size (MS is less significant and negative). In the export-oriented sector, the relative market size does not have this negative impact, thus the estimates are nonsignificant in the $C4$ equation. A significant and positive impact of domestic market size in the Hd equation suggests that scale economies of the domestic market are conducive to the large firms to export (with low marginal costs) and to gain large market shares of total sales.

(3) Capital requirement barriers have, as expected, a significant and positive impact in the export-oriented concentrations (both Hd and $C4$) equations, while they do not have a significant impact in domestic-oriented concentration. It is related to the choice of technology and should be further discussed below.

The impact of international linkages is considered. To further investigate the effects of international linkages on concentration, a F-statistic is applied. Table 6.4 provides a set of F-statistics to test the null hypothesis that concerns individual or combined international linkages are equal to zero. Only the coefficient of import ratio (K_5) is significant and positive in the export-oriented $C4$ equation, others cannot reject the null hypothesis (coefficients being zero). This may imply that imports as inputs of processing exports are more concentrated, particularly among the largest firms. Additionally, another possible explanation for nonsignificant impacts of other international linkages on export-oriented concentration is the poor measures of concentration. However, no significant impact of international linkages in the domestic-oriented sector seems to indicate that it is a sector protected from import and foreign firms' competition.

Table 6.4

Testing the existence of international linkages in the concentration equation (F-statistics).[a]

Null hypothesis[b]	Export-oriented sector Hd	$C4$	Domestic-oriented sector Hd	$C4$
$Ho(K_6 = 0)$	1.63 (1,40)	3.49 (1,40)	1.09 (1,69)	2.89 (1,69)
$Ho(K_6 = K_7 = 0)$	1.03 (2,40)	2.22 (2,40)	0.54 (2,69)	1.60 (2,69)
$Ho(K_7 = 0)$	0.42 (1,41)	0.90 (1,41)	0.00 (1,70)	0.30 (1,70)
$Ho(K_5 = K_6 = K_7 = 0)$	0.85 (3,40)	3.18 (3,40)	0.48 (3,69)	1.36 (3,69)
$Ho(K_5 = 0)$	0.50 (1,42)	4.80 (1,42)	0.37 (1,71)	0.86 (1,71)

[a] A pair of degrees of freedom for F-statistic is given in the brackets.

[b] K_5, K_6 and K_7 denote the coefficients of $Tm1, Tx$ and FDI included in a vector of F in eq. (1).

The right part of table 6.4 shows the estimates of the regression coefficients associated with eq. (1). Only import ratio is maintained in the export-oriented $C4$ equation. All estimates are the same as that of eq. (1) shown in the left part of table 6.4. No further comments are called for. Note, however, one exception: the estimated coefficient associated with KR is now negative and significant in the domestic-oriented Hd equation. This is in opposition with most previous findings. It may be argued that this variable is correlated with the choice of technology. As we know, excessive capital-using technology probably characterizes most domestic-oriented industries. If the high value of KR is derived from this kind of technology, it could not be an effective barrier. Whether this is true or not is still an open question requiring further investigation.

The PCM equation

Table 6.5 provides the estimates of the regression coefficients associated with eq. (2). Two estimated values of variable CR (Hd and $C4$) are used to indicate different behaviors of two dichotomous sectors. Furthermore, it is assessed whether the coefficients (individual or combined) of the international linkage variables in these equations are equal to zero. Then only foreign direct investment (FDI) is maintained in the equations whose estimates are also given in that table.

The first result is that there is a strong positive relationship berween the degree of concentration (measured by the Herfindahl index) and the PCM only for the domestic sector; such a degree of concentration is not linked with the Lerner index in the export sector. Furthermore, in the domestic-oriented sector, it can be found that the esimate of Hd rather than $C4$ is more significant and positive. This seems to reveal that the firms (the industries) within the domestic-oriented sector display the Cournot type of conduct. The estimates of both specifications in the export-oriented sector are nonsignificant. However, the Concentration Ratio ($C8$) of eight firms is used in preliminary tests but is not included here because it brings no improvement in the estimated results.[16] Again, the result shows that, for the domestic sector, the market structure variables ($Hd, C4$ and $MESS$) have significant effects on PCM, while for the export sector, they are not significant. This result indicates, on the one hand, Taiwan's export sector behaves as a pure competitor in the world market. On the other hand, the domestic sector is protected from foreign competition so that domestic structure variables are still important factors.[17]

Secondly, most of the elements of the domestic market structure have the expected signs in the two regimes. (1) Scale economies barriers ($MESMS$) are significant with the expected (positive) sign in the domestic-oriented sector while they have no significant impact for the export-oriented sector. (2) The rate of growth ($GROWTH1$) is nonsignificant in influencing profits. (3) the impact of capital-intensity

Table 6.5

Determinants of industry profitability in export-oriented and domestic-oriented sectors in 1976.[a]

Independent variables	Without adjustment of international linkages				With adjustment of international linkages			
	X-sector	D-sector	X-sector	D-sector	X-sector	D-sector	X-sector	D-sector
Intercept	3.13 (2.70)	17.93 (6.34)	0.72 (0.33)	8.69 (0.91)	2.49 (1.63)	17.98 (6.72)	2.59 (0.67)	1.71 (0.16)
$\hat{H}d$	16.30 (1.34)	41.61 (2.31)			19.13 (1.06)	49.48 (2.30)		
$\hat{C}_4$			11.52 (1.52)	31.21 (1.33)			2.97 (0.28)	53.16 (1.77)
$MESMS$	−95.18 (−0.91)	1,079.51 (3.41)	−71.65 (−0.73)	1,108.60 (3.27)	−96.84 (−0.86)	1,083.11 (3.40)	−43.70 (−0.43)	1,112.99 (3.46)
$GROWTH1$	0.0002 (1.11)	0.07 (0.84)	−0.0002 (−0.09)	0.05 (0.57)	0.0003 (0.12)	0.06 (0.79)	0.0001 (0.05)	0.04 (0.53)
KY	2.95 (3.38)	−11.06 (−10.59)	3.18 (4.04)	−11.21 (−10.21)	3.06 (3.67)	−11.02 (−10.66)	3.35 (3.92)	−11.25 (−10.49)
PE	−4.96 (−1.68)	8.82 (1.59)	−5.99 (−1.86)	9.73 (1.36)	−5.48 (−1.53)	7.6 (1.28)	−3.46 (−0.96)	2.52 (0.27)
$Tm1$	−0.001 (−0.81)	−0.003 (−0.33)	−0.002 (−1.25)	−0.01 (−0.60)				
FDI	0.67 (3.75)	−0.97 (−2.80)	0.53 (3.03)	−0.67 (−2.06)	0.53 (3.21)	−1.18 (−2.83)	0.58 (3.33)	−0.88 (−2.40)
N	48	77	48	77	48	77	48	77
R^2	0.42	0.66	0.43	0.64	0.42	0.66	0.40	0.65
F	5.78	21.64	5.92	20.13	6.59	24.49	6.26	24.41
SSR	589.8	9,180.1	582.8	9,643.1	603.7	9,210.8	619.0	9,486.3

[a] t-statistics are given in parentheses.

(KY) is significant and positive (negative) in the export-(domestic-) oriented sectors. As mentioned before, this result relating to the impact of KR on concentration suggests that excessive capital-using technology is used in the domestic-oriented sector while it is not in the competitive export-oriented sector. (4) The impacts of public enterprises (PE) on profits are significant and negative in the export-oriented sector while it is positive but less significant in the domestic-oriented sector.

Thirdly, the relationship between FDI and PCM is significant in both sectors but with different signs. The same result that FDI is negatively associated with PCM in the domestic sector is also found by the author (Chou 1986). However, for the export sector, FDI is found to be a significant determinant of PCM. FDI may be reflecting not only the efficiency of foreign subsidiaries, but also other complex factors. FDI in Taiwan tends to occur because labor cost is low compared to the home countries of foreign firms. To the extent that FDI occurs more in the sector where labor cost is far below the world price, FDI should have a positive relation with PCM.

Finally, let us consider the impact of international linkages. Tests are similar to those examined in table 6.4 and given in table 6.6. To search for any possible impact of international linkages, the variable Tx is also included in eq. (2). F-statistics confirm that only the impact of foreign direct investment (FDI) is significant. Thus, in both sectors import competition does not influence profits.[18] The absence of import penetration in the domestic-oriented sector is probably the result of import control policy. Therefore, only FDI is maintained in eq. (2). This does not change the estimates of other coefficients: only the impact of PE becomes nonsignificant. If domestic-oriented industries dominated by public firms experiment significant increases of prices (Chou 1985, ch. 4), the nonsignificantly positive impact on profits now could indicate a situation of low efficiency. On the other hand, it is confirmed that the impact of FDI is significant and positive (negative) in the export-(domestic-)oriented sectors. Thus, competition between domestic and foreign subsidiaries seems vigorous in the domestic-oriented

Table 6.6

Testing the existence of international linkages in
the profitability equation (F-statistics).[a]

Null hypothesis[b]	Export-oriented sector Hd	$C4$	Domestic-oriented sector Hd	$C4$
$Ho(\phi_8 = 0)$	1.94 (1,39)	2.00 (1,39)	0.35 (1,68)	0.56 (1,68)
$Ho(\phi_6 = \phi_8 = 0)$	1.05 (2,39)	1.48 (2,39)	0.19 (2,68)	0.23 (2,68)
$Ho(\phi_6 = \phi_7 = \phi_8 = 0)$	4.14 (3,39)	4.78 (3,39)	2.74 (3,68)	2.09 (3,68)
$Ho(\phi_7 = 0)$	10.30 (1,41)	10.94 (1,41)	8.02 (1,70)	5.80 (1,70)

[a] A pair of degrees of freedom for F-statistic is given in the brackets.

[b] ϕ_6, ϕ_7 and ϕ_8 denote the coefficients of $Tm1, FDI$ and Tx included in a vector of F' in eq. (2).

sector while it is not in the export-oriented sector. Domestic-oriented foreign firms could restrain market power of domestic firms. It is also proved for other LDCs that export-oriented foreign firms are more profitable (Caves 1980a).

Concluding remarks

The presented results suggest that there is a two-regime situation since estimated coefficients are statistically different between the two types of sectors. However, the identification of market conducts in the two sectors requires furhter investigation. Nevertheless, two dichotomous sectors with the partition of export intensity is proven to be true in Taiwan. For the export sector, the effect of domestic sector and market structure variables have significant effect on PCM, because this sector is protected from foreign competition by protective measures.

So far as industrial policies are concerned, this study suggests, among other things, (1) that international linkages (imports and foreign subsidiaries) do not exercise a significant influence on Taiwan's market concentration, and (2) that foreign subsidiaries stimulate competition in domestic-oriented sectors and improve profitability in export-oriented sectors. Therefore, different policy criteria, market structure versus performance, could lead to the use of different policy instruments. For example, if the policy goal is to reduce concentration rather than performance (in order to continue the manipulation of 'domestic sales subsidizing export sales' policy), it does not appear to be useful to encourage domestic-oriented foreign subsidiaries. On the contrary, this kind of foreign firm is welcome to restrict high monopolized profits in the domestic sector.

However, it should be underlined that the above conclusions are obtained under the existing import-control policy. If the policy measures were changed, the conclusions could be enormously different, as suggested by the experiment of Chile (de Melo and Urata 1984).

This study also suggests that public enterprises are powerful enough to influence domestic concentration. Furthermore, the low efficiency of public firms is revealed by their high prices with nonsignificant impact on profits at home. Also, the negative impacts of KR on concentration and KY on profits in the domestic-oriented sector indicate that there is an excessive capital-using technology leading to a very low value of marginal product of capital. However, an inefficient PE and inappropriate technology should be modified to better economic peformance in Taiwan. This requires further investigation.

Notes

1. There are 134 SIC four-digit industries in Taiwan. Of the nine industries deleted from the sample, three (3702, 3706 and 3909) were dropped due to lack of concentration data. The six remaining industries (2011, 2521, 2529, 3501, 3708, and 3709) could not

be used because of the somewhat aggregated presentation of the foreign trade data.

2. No attempt is made, here, to argue the causal relationship between market power and inflation, see Heusz (1977).
3. Usual deficiencies in the empirical measurement of PCM also remain here. For critiques on these, see Feinberg (1980).
4. Donsimoni et al. (1984) present this view very clearly.
5. This is similar to the method of Geroski (1982). He indicates that actually observed PCM do not in general equilibrium (maximum) PCM due to the intervening influence of additional market structure factors. As a result, concentration (being a proxy for equilibrium PCM) and additional structural factors are determinants of actually observed PCM. This, as shown in (2) below, is the profitability equation.
6. For surveys of the various theories of the determinants of industry concentration, see Ornstein et al. (1973) and Curry and George (1983).
7. See Jacquemin et al. (1980): 'Sectors characterized by a systematic high share of imports are expected to be also characterized by a high degree of defensive concentration of domestic producers, as long as imports are close substitutes for domestic product,' (p.135)
8. However, the impact would be negative if inefficient producers improve their productive efficiency in response to an increase in imports, see de Melo and Urata (1984).
9. The effect of imports should be influenced by trade policy as in the case of Chile (see de Malo and Urata 1984).
10. This hypothesis seems similar to the argument of Porter's strategic group.
11. For instance, in the contrary case where domestic firms are treated as the competitive fringe, the relation becomes positive. And in the mixed case where both domestic and foreign firms form a cartel, the relation is ambiguous, see Geroski and Jacquemin (1981).

12. Urata (1984) shows that the relationship is likely to be positive, if the implicit collusion between domestic firms is lower than that between domestic and foreign firms and if domestic concentration is low. De Melo and Urata (1984) also indicate that the profitability can also be positively associated with the import intensity in a model where an oligopolistic firm is engaged in both production and imports simultaneously.
13. Also see the argument of Esposito and Esposito (1977) in their discussion of the influence of aggregation level on structure-profitablilty relatonship.
14. The values of $SSRU$ are 1.267, 4.254, 9443.5 and 9779.7 corresponding to the first row in table 6.2.
15. For the domestic sector, $MESS$ has a significant positive relation with the Hd but not with $C4$. This perverse result could be, as suggested by the referee, interpreted by the meaning of Hd index which can be decomposed into two factors: the number of firms (n) and variance of firm size. This implies that (i) large $MESS$ leade to small n or (ii) large $MESS$ leads to large variance of firm size. Therefore, it seems that, in Taiwan, the presence of small firms has a close relstion with $MESS$. If the industry with large $MESS$ tends to be dominated by very large firms, the Hd will be more sensitive to $MESS$.
16. The t-statistics of estimated coefficients of $C8$ are 1.52 and 0.69 in export- and domestic-oriented sector respectively. After adjusting the effect of international linkages, t-statistics in the two sectors are 0.83 and 1.67 respectively.
17. Thanks are due to a referee's mention for these important points.
18. This nonsignificance is very much possible due to a simultaneity of PCM and imports. This was found by the author (Chou 1986).

Appendix

Appendix 6.1 Sources and definitions of variables

Variable[a]	Source[b]	Definition
PCM (10.52, 15.74)	(1)	'Production value minus intermediate expenses minus wages' divided by sales. (%)
HD (0.12, 0.18)	(4)	Herfindahl indes of concentration in terms of sales.
$C4$ (0.43, 0.25)	(4)	The four-firm concentration ratio in terms of sales.
$C8$ (0.55, 0.25)	(4)	The eight-firm concentration ratio in terms of sales.
Tx (29.18, 28.33)	(1)	Exports divided by sales. (%)
Tm (65.57, 141.00)	(1) & (2)	Imports divided by sales. (%)
$Tm1$ (123.41, 381.14)	(1) & (2)	Imports divided by domestic sales (sales minus exports). (%)
FDI (2.35, 5.18)	(1)	The ratio the number of foreign enterprises unit to the total number of enterprise unit. (%)
PE (0.11, 0.32)	(1)	A dummy having the value of one if the percentage of sales from public enterprise is above the average level of 3-digit industry.
MS (5.37, 10.02)	(1) & (2)	Sales plus imports minus exports. (NT$ M.)
MES (0.13, 0.03)	(1)	The average size of the largest plants accounting for 50% of industry value-added. (NT$ M.)
$MESS$ (0.18, 0.09)	(1)	The average size of the largest piants accounting for 50% of industry sales. (NT$ M.)
$MESMS$ (0.34, 0.52)	(1)	MES divided by MS. (%)

Variable[a]	Source[b]	Definition
KR (28.00, 128.46)	(1)	MES times (assets divided by sales).
$GROWTH1$ (21.12, 36.16)	(5)	The average growth rate of industry production value between 1971 and 1976, at 1976 prices. (%)
$GROWTH2$ (98.94, 84.18)	(1) & (3)	The average growth rate of industry value-added between 1971 and 1976, at current prices. (%)
KY (1.28, 1.15)	(1)	Assets divided by production value.
KL (684.5, 986.6)	(1)	Assets divided by employment. (NT$ thousand per person)
SK (0.35, 0.16)	(1)	The skilled workers divided by total workers.

[a] Mean and standard deviation shown in parentheses.

[b] Data sources are: (1) The Committee on Industrial and Commercial Censuses of Taiwan, R.O.C. (1976), *General Report of Industry & Commerce Census of Taiwan*. (2) Statistical Department, Inspectorate General of Customs (1976), *The Trade of China, Taiwan District*. (3) The Committee on Industrial and Commercial Censuses of Taiwan, R.O.C. (1971) *General Report of Industry & Commerce Census of Taiwan*. (4) Hsiao (1982). (5) Department of Statistics, Ministry of Economic Affairs (1982), *Taiwan Industrial Production Statistics Monthly, Republic of China*.

References

Adams, W.J. (1980), "Producer Concentration as a Proxy for Seller Concentration: Some Evidence from the World Automobile Industry," *in* R.E. Caves, ed., pp.185–202.

Aharoni, Y. (1980), "The State Owned Enterprise as a Competition in International Market," *The Columbia Journal of World Business*, 15 (1), pp.14–22.

Caves, R.E. (1980), *Multinational Enterprise and Economic Analysis*, Cambridge University Press, Cambridge.

Caves, R.E., ed. (1980b), "Symposium on International Trade and Industrial Organization," *Journal of Industrial Economics*, 29 (2), pp.113–218.

Chou, T.C. (1985), *Industrial Organization in the Process of Economic Development, the Case of Taiwan*, Ph.D. dissertation, Université Catholique de Louvain, CIACO, Louvain-la-Neuve.

——— (1986), "Concentration, Profitability and Trade in a Simultaneous Equation Analysis: The Case of Taiwan," *Journal of Industrial Economics*, 34 (4), pp.429–33, Also the chapter 5 of this book.

——— (1988), "The Evolution of Market Structure in Taiwan," *Rivista Internazionale di Scienze Economiche e Commerciali*, 35 (2), pp.171–194, Also the chapter 4 of this book.

Curry, B. and K.D. George (1983), "Industrial Concentration: A Survey," *Journal of Industrial Economics*, 31 (3), pp.203–56.

De Ghellinck, E., P. Geroski and A. Jacquemin (1984), "Inter-industry and Inter-temporal Variations in the Effect of Trade on Industry Performance," *Working paper 8401*, Institute des Sciences Economiques, Universite Catholique de Louvain, Louvain-la-Neuve.

De Melo, J. and S. Urata (1984), "Market Structure and Performance: The Role of International Factors in a Trade Liberalization," R-142/JDD/d6, The World Bank, Washington, DC.

Donsimoni, M.P., and V. Leoz-Arguelles (1981), "Strategic Groups: An Implication to Foreign and Domestic Firms in Spain," *in* P. Geroski and A. Jacquemin, eds., pp.291-306.

———— P. Geroski and A. Jacquemin (1984), "Concentration Indices and Market Power: Two Views," *Journal of Industrial Economics*, 32 (4), pp.419-34.

Esposito, L. and F.F. Esposito (1977), "Aggregation and the Concentration-Profitability Relationship," *Southern Economic Journal*, 44 (2), pp.323-32.

Feinberg, R. (1980), "The Lerner Index, Concentration and the Measurement of Market Power," *Southern Economic Journal*, 46 (4), pp.1180-86.

Geroski, P. (1982), "Simultaneous Equations Models of the Structure-Performance Paradigm," *European Economic Review*, 19 (1), pp.145-58.

———— and A. Jacquemin, eds. (1981), "Symposium on Industrial Organization and International Competition," *Recherches Economiques de Louvain*, 47 (3-4), pp.197-355.

———— and ———— (1981), "Imports as a Competition Discipline," *in* P. Geroski and A. Jacquemin, eds, pp.197-208.

Heusz, E. (1977), "Oligopoly and Inflation," *in* A. Jacquemin and H.W. de Jong, eds. *Welfare Aspects of Industrial Markets*, Nijhoff, The Hague, pp.89-99.

Hsiao, F.S. (1982), "The Measurement of Industry Concentration in Taiwan," *Taipei City Bank Monthly*, 13 (5), pp.43-56 (in Chinese).

Jacquemin, A., E. de Ghellinck and Ch. Huveneers (1980), "Concentration and Profitability in a small Open Economy," *in* R.E. Caves, ed., pp.131–43.

Ornstein, S.I., J.F. Weston, M.D. Intriligator and R.E. Shrieves (1973), "Determinants of Market Structure," *Southern Economic Journal*, 39 (4), pp.612–25.

Porter, M.E. (1979), "The Structure within Industries and Companies Performance," *Review of Economics and Statistics*, 61 (2), pp.214–27.

Pugel, T.A. (1980), "Foreign Trade and U.S. Market Performance," *in* R.E. Caves, ed., pp.119–29.

Urata, S. (1984), "Price-Cost Margins and Imports in an Oligopolistic Market," *Economics Letters*, 15 (1–2), pp.139–44.

Part III
Large, Small and Foreign Firms

7 Aggregate Concentration Ratio and Business Groups*

Introduction

Aggregate concentration ratios (ACR) are often used to indicate to what extent national economic activities are controlled by the largest firms in the economy. Thus, the level and the trend of ACR are a real concern for industrial economists. The first purpose of this study is to document ACR in Taiwan during the 1970's. As a result, we find that a non-growing trend of ACR occurred in the manufacturing sector during that period. This trend is, surprisingly, in contrast to the experience of some industrialized countries, for instance, the United States of America and the United Kingdom.

Besides the general limitations of aggregate concentration data as mentioned by White (1981a), the second purpose of this study is to show the limitations of ACR when it is used to indicate the true percentage of Taiwan's largest firms, and to see an organizational feature of large business in Taiwan. As it will be shown that Taiwan's entrepreneurs do not prefer to increase their business activities by means of a single large company. In contrast, they prefer to set-up a number of member-companies under the control of common directors. This is a so-called "business group" in Taiwan. Consequently, business in Taiwan is organized on the basis of a multi-companies group instead of a

---

*This paper was reproduced from *Taiwan Economic Review*, Vol. 16, No. 1, March 1988, pp.79–94, with permission of the publisher.

large multidivisional company with a lot of subsidiaries. This dispersed organization not only understates the real influence of large firms, but also leads the share of the large firms in units of a single corporation do not increase. However, during the same period, we find an increasing trend of a share of the large firms in units of business groups.

The third purpose of this study is to go more deeply into the inside story of business groups, particularly, their diversification. It is evident that giant Taiwanese enterprises adjust their business activities by way of establishing new companies and/or closing existing ones. Conglomerate groups with higher and higher degrees of diversification are also found. To complete the whole story, it is necessary to search for reasons as to why business groups are formed, after we understand that the organization of business groups is closely related to aggregate concentration. Thus, the last purpose of this study is to provide some reasons as to why business groups are formed.

In section 1, the measures of ACR in the 1970's are presented. The reasons explaining the short-term fluctuation and a stable trend of ACR are provided. In section 2, the characteristics of Taiwan's business organizations, and business groups, are discussed. In section 3, their diversification is shown to indicate the internal growth of Taiwan's large firms. In section 4, reasons for forming business groups are discussed. Finally, some concluding remarks are presented in section 5.

Aggregate concentration ratios in the 1970's

The last forty years of evolution of Taiwan's large (e.g., the hundred largest) industrial enterprises is largely unknown. Unfortunately, the data before 1970 was not available, and thus only the data covering one decade (1970–80) can be used to measure ACR. To start, we report the shares of the fifty, one-hundred and two-hundred largest firms in terms of turnover, assets and employment in manufacturing industry. We then discuss factors influencing the changes in ACR over the last decade. Two views could be advanced. On one hand, the short-term fluctuations can be possibly explained by business cycles. On the other hand, business groups organized to realize the internal growth of large firms could be a significant factor in explaining a stagnant level of ACR.

The measures and the trends

There are two approaches to measure aggregate concentration in the manufacturing or the total private sector. One is the 'disaggregated approach', the other the 'aggregate approach'. The disaggregated approach measures the shares of the top 3 (or any special number) largest enterprises in each industry, then estimates the simple or weighted average of these industry concentration ratios. (See, for example, British industry, by Hart and Clarke, 1980.) The aggregate approach measures the shares of the top 50, 100 or 200 (so-called ACR 50, ACR 100 or ACR 200 respectively) enterprises in the manufacturing industry or in the total private sector. (For example, see Prais, 1981 for the British case, and see White, 1981a, 1981b for the U.S. case.)

In the published Census Report, there were no individual firm's data ranked by their size in any individual, nor in the whole manufacturing industry. Also, the original Census data before 1976, (i.e. 1954, 1961, 1966, 1971) was not available. Therefore, the Census data in Taiwan can't provide information needed for either the aggregate or the disaggregated approach. Fortunately, other data sources allow us to make use of the aggregate approach. We collect the data of the largest firms from *Top Private Enterprises*, which has been published annually by China Credit Information Services ever since 1970. Therefore, ACR in the 1970's (1970–80) can be calculated. Yet, from such source, only the data of operating revenues, employment and assets of the largest firms are available. Accordingly, the data of production value and assets in the manufacturing industry are compiled from the Industrial and Commercial Survey,[1] and the data of employment from Labor Statistics.

To use different data sets simultaneously causes some difficulties, particularly if the definition of a variable is not identical. The 'operating revenues' in Top Enterprises data and the 'value of production' in the Survey data is a case in point.[2]

Table 7.1 highlights several interesting changes over time of Taiwan's manufacturing ACR in the 1970's. First, there are concurrent trends among ACR 50, ACR 100 and ACR 200 in each index respectively. Only one exception occurred during 1973–75 between the shares of assets held by the 50 largest firms, and the 100 (also 200) largest firms. This reveals that the changes among the groups of the leading 50, 100 and 200 are moving in the same direction, and are largely of the same order of magnitude. Therefore, to save space, from now on, we will limit our discussion to the ACR 100 only.

Second, there are significant differences of ACR 100 among the three indices. Specifically, the percentage of assets controlled by the 100 largest firms in the manufacturing industry is larger than the percentage of their output, which in turn is greater than the percentage of the employment they created (see Figure 7.1).

On the average, in the 1970's, the one-hundred largest enterprises controlled one quarter (26.7%) of assets, produced 23% of production, and employed only 11% of laborers in the manufacturing industry. It is evident that the large firms tend to be more capital-intensive or less laborintensive in their production processes than their smaller counterparts.[3] Therefore, the measures of ACR in terms of employment or assets may understate or overstate the relative importance of large firms.

Finally, the evolution of ACT 100 in the 1970's should be examined in detail. The shares of turnover maintained a stagnant trend during the entire period with a mean value of 22.5%, and little short-term fluctuation. Specifically it was growing in 1970–73 (+4.2 percentage points), declining in 1973–76 (−4.5 percentage points), moving-up again in 1976–78 (+2.5 percentage points), and declining again in 1978–80 (−1.3 percentage points). There was a similar trend of ACR 100 in

Table 7.1

Aggregate concentration ratios in the manufacturing industry

	1970	1971	1972	1973	1974	1975	1976	1977	1978	1979	1980
A. Percentage of total manufacturing											
% share of turnover											
Largest 50	—	16.2	—	17.2	16.9	15.8	15.1	15.2	17.3	16.1	16.4
Largest 100	21.0	23.2	22.7	25.2	23.4	21.7	20.7	22.4	23.2	21.7	21.9
Largest 200	—	—	—	33.2	31.2	28.7	27.0	28.9	30.0	28.0	28.2
% share of employment											
Largest 50	—	7.6	—	7.6	6.8	7.2	6.8	7.3	7.4	8.3	7.8
Largest 100	11.1	11.1	11.1	10.9	9.1	10.8	10.1	10.6	10.4	11.2	10.6
Largest 200	—	—	—	16.0	14.5	15.8	14.6	14.9	14.3	15.7	14.8
% share of assets											
Largest 50	—	19.0	—	18.2	16.4	18.2	18.2	19.5	21.5	23.3	19.3
Largest 100	21.6	26.3	22.9	26.8	32.3	26.8	26.1	25.6	28.7	30.8	25.9
Largest 200	—	—	—	35.0	42.8	35.6	36.0	32.9	37.3	39.7	32.9
B. Percentage of private manufacturing											
% share of turnover											
Largest 50	—	20.8	—	19.7	20.3	19.3	17.8	18.1	20.7	19.0	20.4
Largest 100	—	29.7	26.4	28.7	28.1	26.4	24.4	26.8	27.8	25.6	27.4
Largest 200	—	—	—	37.8	37.5	34.9	32.4	34.5	35.9	33.0	35.3
% share of assets											
Largest 50	—	24.7	—	22.6	20.9	24.9	25.9	27.0	32.0	33.6	26.3
Largest 100	39.2	34.1	29.2	33.3	40.8	36.7	37.2	35.4	42.6	44.4	35.4
Largest 200	—	—	—	43.5	54.3	48.7	51.4	45.5	55.4	57.2	44.8

Sources: China Credit Information Services, *The Largest Industrial Corporation in the R.O.C.*, various years.

Department of Statistics, Ministry of Economic Affairs, *Report on Industrial and Commercial Survey*, various years.

DGBAS, Executive Yuan, *Yearbood of Labor Statistics, R.O.C.*, various years.

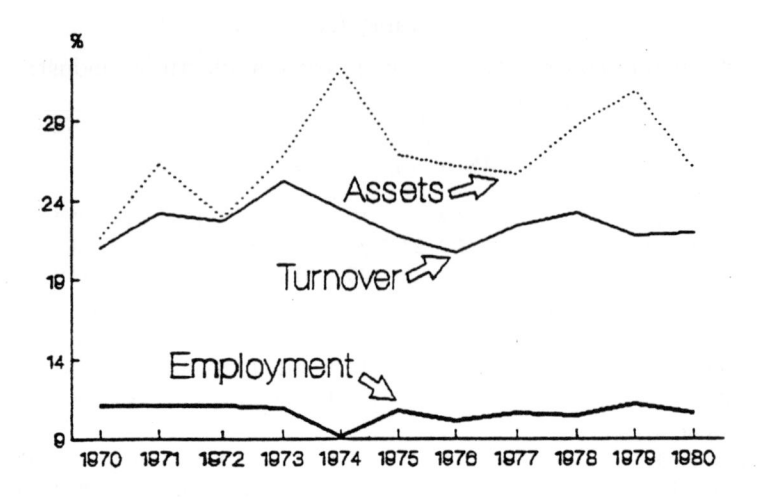

source: Table 7.1

Figure 7.1   ACR 100 in terms of turnover, employment and assets, 1970–80

terms of assets after 1974, fluctuations having only a one-year lag, i.e. declining in 1974–77 (−6.7 percentage points), moving-up in 1977–79 (+5.2 percentage points), and declining again in 1978–80 (−4.9 percentage points). Viewing the period as a whole, we find that the trend of ACR 100 in terms of turnover or employment is relatively stagnant with little volatility. The factors influencing the short-term fluctuations and causing a stagnant trend of ACR 100 in the 1970's form the subject matter of the following subsection.

Some possible explanations

Many factors are used to explain the long-run evolution of ACR. For example, Prais (1981) examines the change in plant-sizes, operation, financial factors, and stochastic shocks. He finds that stochastic forces, variability in the growth rate of firms, can sufficiently explain much of the developnents in the first half of this century, of the share of the largest firms in the U.K. Also, the evolutionary changes in the ownership of capital, and associated financial development seem to carry great weight in explaining the rise of aggergate concentration in the past half century. Finally, the increasing diversification of large firms across several industries can be seen as another factor which links the evolution of aggregate concentration with industrial concentration (see Utton, 1979). Furthermore, Prais (1981) also cites other factors to explain a slowing-down of British aggregate concentration in the period from 1970 through 1976. Among others, the increasingly heavy strikes experienced by the very largest manufacturing plants have played a significant role in restraining the growth of the very largest enterprises. This factor is not relevant for Taiwan because, so far, there have been no strikes. On top of the factors suggested above, a wave of mergers of large companies has also been emphasized by many studies[4] to explain the change in aggregate concentration.

After a brief review of explanations in the U.K. and U.S., we turn our attention to the case of Taiwan. Since data for only one-decade is available, we confine ourselves to the short-run factors, rather than the long-run stochastic forces influencing aggregate concentration. Basically, ample export opportunities enjoyed by small firms may help lead to a stagnant trend, as opposed to what has been observed in industrialized countries. Nevertheless, two factors: business-cycle fluctuations and the organization of large firms may account for fluctuations and a stagnant trend of aggregate concentration in manufacturing in the 1970's, respectively.

On one hand, oil shocks significantly worsened the growth of the economy, particularly the first shock in late 1972. Taiwan suffered low growth rates in 1974 and 1975 (1.1% and 4.2% compared to the average growth rate of 10.8% in 1963–72, and 8.3% in 1973–81). Again, the second shock led to a worldwide recession in the late 1970's. This also lowered the growth rate of the economy in Taiwan, (i.e. 6%, 4.6% and 3.6% in 1979, 1980 and 1981 respectively). It seems that the business-cycle caused by oil shocks may partially explain fluctuations of the shares of the largest firms. In other words, recession seems to hurt the large firms much more than the smaller firms, probably because of the low adjusting capablilty of the large firms.

On the other hand, we turn our attention to the behavior of the large enterprises themselves. Increases in aggregate concentration are mainly determined by the growth of the largest firms. Viewed from this perspective, one eminent, if not unique, characteristic of business organization should be focused on: the growth of the large firms and their diversification across sectors. Unlike the U.K. case (Utton, 1979), businessmen in Taiwan expand their businesses primarily by establishing new firms within a group, rather than through mergers or acquisitions. As a result, in contrast to the big parent company with many subsidiaries, or large multidivisional corporations in the U.S. (Chandler, 1977), Taiwan's business groups are constituted of a number of separate member-companies. By not keeping a unified account for member companies, and not consolidating their operations, the internal growth of large firms goes unreported. This may help explain a stagnant trend of ACR emerging in the 1970's. This is of great significance for Taiwan's business organizations, and additional explanations are in order. We now turn to this.

Business group: organization

According to the definition of Leff (1978, p.633), a business group is "a multi-company firm which transacts in different markets but which does so under common entrepreneurial and financial control." In Taiwan, the common control for a business group is from its *common directors*. Furthermore, one common basis of the interlocking (or common) directorship is the family. This can be confirmed by examining the list of directors (see note 5). Thus business groups in Taiwan are primarily based on family relations (i.e. nepotistic practices). As they have no legal status, business groups are not identified in official data.

The relevant information has been collected and surveyed only by a private institution (China Credit Information Service) every two years since 1972.[5] According to their classification, Taiwan'a business groups are distinguished as "Sister" type, "Mother-Son" type, and "Marriage" type in terms of the personal relationship of directors.

This kind of organization is similar to French (or Continental European) industrial groups which are constituted of legally distinct companies without requiring the publication of a consolidated statement, and whose major capital is in the hands of key family members.[6] However, there are some distinctive characteristics in comparing Taiwanese business groups with their French counterparts. First, the capital tie or ownership of capital within a group in Taiwan is mostly connected through personal, rather than institutional investment. As a result, there is no clear, legal relationship between the controlling (parent) corporation and the controlled corporation (its subsidiaries of affiliates). That is why the term 'member-companies' is used here. Secondly, the fabric of internal organization is quite loose and mostly based on personal terms. Only a few share a general head office, which is not a legal entity, to coordinate and monitor all member companies. In other words, business groups are organized in a covert way with the possible exception of some eminent groups. Therefore, the names of business groups are hard to come by, unless the list of their directors is carefully examined.

Carefully comparing the list of Top Enterprises and business groups, we find that business groups are widely formed among giant enterprises. For instance, the Top 50 private enterprises in 1981 were related to 25 groups.[7]

Most of the giant enterprises prefer establishing new member companies rather than acquiring or merging existing ones to expand their business. This can be shown by the drastic changes in the number of menber-companies within each group. Between 1972 there were 65 groups with the same name, between 1976 and 1982 there were 50

Table 7.2

Changes in the number of companies within 65 groups between 1972–76, and 50 groups between 1976–82

Increase of the number of companies	Changes between 1972–76 (number of groups) Increase	Decrease	Changes between 1976–82 (number of groups) Increase	Decrease
0	21	37	12	19
1	18	12	8	13
2	7	8	8	9
3	5	5	12	4
4	5	1	3	1
5	2	1	3	1
6	2	1	0	2
7	2	0	1	1
8	1	0	2	0
9	0	0	0	0
10	2	0	1	0
Total	65	65	50	50

Sources: China Credit Information Services, *Business Groups in Taiwan*, 1972, 1976 and 1978.

groups. Table 7.2 shows the changes in the number of their member-companies. Only 21 groups did not increase their member-companies in 1972-76. Two groups were witnessed to build 10 companies respectively over those four years. The total number of new companies amounted to 131 in that period. From 1976 to 1982, the number of new companies in the 50 groups totalled 120. Table 7.2 also reveals one surprising phenomenon, that many member-companies folded. This tells us the whole story: the giant enterprises adjust their business activities by way of establishing new companies and/or closing existing ones. Therefore, business groups instead of single corporations seem to be a more appropriate analytical unit, especially in the study of the share, or the power of giant enterprises in this country.

Table 7.3

Diversification of business groups, 1972 and 1978

No. of 2-digit industry engaged by one business group	Number of groups, 1972			Number of groups, 1978		
	Within all sectors	Within mfg. sectors	Within other* sectors	Within all sectors	Within mfg. sectors	Within other* sectors
0	0	0	39	0	0	24
1	13	30	42	7	34	47
2	22	32	10	31	30	14
3	25	22	4	17	16	9
4	22	9	2	20	10	3
5	8	2	0	9	5	2
6	2	1	0	3	2	0
7	3	0	0	8	1	0
8	1	1	0	0	1	0
9	1	0	0	2	0	0
10	0	0	0	2	0	0
Total	97	97	97	99	99	99

Sources: China Credit Information Services, *Business Groups in Taiwan*, 1972 and 1978.

Notes: *, Other sectors include mining, construction, commerce and transportation.

As shown by Encauoa and Jacquemin (1982), if the data of group members are consolidated, market concentration will increase. Therefore, the ACR here should be understated because of the use of data of individual firm. If we want to know whether the largest firms in Taiwan grow, and increase their shares of economic activities, the data of consolidated groups rather than legally distinct companies should be used.

Unfortunately, no suitable variable could be measured as ACR, because business groups engage in economy-wide activities (see Table 7.3) in which assets and turnover have obvious double-counting problems

(White, 1981a). This problem seems not to be serious to compare the changes over time, if the magnitued of double-counting does not change significantly. Then, we find an increasing trend in the share of turnover of the 'one hundred' business groups in GNP,[8] (i.e. from 27% in 1974, 28% in 1976, 31% in 1978 to 32% in 1980). This seems to reveal that the share of large firms in terms of business groups increased more significantly than in terms of a single corporation.

Business group: diversification

Diversification is an integral part of the growth of firms and of the continuous adjustment process that they undergo against an ever changing environment. the explanations of diversification and their effects on aggregate concentration were studied by Utton (1979) and Prais (1981). However, here we center on the measures of diversification in Taiwan's business groups. By doing so, it is hoped that we can have a clearer idea of the growth of giant firms within business groups. Similarly, we might be able to supplement the inside story benind aggregate concentration trend.

A summary index of diversification should measure both the spread and the relative importance of a firm's activities in different industries. Utton (1979, Ch. 2) derives one 'number equivalent' index to incorporate these two characteristics. Another measure having somewhat similar properties is the Herfindahl index.[9] Both measures require the data. (e.g., employment or value-added) of a firm's activities across industries. Due to the intense calculation work, and lack of well-disciplined classification, we decided to measure diversification without using such an index. As an alternative, the number of secondary industries in which firms are active will be used with little modification.[10]

The data of China Credit Information Services is the only source we can find. In these data, the name and activities of business groups including every member-company are recorded, but the classification of each company's business activities is not well-disciplined. Also, only the main activity, and not all of them are reported. Limited by the availability of data, our measures are primarily based on two-digit level classification with some arbitrary judgment. This should be kept in mind, particularly, when an attempt at conducting a cross-country analysis is made. However, the bias of these arbitrary judgements will be minimal when comparison is made over time for a specific country. Two years, 1972 and 1978, are chosen because they were little affected by oil shocks.

Again, it should be mentioned that our diversification measures are based on a business group instead of a single enterprise. The possibility of diversification within one enterprise can be neglected because the large firms prefer a multi-companies group rather than a multi-units enterprise to conduct business.[11]

The index of diversification in business groups is defined as: the number of industries in which groups are actively engaged. Also, diversification both within the manufacturing sector and across other sectors (e.g., mining, construction, commerce and transportation services) is completely considered. Therefore, three categories of diversification indices are measured: (1) the total number of industries in which business groups are active, (2) the number of manufacturing industries in which business groups are active, and (3) the number of non-manufacturing industries in which business groups are active. There were one hundred groups in 1972 and 1978 respectively. Among them, a few groups having no business activities in the manufacturing industry are excluded. As a consequence, the samples were 97 groups in 1972 and 99 groups in 1978. The measures of diversification are presented in Table 7.3.

Table 7.3 shows that the degree of diversification in the manufacturing sector was not as high in 1972 and in 1978. In 1972 there were 62 groups (64%) active in 1 to 2 industries, and 31 groups (32%) in 3 to 4 industries. Data is similar in 1978. In total, only slight increases in diversification occurred between 1972 and 1978.

If we focus on diversification of business groups in the non-manufacturing sector, it is found that groups engaging in inter-sectoral diversification increased significantly from 1972 to 1978. The number of groups with no inter-sectoral diversification decreased from 39 (40%) in 1972, to 24(24%) in 1978. At least 43% in 1972, and 48% in 1978 of the sampled groups were active in one non-manufacturing sector. As a consequence, conglomerate groups seem more and more popular, and these groups are diversely engaged in many less-relative sectors.

Reasons to form business groups

After we know that the organization of business groups is an eminent factor in influencing the level of ACR, it is natural to ask: why do entrepreneurs in Taiwan prefer a multi-companies group, rather than a single multi-divisional corporation or a parent corporation with several subsidiaries? The survey conducted by Liu et al. (1981, p.12–13) sheds some light on this issue. Among other things, Liu et al. mentions the following factors (1) engaging new industries (100%),[12] (2) training successors (80%), and (3) receiving tax benefits (80%). The first factor re-confirms the claim made by the multi-companies group that the large firms use business groups to diversify their business activities across different industries. The other reasons can be further explained as follows.

First, receiving tax benefits as mentioned by Liu et al. is an important reason for organizing business groups. To encourage investment, the government exempts new enterprises from business income tax for the five years (instituted in the Statute for Encouragement of Investment in 1960). This encourages the enterprises to build new companies and close existing ones within a short space of time, i.e. five years. To be entitled for this tax benefit, some units of a large corporation are dispersed into a certain number of small separate ones; alternatively, the existing corporation can be closed and replaced by a new one. In either case, a multi-company group emerges.

Second, another incentive similar to taxation privileges, is the evasion of tax payment. Profit transferring within a group provides such an opportunity. It is hard to have solid evidence concerning this matter. However, indirect evidence is gained by observing whether or not the largest firms issue stocks in stock market. Issuing stocks publicly will lead to much more monitoring and supervision by the government, and thus reduce the possibility of behind-the-scenes maneuvers, and profit transferring manipulations. Only one-half of the 50 largest enterprises issue their stocks publicly.[13]

Third, an incentive in dispersing business activities (even in the same industry) by building different companies, is to evade the constraint of maximum credit lines imposed by banks. According to the operating rules of the banks, the maximum credit line to an individual corporation can't exceed a certain percentage of net worth of the banks. This rule, of course, is applicable only to a firm. Thus, evasion of the measures of selective credit control, is also a possible cause for formming a business group.

Fourth, in a dispersed multi-companies group it is much easier to arrange opportunities for members of a family or a group to learn entrepreneurship. A unequal distribution of status within famliy members could be well arranged within a business group. In a Chinese family, the status of a son (particularly, an eldest son) is quite different from a daughter or a son-in-law. Therefore, the big or main companies can be managed by the former, and the smaller ones by the latter. All of them can learn in a completely separate corporation. It is not easy to make such an arrangement in a large multi-units corporation.

Finally, one may ask: is the organization of a multi-companies group (in which some member-companies are built and closed in a short period) disadvantageous to the accumulation of intangible assets? It seems to be not very serious, because the good-will of enterprises in china is closely tied to the personal reputation of the entrepreneur. In sum, the reasons listed above suggest that Taiwan's entrepreneurs prefer to organize multi-company groups, in the wake of expanding and adjusting their business activities.

Concluding remarks

In this paper we have examined the relationship between business groups and the measures of ACR. Our analysis suggests that ACR in Taiwan should be calculated by the unit of a business group, instead of the unit of a single firm. Our findings can be summarized as follows: First, we find a stagnant trend of ACR in the 1970's (on the average, the ratio of ACR 100 in terms of the turnover amounted 23%). Second, a multi-companies group in which new companies are established and existing ones are closed is preferable to Taiwan's entrepreneurs. Because it hides the true position of the large firms. In contrast to the stagnant trend of the aggregate concentration ratio, the shares of business groups in the whole economy increased, (i.e. its turnover share increased from 27% in 1972 to 32% in 1980). Third, the conglomerate business groups are growing, but they also are not accounted for by calculating aggregate concentration. Fourth, profits transferring, receiving tax benefits, evading credit constrain and training family members are possible reasons as to why business groups are formed in Taiwan.

Notes

1. The Survey has been held every year since 1967. The population of the Survey comes from the Census. Of course, the sample of Survey shuld be changed, because (1) Census definitions and coverage are modified over time, and (2) the sampling method and ratios are changed, partly in response to changes in economy.
2. The main differences between two variables are (1) changes in inventories and (2) products purchases. Both are accounted for in the value of production but not in operating revenues.

3. The capital-labor ratio of the top 200 enterprises was, in 1973-80, 3.6 times greater of those firms outside of the top 200. But the ratios are almost the same among the three groups of the top 50 top 100, and top 200 firms (calculated from Table 7.1).

4. For instance, to explain industrial concentration in the U.K., see Hart and Clarke (1980, Ch.5), to explain aggergate concentration in British manufacturing, see Prais (1981). However, an exception is White (1981a), who finds there was a virtual absence of any increase in aggregate concentration after merger waves of the late 1960's in the U.S.

5. There were 15,000 firm's data and more than 5,000 personal files of entrepreneurial directors in the data bank of China Credit Information Services in 1971. The main source of information on group membership is the list of directors (in particular, executive directors). A survey of the directors concerned was done to identify group membership. This is the source and procedure by which to define business groups in Taiwan. Around one-hundred groups are listed in the published data (see note 8 below).

6. For the case of France, see Encauoa and Jacquemin (1982); for the case of West Germany, see Cable and Dirrheimer (1983). This kind of organization is to a certain extent different from American multidivisional large corporations which are called "Hierarchies" by Williamson (1975).

7. Among the 50 largest firms, only 15 are a single-corporation type without belonging to any business group. Among the rest, 18 firms are controlled by one group and 17 firms can be "consolidated" into 7 groups (see Appendix 7.1).

8. There were 111 groups (793 firms) in 1974, 106 groups (673 firms) in 1976, 100 groups (653 firms and 645 firms) in 1978 and 1980 respectively.

9. Utton's index is $\sum_i i(P_i)$, where the activities have been arrayed in order of their importance (the largest first) and P_i is the proportion of the total employment (or other variables) in the i-th activity. The Herfindahl index is $1/\sum_i P_i^2$.

10. It is an evident shortcoming that this measure makes no allowance for the relative importance of the different industries in the firms' total activities. However, it is convenient to use this measure for easy calculation.

11. More evidence concerning this preference can be found. For example, in 1972 there were 13 groups who specialized only in one industry (see Table 7.3), but those groups also have a number of separate, legal, member companies. This confirms the claim of "multi-companies group" and leads us to use the group as an analytical unit here.

12. The brackets denote the multiple-choice percentage that managers recognize, that is, at least, a factor considered in organizing business groups.

13. Only 25 companies arrayed in the Top 50 enterprises issued their stocks publicly in 1975, 28 companies in 1980 and 29 in 1981. Also in the Top 25 enterprises list, only 12 companies issued their stocks on the stock market in 1975, 16 companies in 1980 and 1981. More importantly, without exception, within each group there is at least one member-company which does not issue its stocks publicly.

Appendix

Appendix 7.1
Listing of the 17 giant firms and their related business groups, 1981

17 giant firms in 1981	Related business groups
Nan-Ya Plastics Corp. (1) Formosa Plastics Corp. (2) Formosa Chemicals Fibre Corp. (4)	Formosa Plastics
Yue Loong Motor Co., Ltd. (3) Tai Yuen Textile Co., Ltd. (20) China Motor Co., Ltd. (25)	Yue Loong Motor
Far Eastern Textile Ltd. (6) Asia Cement Co. (13)	Far Eastern
President Enterpriese Corp.(9) Tainan Spinning Co., Ltd. (43) Universal Cement Corp. (47)	Tainan Spinning
Sampo Corporation (11) Shinlee Corp. (35)	Sampo

Pacific Electric Wire
  Cable Co., Ltd. (24)
Walsin Lihwa Electric Wire
  Cable Corporation (26)
	Pacific Electric Wire

China Rebar Co., Ltd. (31) China Hsin Flour Feed Vegetable Oil (38)	China Rebar

Sources: 1. China Credit Information Service (1983), *Business Groups in Taiwan.*

2. China Credit Information Service (1982), *The Largest Industrial Corpsrations in the Republic of China.*

Note: The figures within brackets indicate the rank of the top firms in 1981.

References

Cable, J. and M.J. Dirrheimer (1983), "Hierarchies and Markets: An Empirical Test of the Multivisional Hypothesis in West Germany," *International Journal of Industrial Organization*, 1 (1), pp.43–62.

Chandler, A.D. (1977), *The Visible Hand: The Managerial Revolution in American Business*, Belknap Press, Cambridge.

Encaoua, D. and A. Jacquemin (1982), "Organizational Efficiency and Monopoly Power: The Case of French Iudustrial Group," *European Economic Review*, 19 (1–2), pp.25–52.

Feinberg, R.M. (1981), "On the Measurement of Aggregate Concentration," *Journal of Industrial Economics*, 30 (2), pp.217–22.

Hart, R.E. and R. Clarke (1980), *Concentration in British Industry 1935–75*, Cambridge University Press, Cambridge.

Leff, N.H. (1978), "Industrial Organization and Enterepreneurship in the Developing countries: The Economic Groups," *Economic Development and Cultural Change*, 36 (4), pp.661–75.

Liu, S.S., K.M. Kuo, C.E. Huang and T.S. Stzutu (1981), "Causes, Operations and Effects of Corporate Groups in Taiwan," *Medium Business Bank of Taiwan Quarterly*, 4 (3/4), pp.5–19 and 5–23. (in Chinese)

Prais, S.J. (1981), *The Evolution of Giant Firms in Britain*, Cambridge University Press, Cambridge. lst ed. in 1976.

Utton, M.A. (1979), *Diversification and Competition*, Cambridge University Press, Cambridge.

White, L.J. (1974), *Industrial Concentration and Economic Power in Parkistan*, Princeton University Press, Princeton.

―――― (1981a), "What Has Been Happening to Aggregate Concentration in the United States." *Journal of Industrial Economics*, 29 (3), pp.223–30.

―――― (1981b), "On Measuring Aggergate Concentration: A Reply," *Journal of Industrial Economics*, 30 (2), pp.23–24.

Williamson, O.E. (1975), *Market and Hierarchies: Analysis and Antitrust Implications*, McMillan, London.

8 The Experience of SMEs' Development*

Introduction

This paper tries to analyse the elements of Taiwan's success in economic development from the industrial organization's point of view. As we know, a package of export-led industrial strategies adopted in the late 1950s has made export an engine of Taiwan's economic growth (Chou, 1985). However, what kind of business organization or firm size starts this engine still remains unclear. The purpose of this study is to fill up this gap by examining the relationship between firm size and export performance.

Taiwan's manufacturing sector accounts for 43% of the economy, and has given an important contribution to economic growth. The percentage of manufactures in total exports has risen from a mere 8% in 1953 to nearly 94% in 1985. If we analyze further, we find that small-and-medium enterprises (SMEs) play a very distinguished role in Taiwan's export business. In 1985, 65% of manufacturing exports came from SMEs. In other words, in exports — the engine of Taiwan's rapid growth — more than 60% of industrial goods are produced by SMEs. Moreover, Taiwan's SMEs have a higher relative export-intensity (i.e. 71% of their products were exported in 1985) than large firms

---

*This paper was reproduced from *Rivista Internazionale di Scienze Economiche e Commerciali*, Vol. 39, No. 12, December 1992, pp.1067–1084, with permission of the publisher.

and contribute with a higher percentage to total exports. This is a distinctive feature of Taiwan's economic development, and is contrary to the experience of many industrialized countries, such as the U.S., Belgium, France, and Japan[1]. In these countries, large firms rather than SMEs give a high contribution to exports. This could induce us to see a relationship between firm size and export performance.

However, we must consider that most of Taiwan's SMEs take care only of manufacturing goods and export them without bothering how to market them abroad. By cooperating with Japanese general trading companies, multinational trading companies and foreign importers, SMEs in Taiwan have been able to avoid being restricted by economies of scale in international marketing, and still have managed to sell their manufacturing products in the whole world. This is also the fundamental driving force behind Taiwan's economic development with her export-led growth.

The role of SMEs in Taiwan's economy and trade is respectively discussed in Section II and III. In Section IV, the relationship between firm-size and export-performance is examined and tested by the evidence of Taiwan's manufacturing firms. The prospects of highly export-oriented SMEs are discussed in Section V. Concluding remarks are in Section VI.

The role of SMEs in Taiwan's economy

Since Taiwan's decolonization in 1945, the industries that the government took over from the Japanese have become public enterprises. The remaining private sectors were few in number and all small in scale. In 1949, private enterprises had only a one-third share of total production and most of them were light industries. Following the implementation of land reform in 1949, the stock of the four big companies - i.e. Taiwan Cement Co., Taiwan Paper Co., Mining Co., and Agriculture and Forest Co. – was offered instead of cash to the landlords at the land price, and then the four companies were transformed into private businesses. Thanks to the economic reforms carried out at the end of the 1940s, private enterprises gradually grew and later on began to play a major role in the process of economic development. These enterprises have had a very different role from public ones in the development process since most of them started small or medium-sized. Although after thirty years several private enterprises have expanded and become large-scale enterprises, SMEs still dominate Taiwan's industry, regardless of the indicator used, be it the number of firms, the volume of production, employment, or even the export share.

As for the law regarding the assistance offered to SMEs, i.e. the "SMEs Assistance Guideline", enacted by the Executive Yuan on Sep. 14, 1967, these guiding principles were revised 5 times — first on July 8, 1968, and then on March 6, 1973, August 2, 1977, Feb. 21, 1979, and July 14, 1982. The most sweeping of these revisions, was made in August, 1977[2]. The "SMEs Development Act" was enacted into law in February 1991.

The definition and scope of SMEs have themselves varied with the revisions of the SMEs assistance guidelines. In September 1967, SME was defined as "a manufacturing enterprise having total assets of less than NT$ 5,000,000, with no more than 100 persons regularly employed[3]; or a commercial firm having an annual turnover of no more than NT$ 5,000,000, with less than 50 persons regularly employed". To date, this definition has been changed four times (1973, 1977, 1978, 1982). According to the latest version (issued on July 14, 1982), SME is "a manufacturing, processing or handicraft enterprise having a paid-in capital of less than NT$ 40,000,000, and having total assets of no more than NT$ 120,000,000; an importer/exporter, a commercial firm, a transportation company or other service establishment having an annual turnover of no more than NT$ 40,000,000; or a mining enterprise having a paid-in capital of less than NT$ 40,000,000" (see Table 8.1).

During different periods, SME has had different definitions. Therefore, whenever we discuss the role that SMEs play, we need to use the

Table 8.1

Criteria for small and medium enterprises in various periods

Date	Manufacturing processing, & handicraft	Commercial, transportation, & other services	Mining
Sep. 14, 1967	1. Total assets of no more than NT $ 5,000,000 2. Under 100 persons regularly employed	1. Annual sales of no more than NT $5,000,000 2. Under 50 persons regularly employed	
March 6, 1973	1. Registered capital of less than NT $ 5,000,000, total assets of no more than NT $ 20,000,000 2. Registered capital of less than NT $ 5,000,000 number of regularly employed persons as follows: (1)clothing, footwear, and electrical industry - less than 300 persons (2)food-processing industry - less than 200 persons (3)other industries - less than 100 persons	1. Annual sales of no more than NT $ 5,000,000 2. Under 50 persons regularly employed	
August 2, 1977	1. Paid-in capital of less than NT $ 20,000,000; total assets of no more than NT $ 60,000,000 2. Less than 300 persons regularly employed	1. Annual sales of no more than Nt $ 20,000,000 2. Less than 50 persons regularly employed	

Table 8.1   (continued)

Date	Manufacturing processing, & handicraft	Commercial, transportation, & other services	Mining
Feb. 21, 1979	1. Paid-in capital of lesss than NT$ 20,000,000: total assets of no more than NT$ 60,000,000 2. Less than 300 persons regularly employed	1. Annual sales of no more than NT$ 20,000,000 2. Less than 50 persons regularly employed	1. Paid-in capital of less than NT$ 20,000,000 2. Less than 500 persons regularly employed
July 14, 1982	Paid-in capital of less than NT$ 40,000,000; total assets of no more than NT$ 120,000,000	Annual sales of no more than NT$ 40,000,000	Paid-in capital of less than NT$ 40,000,000

Source: *Small and Medium Enterprises Overview in Taiwan*, 1986, p.18, in Chinese.

current definition to define our scope. Table 8.2 shows the number and ratio of the SMEs from 1961 to 1988. We can see from this table that the ratio is over 97% every year, and for three years the ratio is even more than 98%, which indicates the huge number of SMEs. If we look at the breakdown according to industries, the ratio of the electicity, gas & water industry is the lowest one, followed by that of the construction industry. As to the remaining industries, the number and ratio of SMEs are very high. For the industries within the manufacturing sector, the number and ratio of SMEs also exceed 90% (see *Small and Medium Enterprises Overview in Taiwan*, 1986, pp.24–29).

Table 8.3 shows the output ratios of SMEs from 1971 to 1989. In manufacturing, for instance, SMEs' output represented 27% of the total, rose to 47% in 1976, and the ratio was still as high as 45% in 1981 and in 1989. The main reason why the ratio increased by 20 percent in 1976 was because of the change in the definition of SMEs, the number of

Table 8.2

Firm number and ratio of small and medium enterprises[1]

	1961 number	1961 ratio	1971 mumber	1971 ratio	1981 number	1981 ratio	1988 number	1988 ratio
Mining & Quarring	881	96.7	—	—	931	98.6	1,902	98.1
Manufacturing	51,389	99.7	40,739	95.4	90,580	98.9	152,871	98.6
Electricity Gas & Water	147	94.2	120	80.5	31	52.5	132	88.0
Construction	4,261	98.9	5,018	85.4	11,297	90.1	22,955	95.2
Commerce	91,389	99.6	161,734	99.9	314,442	99.7	455,350	97.4
Transport Storage & Communications	1,549	96.3	—	—	14,412	85.3	47,852	98.3
Financing, Insurance, Real Estate & Business Services	29,122	100.0	—	—	14,618	97.3	21,735	93.4
Others	178	90.8	66,751	98.3	62,473[2]	99.5	68,146	99.7
Total	178,916	99.6	274,362	98.3	508,784	99.1	770,331	97.7

Sources: 1. *Small and Medium Enterprises Statistics*, 1988.

2. *Small and Medium Enterprises Overview in Taiwan*, 1988.

Notes: 1. For the definition of SMEs in every year, see *Small and Medium Enterprises Overview in Taiwan*, 1988.

2. Social community and personal services.

Table 8.3

Value and share of output of small and medium enterprises

	1971 NT$ millions	%	1976 NT$ millions	%	1981 NT$ millions	%	1989 NT$ millions	%
Mining & Quarring	—	—	3,571	46.3	9,418	53.1	11,488	83.0
Manufacturing	64,957	26.7	386,087	47.1	916,212	44.8	1,833,897	44.7
Electricity, Gas & Water	110	1.2	47	0.2	55	0.0	2,911	1.7
Construction	5,191	37.0	14,129	26.4	56,714	32.9	—	—
Commerce	90,489	89.7	70,194	84.2	—	—	363,670	72.4
Transport Storage & Communications	—	—	13,607	18.3	—	—	26,896	50.6
Financing, Insurance, Real Estate & Business Services	—	—	25,948	34.5	—	—	16,389	83.2
Others	18,748	35.7	—	—	75,570	25.8	—	—
Total	—	—	513,583	44.9	—	—	2,255,251	46.4

Sources: 2. *Small and medium Enterprises Overview in Taiwan*, 1989.

regularly employed persons having increased from less than 100 persons to no more than 300 persons. From Table 8.2, we can see that the number and ratio of SMEs was almost 99% (in 1981), but the output ratio, as shown in Table 8.3, was only 45%. Therefore we can clearly see that the average scale of operations (represented by output) of large enterprises was 400 times than that of SMEs. SMEs engaged in Mining & Quarrying and Business Services had a similar size distribution. As to the commercial sector, there was a different pattern. The output ratio of SMEs was 84% (in 1976), and the firm number ratio was also over 99%. In other words, commercial business in Taiwan is almost completely dominated by SMEs. In fact, large enterprises are not only few in number but also low (16%) in terms of the volume of output ratio. On the other hand, in the utilities (electricity, gas & water), transport, storage & communications industries, large enterprises have a higher ratio in both firm number and output. These industries are always regulated by the government and may operate only as public enterprises. Therefore, large enterprises play a more dominant role in this regard.

All scholars who have studied SMEs agree that SMEs contribute significantly to employment. SMEs create job opportunities, thereby making social policy targets (such as social stability, fair income distribution, and balanced urban-rural development) more easily achievable. Unlike those in Korea (Ho, 1980), SMEs in Taiwan are relatively well dispersed, and this dispersion helps reduce the gap between urban and rural development. This is one of the features of Taiwan's industrial development. Ho (1980) has also pointed out that SMEs in Taiwan tend to specialize in labor-intensive production, which contributes substantially to employment and exports.

Table 8.4 shows the number and share of employed persons in SMEs. If we take 1976 as an example, we can find that those employed in SMEs accounted for 61% of the total number of employees, and this proves the great contribution of SMEs to employment. If we look further at the classification by industry, we note that commercial operations are almost all of small or medium scale, with 89% to 96% of the employment of the whole industry to be ascribed to SMEs. This is followed by manufacturing, services, mining, and construction. As for utilities (i.e. electricity, gas & water), since very few SMEs are found in this sector, their contribution to employment is, obviously, very low. In manufacturing, the employment share of SMEs ranged from 43% to 68% through the period from 1966 to 1986. From 1976 to 1986, SMEs grew rapidly, providing more than 68% of total employment. This shows how much SMEs have contributed to employment.

Table 8.4

Number and share of employees in small and medium enterprises

units: persons; %

	1966		1976		1986	
	persons	%*	persons	%*	persons	%*
Mining & Quarrying	—	—	30,439	49.1	18,584	73.8
Manufacturing	251,877	42.7	1,136,766	59.6	1,695,609	68.3
Electricity, Gas & Water	1,390	7.3	147	0.5	—	—
Construction	44,237	24.2	81,929	26.5	86,435	58.0
Commerce	288,476	95.9	710,715	89.3	487,510	73.2
Transport Storage & Communications	—	—	83,579	30.6	128,429	45.3
Financing, Insurance, Real Estate & Business Services	—	—	218,346	66.2	170,635	41.4
Others	220,381	61.6	—	—	—	—
Total	—	—	2,261,011	61.0	2,587,202	64.4

Sources: 1. *Small and Medium Enterprises Overview in Taiwan*, 1989.

*: Share of SMEs.

The role of SMEs in Taiwan's export

Many studies show that export is the most important source of Taiwan's economic development. This can be evidenced by the percentage of exports to GDP in Taiwan which is said to have reached in 1985 the record of 55.4%. This is one of the highest figures in the world. A large contribution to export has obviously an important role in economic development. After examining the role of SMEs in Taiwan's economy, we turn our attention to their role in Taiwan's trade.

Studies of Taiwan's trade development indicate that the main reason why Taiwan's trade has grown so fast is that it is based primarily on the principle of comparative advantage, which stresses full utilization of the relatively abundant labor force. This outward-looking development strategy has resulted in a highly specialized manufacturing and industrial-product structure (product concentration), especially in labor-intensive industries. Table 8.5 shows the number of SMEs in 20 sub-industries of manufacturing. Apart from the years 1985 and 1987, the shares of SMEs in the petroleum & coal-product industries were 92.9% and 94.4%, and in none of the other industries did SMEs have a share of less than 95%. Therefore, with such a trade-oriented pattern of industrial development, the contribution of SMEs to exports is well worth studying.

The percentage of SMEs to total export earnings is our main indicator. According to the estimates made by the Medium and Small Business Administration, Ministry of Economic Affairs, (see *Small and Medium Enterprises Overview in Taiwan*, pp.192–193) the total export earnings of SMEs in 1978 was 8,098 million US dollars, which accounted for 63.8% of the total export earnings. This figure jumped to 10,337 million US dollars, or 64% in 1979, and in 1980 this amount increased to 12,876 million US dollars, or 65% of the export earnings. From 1981 to 1985, the export earnings of SMEs and the corresponding shares are shown in Table 8.6 (68.1%, 69.7%, 63.4%, 59.2% and 61.2%). The data tell that the contribution of SMEs to exports seems to have had an

Table 8.5

Number and share of SMEs in manufacturing (1983, 1985, 1987)

unit: number; %

Industry	1983 number	ratio	1985 number	ratio	1987 number	ratio
Food & Kindred products	10,096	99.2	9,247	98.6	19,079	99.1
Beverage & Tobacco Manufactures	162	97.0	124	94.7	148	94.3
Textile Mill Products	6,783	97.4	6,582	95.9	7,731	96.2
Apparel & Other Textile Products	7,140	99.6	6,942	99.3	6,025	99.2
Leather, Fur & Related Products	1,241	99.5	1,275	98.8	1,618	98.4
Paper & Paper Products; Printing & Publishing	9,474	99.6	9,619	99.4	10,927	99.2
Industrial Chemicals	1,847	96.3	1,698	95.1	1,493	94.3
Chmeical Products	2,129	98.2	1,911	96.7	2,003	95.7
Petroleum & Coal Products	81	96.4	52	92.9	51	94.4
Rubber Products	1,239	99.3	1,295	98.3	1,857	98.4
Plastic Products	9,857	99.7	9,950	99.4	13,658	99.2
Primary Metal Industries	5,856	98.8	5,803	97.9	6,254	97.7
Fabricated Metal Products	26,690	99.8	26,244	99.7	31,389	99.6
Machinery, excluding Electrical Equipment	7,177	99.7	7,220	99.2	8,321	98.9
Electrical & Electronic Equipment	5,857	97.9	6,013	96.5	7,773	96.1
Transportation Equipment	2,647	98.3	2,699	97.3	3,879	97.8
Precision Equipment	834	99.3	884	98.7	1,156	98.1
Wood & Bamboo Products, Non-metallic Furniture	10,302	99.7	9,481	99.5	9,283	99.4
Non-metallic Mineral Products	4,433	98.9	4,203	98.5	4,357	97.8
Miscellaneous Manufacturing Industries	6,980	99.8	7,831	99.6	8,122	99.4
Total	120,844	99.3	119,073	98.8	145,124	98.7

Sourcds: 1. *Small and Medium Enterprises Statistics*, 1988.
2. *Small and Medium Enterprises Overview in Taiwan*, 1988.

235

Table 8.6
Export sales earnings of small and medium enterprises, 1981–1985

unit: NT$ millions; %

Year	Manufacturing companies earnings	%	Trading companies earnings	%	Total earnings	%
1981	10,559	71.8	4,832	61.1	15,391	61.8
1982	10,613	73.5	4,858	62.5	15,471	69.7
1983	10,926	66.9	5,001	56.9	15,927	63.4
1984	12,379	62.5	5,666	53.2	18,045	59.2
1985	12,897	64.6	5,903	54.9	18,800	61.2

Sources: 1. *Small and Medium Enterprises Statistics*, 1988.
2. *Small and Medium Enterprises Overview in Taiwan*, 1988.

increase before 1982, and then to have declined. However, from 1978 to 1985, SMEs' contributions to exports were all over 60%. In other words, in the export sector — the prime mover behind Taiwan's rapid growth — more than 60% of the industrial products derived from SMEs which clearly shows the great contribution of SMEs to trade and economic growth. All in all, Taiwan's rapid economic development is largely a story of how numerous SMEs have, in line with the principle of comparative adventage, employed labor-intensive methods to process products for export to overseas market.

In addition, Table 8.7 shows the export ratios and the domestic sales ratios for SMEs. As the data show, the ratio of export sales earnings to total sales earnings was 53% in 1975, 67% in 1980 and 71% in 1985. However, this increasing trend started changing in 1986[4]. It is surprising that the export-intensity of SMEs was reversed from 71% in 1985 to 33% in 1989. Due to such a drastic change in this short period, the credibility of this figure must be carefully checked. However, this could reveal that the impact of NT dollar revaluation since 1986 on SMEs' exports was still incredibly huge and also could change the export behavior of SMEs.

Table 8.7

Shares of export and domestic sales in SMEs

	1975	1980	1985	1989
Total Sales Earning	100.0	100.0	100.0	100.0
Domestic	47.0	33.3	28.9	63.3
Export	53.0	66.7	71.1	32.7

Sources: Industrial Financial situation Survey, volumes 15-27, Economic Research Department, Bank of Taiwan.

Nevertheless, it is cautious to say that the observed period is too short to determine whether the export intensity of SMEs is completely changed. This should be studied in the future. It is also clear that before the mid-1980s SMEs have heavily depended on foreign markets, and 70% of the sales earnings of all SMEs have come from foreign markets. Owing to the great differences existing between domestic and foreign markets as regards marketing systems, financing situations, pricing policies, and trade features (see Chou, 1984), high marginal costs will mean that a firm cannot make a profit in both markets unless its scale of operations reaches some optimal level. Therefore, when choosing a market, SMEs have to consider the trade-off between the foreign and the domestic market. If this inference is correct, the export sales earnings ratios of SMEs which depend largely on foreign markets must be higher than those just mentioned above. That is to say, in Taiwan, more than 60% of the exports of manufactured products are those of SMEs which largely depend on exports and which have more than 70% of their sales earnings coming from export. Therefore, the pattern of the interaction between SMEs and export trade is seen to take shape.

In an economy that greatly depends on export-oriented SMEs, the main features include a sensitive response and flexibility in adjusting to market variations, which is also one of the major reasons why Taiwan's trade and economy have grown so rapidly (see Wu, 1986). Of course, this kind of industrial organization pattern makes Taiwan's export market almost fully competitive, but without significant market power. In contrast, the structure of the domestic market is much different. We can refer to this as a kind of "dichotomous market structure"[5].

Firm size and export performance: proposition and evidence

What are the underlying reasons why SMEs continue to prosper in Taiwan and play a vital role in promoting export and economic growth? At the outset, we should say that whether the smallness of scale is optimal or not is a key point in answering this question. When SMEs are operating inefficiently due to their small scale, this is an indication that the industries in which SMEs are involved should have significant economies of scale. There are two possibilities in this case. One is that the small firms are new entrants with relative small-scales of operations when they enter. If this is the case, however, in the long run those small firms ought to grow and the relative share of SMEs should decline. From the evidence of the steadily increasing share of SMEs in Taiwan, this deduction seems to be unfounded. The other possibility is that small firms operate inefficiently with high barriers to entry. In other words, inefficient SMEs keep themselves going due to high protective barriers. As is well known, protective measures are only effectively realized for the domestic market as opposed to the export market. This means that if inefficient SMEs do in fact exist in Taiwan, they should be mainly domestic-market oriented. However, the above evidence does not support this argument. On the contrary, the high export-orientation of SMEs may be seen in Table 8.6. Therefore, SMEs in Taiwan cannot be thought of as inefficient.

From the viewpoint of industrial economics, SMEs can operate efficiently because the industries in which they engage do not have significant economies of scale. What are the industries operating through

SMEs in Taiwan? Considering how much SMEs contribute to Taiwan's exports, it seems that most of those industries are export-oriented. However, this seems to go against the general proposition that export businesses have significant economies of scale. The evidence gathered from industrialized countries, e.g. Japan, France and Belgium, shows that large firms rather than small ones play a vital role in the export business. In sum, the central question is how Taiwan's SMEs can operate prosperously and efficiently in the export market without economies of scale. This is further discussed in what follows.

Economies of scale in the export business arise largely from the marketing stage rather than the manufacturing stage. Whether the manufacturing stage has economies of scale or not depends on the characteristics of individual industries. Some industries have the advantage of large-scale operations, but others have no such advantage. Thus, it is natural to deduce that SMEs without economies of scale should exist only in those industries without large-scale operations. In general, such industries are labor-intensive and mature in terms of technology. This should be the case with Taiwan's SMEs. On the other hand, scale economies in international marketing occur in every industry. Acquier (1980) builds a theoretical model to show how scale economies in marketing influence export behavior and firm size. He also uses French data to verify this proposition. After making a survey of SMEs in many developing countries, Little (1987) also argues that international marketing implies significant economies of scale. This is the reason why the proposition that large firms perform better than small ones in exporting, or the positive relationship between firm size and export performance, is advances. If so, are Taiwan's SMEs a counter-example to this proposition? There are two steps to answer this question. First, a further empirical test should be made by directly examining the relationship of firm size and export performance. Second, some explanations of the characteristics of Taiwan's business should be given.

We use the micro-data of individual firms in 1986 to verify whether the above proposition is true or not in Taiwan. The original survey

Table 8.8

Export performance of manufacturing firms, 1985

unit: %

Size (sales)	Export contribution	Export intensity
Under NT $ 1 million	62.48	50.22
NT $ 1– 5 millions	33.55	37.81
NT $ 5–20 millions	1.50	4.97
NT $20–50 millions	2.47	7.28
Above 50 millions	0.00	0.02
Total	100.00	33.33

Sources: The original survey data conducted by Statistical Bureau, Ministry of Economic Affairs, 1985.

data conducted by the Statistical Bureau, Ministry of Economic Affairs, can be used to observe export performance by different sizes of firms. The export shares of different sizes of firms to total exports (export contribution) and the export intensity (the ratio of exports to sales) are given in Table 8.8. The table shows that the larger the size of firms, the smaller the export contribution and export intensity. As a result, the above proposition does not seem to be verified in Taiwan. This leads us to the second step.

Why this is the case? Why Taiwan's SMEs can overcome the barrier of scale economies in international marketing? Still, a complete answer to this question has not been found, but some possible reasons can be given. As already mentioned, SMEs have more chance of operating efficiently at the stage of manufacturing rather than that of marketing. This is the experience of Taiwan's SMEs, i.e., most SMEs concentrate only on manufacturing business without bothering to market their products, since the marketing function is performed by Japanese general trading companies and foreign importers. As a result, Taiwan's SMEs cooperate with Japanese general trading companies, multinational trading companies and foreign importers within the framework of the international division of labor, especially when it comes to the marketing stage. The so-called OEM manufacturing pattern is a typical example. Under such circumstances, Taiwan's SMEs can specialize in manufacturing and in the production of mostly labor-intensive products. They do not bother with marketing at all. Even the so-called "export" trading companies in Taiwan only offer their services in terms of communication and paper work and do not practise the real function of marketing.

Therefore, the whole system of Taiwan's rapid industrialization and high economic growth is based on this pattern of the international division of labor. This is the real reason why SMEs in Taiwan have been able to avoid being restricted by the scale economies of international marketing, and have still been able to specialize in manufacturing business. This is also the fundamental driving force behind Taiwan's economic development: her export-led growth.

From the above discussion, it seems clear to us that Taiwan's SMEs are able to successfully exploit their small-scale advantage in production, but in general they cannot enjoy any power in marketing their exports, nor derive any mark-up on their selling efforts[6]. This leads us to another question, which is whether those SMEs could or could not grow into large enterprises. To answer this question, we go further to Section V.

Prospects of export-oriented SMEs

Although their business activities are successful, SMEs often encounter difficulties (which larger enterprises are generally able to avoid) mostly due to a lack of working capital and a lower level of technological know-how and experience. Some of the problems confronting SMEs are: (1) an inability to provide sufficient collateral, the lack of a sound accounting system, and a lack of expertise in capital planning, (2) a lack of management expertise, and a lack of consensus on a suitable and simplified management system, (3) the possession of only limited knowledge and, in many cases, the inability to conduct research and development independently. Moreover, as mentioned earlier, the export-oriented SMEs must confront a disorganized and highly competitive market with a limited capacity of marketing their products, especially in terms of foreign markets, and, consequently, their potential export business is chiefly controlled by foreign trading companies. Under these circumstances, a vicious circle is formed: the lack of financial capital, technology and management expertise restricts SMEs form growing, the smallness of their scale of operations restrains them from engaging in international marketing, their lack of marketing capacity in turn hampers their growth, and so on. Furthermore, Taiwan's SMEs are confined to labor-intensive and mature technology industries. This seems to act as a barrier to upgrading the level of technology in Taiwan.

This situation, has given rise to many public debates on industrial policy. It has been argued by some that in order to break the vicious circle described above, government intervention is necessary, this taking the form of incentive measures to encourage the development of big trading companies and a program to support strategic industries, for example. This is the school of "interventionism". On the other hand, others argue that the above vicious circle is due to the inefficiency of the financial institutions, and therefore improving the functions of the financial market is a fundamental prerequisite to the resolution of this problem. Thus deregulation rather than further intervention in the banking system is seen as an important step towards breaking this cycle. This is the school of "liberalism". However, until now, no consensus has been reached between these two schools. Consequently, many highly export-oriented SMEs are even now still the main contributors to Taiwan's economic development and growth.

Concluding remarks

This paper attempted to show that SMEs have played a significanct role in promoting exports and job creation in the course of Taiwan's economic development. This export-contribution has not only helped the economy to grow rapidly but has also greatly helped to solve Taiwan's employment problem. This industrialization process has been fundamentally achieved by exporting labor-intensive manufactured products and promoting an export-oriented growth strategy. A main requirement for exporting successfully is to overcome the international marketing constraints. However, due to the significant economies of scale that exist in marketing, SMEs have been unable to export without the assistance of other institutions. Fortunately, Japanese and foreign trading companies have taken on this role and have helped Taiwan's SMEs to exploit their relatively small-scale production advantage. Nevertheless, when looked at form another angle, such export-oriented SMEs are restricted to some labor-intensive and mature-technology industries; this restrains SMEs from upgrading their technology, enlarging their scale of operations and promoting their marketing capability. Therefore, most export businesses are chiefly controlled by foreign trading companies, especially by the large Japanese general trading companies. Under such circumstances, some specific problems confronting SMEs are very difficult to overcome. In order to break down this present barrier of small-scale and its limited marketing capacity, some policies ard needed. There has been much debate on this issue, but, there is still no consensus when it comes to proposing a solution. The prospects of SMEs, of course, depend on the kinds of adjustments made in industrial policy, trade policy, financial reform and tax reform and other structural measures which have not yet been formulated and implemented. Predicting the future situation of Taiwan's SMEs seems beyond the scope of this study. Nevertheless, the future development of SMEs should be given further attention.

Notes

1. For the case of Japan, see Rapp (1976); for the case of France, see Acquier (1980); for the case of Belgium, see Jacquemin et al. (1980).

2. This concerns overviewing guidance, i.e., basic purposes, basic principles of assistance guidelines, scope of assistance, etc., see *Small and Medium Enterprises overview in Taiwan*, 1986, pp.246–300 (in Chinese). For a brief historical review of the government assistance system for SMEs, see Appendix 8.1.

3. This is similar to the definition of the World Bank. This definition is also very common, because of the unique quality of the employee variable. in addition, cottage industries which employed less than 5 people are excluded from SMEs (see Naya, 1984, p.41).

4. The figures of SMEs' export intensity were 66% in 1986, 63% in 1987 and 50% in 1988.

5. In a previous work (Chou, 1984) the author studied the export-intensity (ratio of exports to sales) and export-contribution (ratio of exports to total exports) of different organizational patterns (for instance, public enterprises, forgign capital and private large enterprises) and discovered that the scale on which the enterprise operates is negatively related to export-intensity and export-contribution. In general, SMEs dominate the export market and are more competitive. Large enterprises dominate the domestic market and are more monopolistic. We refer to this situation as " market-oriented duality" or a "dichotomous market structure". For further details see Chou (1988).

6. This characteristic has been referred to as a "dichotomous" market stucture, see note 5.

Appendix

Appendix 8.1   Historical Review of the Government Assistance System to SMEs in Taiwan, 1954-1982

Owing to the financial difficulties commonly encountered by SMEs, the government set up a small-loan scheme with the U.S. Aid fund in 1954, and authorized the First Commercial Bank, the Hua-Nan Commercial Bank, and the Chang-Hwa Commercial Bank to issue "small private-enterprise loans", each loan being limited to US $60,000. The purpose of this program was to help SMEs import machinery & equipment for their own use. This was how the government started to finance SMEs (see *Small and Medium Enterprise Overview in Taiwan*, 1986, P.9). In 1965, the Council for International Economic Cooperation and Development sent a team abroad to study the guidance and assistance systems in several countries and to make reports and recommendations. In May 1966, the government accepted the recommendations of the Council for International Economic Cooperation and Development; set up a framework for cooperation with the Ministry of Finance, the Ministry of Economic Affairs, the Central Bank, the Taiwan Provincial Government, the China Productivity Center, the Trade Center, and the Metal Industrial Development Center; and established the "Small and Medium Enterprise Assistance Working Group" to guide assistance work. Thus a foundation for the provision of assistance to SMEs had been laid. The actual institution created to assist SMEs underwent several major structural changes, as described below (see *Small and Medium Enterprises Overview in Taiwan*, 1986, pp.259-63):

  – On September 14, 1967, the Council for Economic Cooperation, Executive Yuan, established the "Medium and Small Enterprises Assistance Administration". This agency was to control institutious, while the Union Industrial Research Laboratories of the Ministry of Economic Affairs were to provide assistance.

– In August 1969, the Medium and Small Business Assistance Administration of the Council for Economic Cooperation was disbanded, and its functions were assumed by the Ministry of Econoimic Affairs.

– On Feb. 25, 1970, the Ministry of Economic Affairs created the Industrial Development Bureau. The Sixth Division of the Bureau was put in charge of assisting SMEs.

– On May 1, 1974, the Ministry of Economic Affairs requested the Industrial Development Bureau to coordinate its efforts with those of the Monetary Department of the Ministry of Finance, the Banking Department of the Central Bank of China, the National Youth Commission of the Executive Yuan, the Board of Foreigh Trade, the Medium and Small Business Association, the Foreigh Trade Development Association, the Metal Industry Development Center, the China Productivity Center, the Taiwan Handicraft Promotion Center and the Industry Design Wrap Center. All of these eleven units got together and formed the "SMEs United Service Center" to ensure that the SMEs received assistance.

– On August 2, 1977, owing to the revision of the assistance standard rule, the Ministry became the controlling institution, while the Industrial Development Bureau only provided assistance. In addition, professional instiutions or experts were called in to implement policy, and the Medium and Small Business Bank and the "Financial Services Sector of the SMEs" were directed to offer financial assistance.

– On Jan. 15, 1981, the Medium & Small Business Administration was set up under the controll of the Ministry of Economic Affairs

– On July 14, 1982, the assistance standard rule was revised again. The Ministry of Economic Affairs remained the controlling institution, and the Medium & Small Business Administration of the Ministry of Economic Affarirs began to act in an assistant capacity. Then the production skill, business management, finance and marketing-assistance system was also set up.

References

Acquier, A.A. (1980), "Sizes of Firms, Exporting Behavior and the Structure of French Industry." *Journal of Industrial Economics*, 29 (2), pp.203–18.

Chou, T.C. (1984), "Theory and Empirical Evidence of Industrialization on Industrial Organization and Structure - The Case of Taewan," *Enterprise Bank Ouarterly*, No. 3 & 4, pp.96–111 and 74–88 (in Chines).

―――― (1985), "The Pattern and Strategy of Industrialization in Taiwan: Specialization and Offsetting Policy;" *The Developing Economies*, 23 (2), pp.138–57, Also the chapter 1 of this book.

―――― (1988), "The Evolution of Market Structure in Taiwan," *Rivista Internazionale di Scienze Economiche e Commerciali*, 35 (2), pp.171–94, Also the chapter 4 of this book.

Ho, S.P.S. (1980), "Small-scale Enterprise in Korea and Taiwan," *World Bank Staff working Paper*, No.384.

Jacquemin, A., De E. Ghellinck and Ch. Huveneers (1980), "Concentration and profitability in a Small Open Economy," *Journal of Industrial Economics*, 29 (2), pp.131–44.

Kuo, P.H. (1986), "A Comparison of the Definitions of SMEs in Taiwan America, Japan and Korea," *Taiwan Economic Research Monthly*, 9 (9), pp.78–80 (in Chinese).

Little, I.M.D. (1987), "Small Manufacturing Enterprises in Developing Countries," *The World Bank Economic Review*, 1 (3), pp.203–35.

Naya, S. (1984), "Small-scale Industries in Asian Economic Development: Problems and Prospects," Asian Development Bank: *Economic Office Report Series*, No. 24.

Rapp, W.V. (1976), "Firm Size and Japan's Export Strcuture: A Microview of Japan's Changing Export Competitiveness Since Meize," in H. Patrick, ed., *Japanese Industrialization and Its Social Consequences*, University of California Press, Berkeley. pp.201–48.

Wu, R.I. (1980), "The Distinctive Features of Taiwan's Development," *Economic Study*, 26, pp.1–26.

9 American and Japanese Direct Foreign Investment in Taiwan*

Introduction

Since the mid 1960s, Japanese firms have rapidly increased their overseas investment (Ozawa, 1979). The distinct features of Japanese firms, which differ significantly from firms in other countries, have attracted the attention of many researchers.[1] Professor Kiyoshi Kojima (1973, 1978, and 1985) has posited that the market orientation of Japanese direct foreign investment (DFI, as same as FDI used in other chapters) is significantly different from that of other countries, especially American DFI. Kojima argues that Japanese DFI is "trade-oriented," while American DFI is "anti-trade-oriented." The implicit assumptions with regard to the differences in market orientation include the differences in the choice of industry, the state of the "product-cycle," the scale of operations, and firm-specific advantage. Furthermore, a corollary of Kojima's hypothesis is that the firm carrying out DFI will choose between different patterns of ownership, ranging from 100% ownership to a joint venture or to a minority interest.

Several studies have in fact shown, by means of applying a structure-conduct-performance paradigm,[2] that the differences in foreign ownership could lead to differences in the determinants of profitability. Accordingly, this study constructs a profitability equation and uses regres-

---
*This paper was reproduced from *Hitotsubashi Journal of Economics*, Vol. 29, No. 2, December 1988, pp.165–179, with permission of the publisher.

sion analysis to examine whether the determinants of the profitability of Japanese and American firms, respectively, are all the same.

In section II, Kojima's hypothesis is discussed in greater detail and a number of null hypotheses concerned with market orientation and other operational characteristics are proposed. These hypotheses are then tested using the 1983 survey data on DFI in Taiwan. The empirical evidence for Taiwan, in contrast to the case of Korea (Lee, 1980), does not seem to support Kojima's hypothesis since both American and Japanese DFI in Taiwan are observed to be export-oriented. However, other results show that differences still remain with regard to the scale of operations, factor intensities and the balance of ownership between American and Japanese DFI in Taiwan.

In section III, a profitability model is set up and then tested by using the data for American and Japanese firms both jointly and separately. Therefater a Chow-test is applied, the results indicating that differences in the determinants of profitability for American and Japanese firms do in fact exist. The empirical results also provide additional information in support of the view that there are significant differences in the behavior of these two kinds of DFI in Taiwan. Concluding remarks are provided in Section IV.

Testing Kojima's hypothesis

The dimensions of Kojima's hypothesis

Before presenting a theoretical discussion and carrying out an empirical evaluation of Kojima's hypothesis, it is first of all important to know something about the situation of DFI in Taiwan. Table 9.1 presents DFI in Taiwan on the approval basis for the 1953-85 period. As shown in the bottom row of the table, American and Japanese DFI together constituted 71% of the total DFI and the remaining 29% was shared by other countries.[3]

Table 9.1

Direct foreign investment in Taiwan, 1953–85 (on approval basis)

unit: thousand US$

Year	(1) U.S.A.	(2) Japan	(3)=(1)+(2) Sub-total	(4) Others	(5) Total
1951-60	23,481	1,681	25,162 (100%)	50 (0%)	25,212
1961-65	55,000	8,171	63,171 (94%)	3,653 (6%)	66,824
1966-70	163,658	79,158	242,816 (80%)	61,412 (20%)	304,228
1971-75	227,844	126,862	354,706 (59%)	243,996 (41%)	598,702
1976-80	306,242	241,784	548,026 (72%)	210,592 (28%)	758,618
1981-85	940,048	672,771	1,612,819 (72%)	618,817 (28%)	2,231,636
1953-85	1,716,273	1,130,427	2,846,700 (71%)	1,138,520 (29%)	3,985,220 (100%)

Sources: Investment Commission, MOEA (1985), *Statistics on Overseas Chinese & Foreign Investment, Technical Cooperation, Outward Investment, Outward Technical Cooperation*, R.O.C., p.9.

However, during the 1953-60 sub-period, U.S. and Japanese DFI accounted for 99.8% of the total DFI for that period. Although their share is declining, it is clear that the United States and Japan remain the predominant investors in Taiwan. It seems reasonable, therefore, to regard Taiwan as a good "laboratory" as far as a comparison of American and Japanese DFI is concetned.

The comparison of American and Japanese DFI should be especially instructive in the light of a recent hypothesis advancd by Kiyoshi Kojima (1973, 1978 and 1985). Kojima argues that Japanes DFI complements Japan's comparative advantage position and is thus "trade-oriented"; in contrast, American DFI displaces the U.S.'s comparative advantage position and is thus "anti-trade-oriented."[4] Clearly, Kojima's hypothesis deals only with the impact of DFI on trade—the effect on the comparative advantage of the countries involved. However, one would also expect DFI to change the growth rate of the host country's economy and thus have a long-run dynamic effect on its pattern of trade. Without specifying the long-run dynamic effect, one cannot, therefore, designate any given DFI as either trade-oriented or anti-trade-oriented. To avoid the possible confusion that might arise due to the ambiguous usage of terminology, *export-oriented and domestic-market-oriented* are used in this paper in place of "trade-oriented", and "anti-trade-oriented," respectively. The former has the apparent advantage of referring to a more immediate effect of DFI which bears no relation to its long-run dynamic effect.

According to Kojima, most Japanese firms that have undertaken DFI have directed their attention towards using the abundant natural resources and unskilled labor of the host country. As a result, Japan's DFI in the manufacturing industries has been mostly confined to such traditional industries as textiles and clothing and to such unskilled labor-intensive processing industries as motor vehicle assembly and electrical apparatus. These industries have been albe to be operated by relatively small-scale firms. On the contrary, American DFI has been directed towards the domestic market of the host country. In addition, American firms have usually undertaken DFI in more highly-sophisticated industries, such as the machinery industry, and in capital-intensive industries such as chemicals, mainly through the medium of large oligopolistic firms.

Moreover, the state of the "product cycle" created by American firms tends to be relatively new, whereas the corresponding one for the Japanese firms tends to be relatively mature. As a result, it can be postulated that Japanese firms are more likely to possess advantages in non-marketable, firm-specific marketing, while the American firms' advantages are rooted in technology and management. Since it is easier to transfer production technology than it is to transfer marketing capability, Japanese investors are more likely to allow the local partners to share in the control of their foreign operations, thus causing them to prefer to enter into a joint venture or opt for a minority shareholding instead of seeking 100% ownership.[5] However, for the Americans

Table 9.2

Some dimensions of Kojima's hypothesis

	Japanese DFI	American DFI
Market orientation	Export-oriented	Domestic-market-oriented
Choice of industry	Conventional	Sophisticated
Firm size	Small	Large
Technology (factor intensity)	Labor-intensive	Capital-intensive
Ownership	Joint-venture & minority control	100% ownership or majority holdings

Source: the author.

the reverse is true. They prefer 100% ownership to joint ventures and minority holdings.

To sum up, the differences in market orientation (export-orientation vs. domestic-market-orientation), the choice of industry (sophisticated industries vs. conventional ones), the factor-intensity of technology (unskilled labor-intensive vs. capital-intensity), the size of the firm (small vs. large scale), and the control of ownership (minority vs. majority holdings) between American and Japanese DFI in Taiwan may be inferred from Kojima's hypothesis which is summarized in Table 9.2.

Empirical tests of Kojima's hypothesis

To see if the choice of industry between American and Japanese DFI in Taiwan is significantly different or not, U.S. and Japanese DFI is broken down by industry in Table 9.3. Because the willingness to invest is the main concern, the data on the approval basis rather than on the arrival basis is used here. Table 9.3 shows 13 manufacturing industries in which U.S. and Japanese DFI was undertaken. Among them, the five leading industries in which U.S. was allocated are electronics & electric appliances; chemicals; basic metals and metal products; machinery, equipment & precision instruments; and food & beverage processing, in descending order of the amount invested. As for Japanese DFI, the only difference in these top five industries is that plastic & rubber products replaces food & beverage processing to take fifth place.

In order to further judge the significance of the order of preference of the different industries on the list, the rank correlation of the amount invested within the manufacturing industries for the two kinds of DFI is calculated. The value of Spearman's correlation coefficinet is found to be 0.791, and thus the null hypothesis that American investment is consistently related to Japanese investment with regard to the choice of industry is rejected at the 1% significance level.[6] Moreover, a similar result (the correaltion coefficient is 0.73) is found by using equity data for U.S. and Japanese firms for the year 1984.

Table 9.3 also shows that the number of investment projects is, in general, larger in U.S. DFI than in Japanese DFI. The exceptions are lumber & bamboo products, machinery, equipment & instruments, and miscellaneous manufactured products. However, to compare scales of operation (or market orientation, factor intensity or ownership control) of the DFI of these two countires, the data needs to be more detailed and on an arrival basis.

Every year, the Investment Commission of the Ministry of Economic Affairs collects annual survey data on DFI. The data are prepared and published in the "Survey Report on Foreign Direct Investment," and in the report can only be read in its fixed format. However, this data cannot completely meet the needs of the hypothesis test. Fortunately, by being able to obtain the original tape for this survey's data, we have been able to make this comparison feasible.

We have decided to use 1983 DFI firm data. Brief definitions and the sources of the variables are given in the Appendix 9.1. The market orientation (EX, EXJ and EXA), firm size and scale of operations ($CAP, SELE, NASS$ and $WORK$), ownership control (OWN), and factor-intensity (KL, RD and IMI) are compared between American & Japanese DFI in Taiwan. The null hypothesis here is that there is no difference in each of those variables between the DFI of the two countries in Taiwan. Accordingly, Kojima's conjecture forms our alternative

Table 9.3

American and Japanese direct investment in Taiwan by industry, 1953-85 (on approval basis)

unit: thousand US$

Industry	U.S.A. Cases	U.S.A. Amount	U.S.A. Average amount	Japan Cases	Japan Amount	Japan Average amount
Food & Beverage Processing	25	48,196	1,928	27	13,098	485
Textile	1	2,224	2,224	29	34,346	1,184
Garment & Footwear	15	4,229	282	38	8,122	213
Lumber & bamboo Products	6	778	130	18	4,709	262
Pulp Paper & Products	3	12,314	4,105	10	1,831	183
Leather & Fur Products	10	2,447	245	9	1,087	121
Plastic & Rubber Products	22	26,914	1,223	70	59,974	857
Chemicals	82	440,577	5,373	94	88,055	937
Non-metallic Minerals	12	8,705	725	41	15,957	389
Basic Metals & Metal Products	45	89,518	1,982	163	112,450	690
Machinery Equipment & Instruments	42	59,440	1,415	90	300,961	3,344
Electronic & Electric Appliances	140	808,316	5,774	220	331,512	1,507
Miscellaneous Manufactured Products	27	14,130	523	58	36,595	631
Sub-total	430	1,517,788	3,530	867	1,008,697	1,163
Services	69	192,929	2,796	27	119,998	4,444
Others 1	9	13,919	1,547	6	1,732	289
Total	505	1,716,333	3,399	900	1,130,427	1,256

Sources: Investment Commission, MOEA (1985), *Statistics on Overseas Chinese & Foreign Investment, Technical Cooperation, Outward Investment, Outward Technical Cooperation, R.O.C.*, p.10.

1. Including agriculture, mining, construction.

1. Including agriculture, mining, construction.

Table 9.4

A comparison of some features between American and Japanese firms in Taiwan, 1983

	U.S.A.	Japan	U.S.A.	Japan	U.S.A.	Japan
Market-orientation	EX		EXJ		EXA	
Mean	61.0	60.0	4.6	29.5	50.5	19.3
S.D.	43.1	43.8	17.0	37.5	40.9	31.9
t-stat.	0.19		8.45***		6.08***	
Firm size & scale	CAP		SALE		TASS	
Mean	83.8	47.7	373	234	297	174
S.D.	123.0	70.3	503	362	253	271
t-stat.	2.66***		2.45***		4.03***	
Scale & ownership	NASS		WORK		OWN	
Mean	155	76	454	261	74.3	60.2
S.D.	219	126	1,130	556	33.2	28.4
t-stat.	3.27***		1.56*		4.03***	
Factor-intensity	KL		RD		IMI	
Mean	73.1	47.0	0.78	0.20	52.2	49.8
S.D.	173.3	75.3	2.49	0.81	33.3	33.5
t-stat.	1.38*		2.18**		0.61	

Source: the original taped data of "the 1983 Survey on Foreign Direct Investment in Taiwan" conducted by the Investment Commission, MOEA.

Significance levels of t-statistics are *** = 1%, ** = 5%, * = 10%.

hypothesis. The mean and standard deviation of the above variables can be calculated for each country's DFI. Then, the t-statistic for the tests of the above null hypothesis are shown in Table 9.4. It is to the results and discussions that we now turn.

Fitst of all, the degree of export-orientation may be explained by the export intensity variable (EX). American firms export 61% of their sales, while Japanese firms export 60%. Both American and Japanese firms are thus highly export-oriented. The t-statistic shows that the null hypothesis cannot be rejected. This seems to be inconsistent with

Kojima's hypothesis conerning market orientation. One possible explanation of this phenomenon is the attitude of the Taiwan government. There are many restrictions imposed on direct investment by foreign investors. However, most of the restrictions are not based on statute law but arise as a result of the procedures for obtaining approval from the Investment Commission of the Ministry of Economic Affairs. Export-oriented foriegn investment is particularly welcome in order to fully utilize the abundant supply of labor in Taiwan and to earn foreign exchange.[7] Of course, another reason for selecting this type of foreign investment is to protect domestic firms from foreign competition.[8] As a consequence, both American and Japanese DFI firms in Taiwan are export-oriented. Cohen's suggestion (1977, p.135) that the principal reason behind the Korean government's encouraging DFI may have been political rather than economic seems to gain empirical support in the case of Taiwan.

However, if we further compare the destination of exports, we find that one half of the American firms' exports (50.5%) are sold back to the U.S., and only 4.6% are sold to Japan (see Table 9.4). In the case of the Japanese firms, only 29.5% of their total exports are sold to Japan, and 19.3% are sold to the U.S. It is unlikely, judging from the results, that Japanese exporters in Taiwan adopt a "circular export strategy" to circumvent restrictive import measures by the U.S. It seems reasonable, therefore, to confirm the above argument that Japanese firms in Taiwan possess firm-specific (and non-location-specific) advantages in marketing (international marketing).[9] The high export intensity and resale ratio to the home country reveal that American DFI in Taiwan is motivated by the international division of labor considerations of large U.S. multinationals which usually have firm-specific, non-marketable advantages in production technology and management.

Second, firm size and the scale of operations can be compared by the following variables: capital, sales, total assets, net assets and employees. Table 9.4 shows that American firms in Taiwan have significantly larger

Table 9.5

Ownership pattern of American and Japanese DFI in Taiwan, 1983

Ownership share	U.S.A. Cases	(%)	Japan Cases	(%)
100%	49	(49.5)	81	(22.5)
50–99%	27	(27.3)	124	(34.4)
0–49%	23	(23.2)	155	(43.1)
Tatal	99	(100.0)	360	(100.0)

Source: The Investment Commission, MOEA (1985), *The 1983 Survey on Foreign Direct Investment it Taiwan.*

scales of operation than Japanese firms in terms of capital, sales, or assets. According to Riedel(1976), however, who carried out research on DFI Taiwan, the most important factor for export-oriented DFI is the availability of relatively inexpensive labor in the host country. Consequently, American firm size in terms of the number of employees is still larger than in the case of the Japanese, but the difference only becomes slightly significant at the 10% significance level.

Third, the null hypothesis which assumes that there is no difference in ownership control between American and Japanese firms in Taiwan is rejected in Table 9.4. American firms significantly have more majority shareholdings (74.3%) than Japanese firms (60%). Again, the t-test is significant at the 1% significance level. Table 9.5 presents a more detailed ownership pattern of American and Japanese DFI in Taiwan. It shows that 76.8% of U.S. investment projects in Taiwan have U.S. ownership of 50% or more, and only 23.2% have U.S. ownership of less than 50%. In other words, more than three-quarters of the U.S. investment projects in Taiwan are controlled by U.S. investors and less than a quarter are controlled by the Taiwanese partners. Table 9.5 also shows that Japanese firms in Taiwan have different patterns of ownership. Slightly over half of the Japanese investment projects in Taiwan (56.9%) involve majority shareholdings whereas the other slightly less than half exercise only minority interests. As shown above, Table 9.5 confirms that American investors in Taiwan prefer 100% ownership to joint-ventures or minority holdings while Japanese investors prefer just the opposite.

Finally, factor-intensity can be compared by capital, labor, R & D expenditure and intermediate goods imported. Table 9.4 shows that American DFI in Taiwan is more capital-intensive and "brain-intensive" than Japanese DFI. The R & D intensity is higher in American DFI in Taiwan than in Japanese DFI at the 5% significance level according to the t-test. American firms in Taiwan are more capital-intensive than Japanese firms, but only at the 10% significance level. Again, the same motivation for export-oriented DFI confirms that the difference in KL between Japanese and American firms in Taiwan is not so significant. Furthermore, the fact that around half of the intermediate goods used to produce these final goods are imported means that similar "export-processing" types of investment projects exist in Taiwan regardless of whether they are undertaken by American or Japanese firms. As was mentioned above, this could be the result of government attitudes to DFI in Taiwan. Only one possible difference is the state of the "product cycle" in that American products are relatively new and Japanese products mature, based on the fact that American DFI has a relatively high R & D intensity. This seems to support the above argument that American DFI possesses an advantage in production technology and management, which is why the American firms prefer majority ownership.

In short, the empirical data together with the t-tests show that (1) both American and Japanese firms in Taiwan are "export-processing-oriented" with no significant differences in distribution according to industry; (2) American firms in Taiwan have larger scale of operation than Japanese firms; (3) American firms tend to adopt more capital-intensive technology at the 10% significance level and more "brain-intensive" technology at the 5% significance level; and (4) American investors prefer majority ownership to minority holdings. In other words, Kojima's hypothesis is only partially verified by the empirical evidence. Specifically, differences in market orientation and choice of industry do not occur in Taiwan yet, but the differences in firm size and ownership control do exist. The reason for the rejection of the other aspects of Kojima's hypothesis may be the result of the government's selective restrictions on DFI, while the reason for the confirmation of the points outlined above may be due to American firms in Taiwan being relatively large and possessing advantages in production technology and management.

The determinants of profitability and foreign ownership

Specification of the profit equation

Most of the determinants of a firm's profitability have been extensively analyzed in the industrial organization literature. Therefore, they will only be briefly examined here. A firm's profitability is determined by both industry and firm characteristics. The industrial concentration ratio (CR) represents market power and industrial growth ($GROW$) represents the dynamic market situation within which a firm operates. These two variables which are basic elements of the market structure are included in the profit equation. A positive sign of concentration on profitability is expected. The influence of industrial growth on a firm's profitabiltiy is indeterminate and depends on the increases in demand or supply, high capacity utilization or new competitors.

Firm aize ($LASS$)[10] and capital intensity ($CAPIN$) are two variables that are used to represent the scale of operations of a firm. Again the relation between profitability and the scale of operations is indeterminate and depends on the relative position of the scale of operations with reference to the minimum efficient scale (MES) and the type of cost function. When the scale of operations is less than the MES, in the case of increasing returns, the larger the scale the higher the profitability; but when the scale of operations is larger than the MES, in the case of decreasing returns, the larger the scale the lower the profitability. Thus, the sign of the scale of operations alone is a priori indeterminate.[11]

As was shown above, the control of ownership (OWN) can indicate the degree of firm-specific advantage in terms of production technology, management and marketing. The higher the share of ownership, the larger the firm-specific advantage and thus the higher the profitability. The financial structure of a firm represents its pecuniary position and does have an influence on its profitability. It is expected, by the same token, that the liability ratio ($RLIA$) will have a negative influence on the profitability.

The final group of explanatory variables included in the profit equation relate to the foreign sector. Because both American and Japanese DFI in Taiwan are export-processing-oriented, three variables, namely, EX, IM, and KL, are included. The high import intensity, as shown in Table 9.4, presents both Japanese and American investors with the need to import intermediate and producer goods from their home countries (or abroad) for the manufacturing process. Consequently, given the prices of export-processing products, the higher the import intensity (which may come about through the use of transfer prices), the higher the costs and thus the lower the profitability. The influence of EX on profitability depends on the firms' export behavior and their degree of monopoly power in the export market. The high proportion of the American firms' products that are resold to the U.S. increases the possibility that they will adopt transfer pricing. If this is the case, a negative relationship can be expected to exist between EX and profitability. The variable KL indicates the appropriateness of operational technology. The more appropriate the technology, the higher will be the profitability.

Table 9.6

Testing the difference between the American and Japanese profitability equations

	U.S.A.	Japan	Total
$\bar{R}^2$	42.9	44.2	36.3
Number of firms	89	348	437
SSR	1.694	2.650	5.117
SSRU, SSRR		4.344	5.117
CHOW-test[1]		7.42	

Sources: Calculated from Table 9.7.

1. F-ratio for $CHOW-test = \frac{(SSRR-SSRU)/K}{SSRU/(NS+NJ-2K)}$, where K, NA, NJ are the number of total, American and Japanese firms, respectively.

The resulting profit equation, with the expected signs indicated below each independent variable, may be specified as follows:

$$PRO = f(\underset{+}{CR}, \underset{+}{GROW}, \underset{-}{LASS}, \underset{-}{CAPIN}, \underset{+}{OWN}, \underset{-}{RLIA}, \underset{+}{KL}, \underset{+}{EX}, \underset{-}{IM})$$

Estimation and Chow-test

As noted above, the firm data was gathered from the original tape of the 1983 Survey on Foreign Direct Investment in Taiwan conducted in 1985 by the Investment Commission, Ministry of Economic Affairs. There were 478 firms in that survey and only the data of 437 firms are valid and used in this study. Among them, 89 are American firms and 348 are Japanese firms. The industry data, the concentration ratio and data on industrial growth are obtained from the 1981 Industry and Commerce Census of Taiwan and aggregated to arrive at the current classification. Brief definitions of the variables are given in the Appendix 9.1.

The first test is to determine whether the coefficients in the profit equation shown above differ statistically between American and Japanese firms in Taiwan. Therefore, the profit equation is estimated by first of all using a data set for all 437 firms, and then by using the 89 American firms and the 348 Japanese firms, respectively. The results are given in table 9.7.

From the results, F-ratio can be computed, as shown in Table 9.6, to perform the so-called "Chow-test" for which the null hypothesis is that the coefficients of the profit equation are the same between the two groups of data, i.e., American and Japanese DFI in Taiwan. Table 9.6 reveals that the F-ratio for the Chow-test is 7.42, which means that we can reject the null hypothesis at the 1% significance level. In other words, the determinants of profitability for American and Japanese firms in Taiwan differ from each other.

Empirical results

As was shown in the second and third columns of Table 9.7, some coefficients in the profit equation are statistically insignificant. Therefore, the Amemiya Prediction Criterion (*APC*) can be used to choose explanatory variables in order to improve the fit of the equation.[12] The improved results are given in the fourth and fifth columns of Table 9.7. As a result, the differences in the determinants of profitability between American and Japanese investors in Taiwan can be broken down into five categories.

First, the profitability of American firms in Taiwan is negatively but insignificantly influenced by the two elements of market structure, namely, industrial growth and industrial concentration. This is probably because foreign investment in Taiwan is restricted by government policy within the confines of the export-processing-oriented type in which the firm's performance is not influenced by market circumstances.[13] However, a significant and positive degree of industrial concentration is found in Japanese firms which conforms with our theory. The highly concentrated industries in Taiwan are domestic-market-oriented and mostly controlled by domestic entrepreneurs with protective measures.[14] Therefore, Japanese firms may enjoy high profits from concentrated

Table 9.7

Determinants of profitability

	Total	U.S.A.	Japan	U.S.A.	Japan
CONST	−28.93	−7.70	−26.50	−23.30	−28.30
	(−2.91)***	(−0.23)	(−2.88)***	(−1.13)	(−3.88)***
CR	0.044	−0.224	0.112		0.114
	(0.69)	(−1.03)	(1.85)**		(2.00)**
GROW	−0.157	−0.270	−0.972		
	(−0.77)	(−0.37)	(−0.54)		
LASS	2.00	1.98	1.54	1.99	1.56
	(4.80)***	(1.69)**	(3.85)***	(1.82)**	(3.95)***
CAPIN	0.0054	−0.204	0.0053	−0.236	0.0053
	(13.22)***	(−4.55)***	(15.78)***	(−7.81)***	(15.83)***
OWN	0.025	0.076	0.021	0.065	
	(1.37)*	(1.42)*	(1.14)	(1.33)*	
RLIA	−0.140	−0.468	−0.139	−0.538	−0.140
	(−3.41)***	(−1.47)*	(−4.10)***	(−1.66)*	(−4.16)***
KL	−0.048	−0.014	−0.029		−0.030
	(−8.91)***	(−0.98)	(−4.08)***		(−4.40)***
EX	−0.027	−0.094	−0.0016	−0.074	
	(−1.94)**	(−2.19)**	(−0.12)	(−1.93)**	
IM	−0.013	0.05	−0.017		−0.016
	(−1.36)**	(0.88)	(−2.17)**		(−2.11)**
N	437	89	384		384
R^2	37.6	48.7	45.7	46.7	45.5
$\bar{R}^2$	36.3	42.9	44.2	43.5	44.5
F	28.5**	8.36***	31.6***	14.57***	48.7***
APC		0.643	0.586	0.610	0.578

t-statistics (one-tail test) are given in parentheses.

Significance levels of coefficients are *** = 1%, ** = 5%, * = 10%.

APC is the Amemiya Prediction Criterion.

industries and share them with local partners through their minority holdings.

Second, both LASS and CAPIN are variables used to indicate the scale of operations of a firm. There is a difference in the variables used to represent the degree of capital intensity between American and Japanese firms in Taiwan. As explained above, Japanese DFI is likely to have low capital intensity in relation to the minimum efficient scale of operations, and for American DFI the opposite situation applies. In other words, American direct investment operates in Taiwan with decreasing returns on capital and Japanese direct investment with increasing returns to capital.

Third, the impact of RLIA on profitability meets the above expectations. The variable OWN in the profit equation is significant only in American firms at the 10% significance level. This seems to indicate that Japanese investors do not obtain higher profitability from more majority holdings, but that American investors slightly gain from firm-specific advantages by means of their majority holdings. As shown above, this is because Japanese investors possess a nontransferable marketing advantage and this advantage can be realized by minority holdings through which Japanese firms seem to enjoy monopoly power.

Fourth, it seems to be the case that Japanese firms in Taiwan not only may enjoy increasing returns to scale by increasing their capital, but also by increasing the labor input. Accordingly, increasing labor, and thus decreasing KL, leads to higher profitability. A positive sign for CAPIN and a negative sign for KL jointly reveal that the scale of operations of Japanese firms in Taiwan is too small to exploit the underlying economies of scale.

Finally, the influence of trade on profitability indicates the possibility that transfer pricing is used, though in different ways, in both American and Japanese DFI. That is, American investors prefer to sell their products at low prices and Japanese investors prefer to procure intermediate goods from abroad at high prices. The reason for adopting transfer pricing is likely to be due to the restrictions on the repatriation of profits under the foreign exchange regulations and/or the high level of tax in Taiwan.

Concluding remarks

Since the Taiwan government has imposed highly selective restrictions on foreign investment, the foreign investment in Taiwan is mostly of the "export-processing-oriented" type.[15] Therefore, significant differences in terms of market orientation and choice of industry between American and Japanese DFI do not exist in Taiwan. Hence, the evidence for Taiwan is in part inconsistent with the so-called Kojima hypothesis. As a result, firm profitability is not significantly influenced by the industrial environment. However, differences still exist in terms of the scale of operations, factor-intensity and ownership control. These differences result in the determinants of profitability being different between American and Japanese firms in Taiwan.

From the profit equation, we find that American investors in Taiwan, on the one hand, seem to make use of more capital-intensive technology, possess firm-specific advantage by means of their majority holdings and tend to sell their products at low prices. The Japanese investors, on the other hand, seem to have less capital-intensive operations, relatively small scales of operation, they do not possess firm-specific advantages in terms of ownership control, and they tend to procure their intermediate inputs from abroad at high prices. It must of course be realized that the above findings may no longer hold following the recent liberalization of foreign investment policy in Taiwan. This is a matter that merits further research.

Notes

1. For instance, see Kojima (1973, 1978, 1985), Kojima and Ozawa (1984), Lee (1980, 1983, 1984), Ozawa (1979), Romer (1976) and Pangestu (1987).
2. With regard to the application of the industrial organization approach to the problem of DFI, see Cave (1971, 1982). For a discussion on profitability and ownership, see Chen (1983), Newfarmer and Marsh (1981) and Donsimoni and Leoz-Arquelles (1981).
3. However, here, overseas Chinese investment is not included in the data. It amounted to US$1,175 million on the approval basis during that period.
4. It is quoted from Lee (1980, note 1, p.26) that "Kojima uses Purvis's definition (1972) of trade-oriented and anti-trade-oriented investment. Accordingly, foreign investment is trade-oriented if it generates an excess demand for imports and an excess supply of exportable at constant terms of trade, and it is anti-trade-oriented if the converse holds."
5. The same argument that Japanese firms are deemed to be more responsive to the formation of joint-ventures with the host country is found in Ozawa (1979).
6. A similar structural pattern of industry exists not only between America and Japanese investment, but also between foreign investment and local investment. By means of the same calculation, Spearman's correlation coefficient is found to be 0.637 for the comparison between American and local firms, and also for that between Japanese and local firms.
7. The requirement of the export ratio is usually a necessary condition for obtaining approval for a foreign investment project. Concerning direct investment policy in Taiwan, see Wu et al. (1980) and Yu (1985). However, it should be noted that the direction of policy was forced to change due to Taiwan's huge trade surplus with the U.S. since 1986.

8. One may therefore say that the policy of approving foreign investment by the Taiwan government is highly selective. This can also explain why there is no significant difference in the choice of industry between Japanese and American DFI in Taiwan.
9. Lee's argument (1980) that Japanese DFI in Korea possesses an advantage in "location-specific" rather than "non-location-specific" marketing techniques seems not to apply to Taiwan.
10. Other variables representing firm size are shown in Table 9.4. They are used to estimate the profit equation in the preliminary estimations and are dropped due to their failure in the statistical tests.
11. If the variable can be computed as the operational scale divided by MES, a positive sign for this variable on the profitability is expected. However, the MES variable cannot be exactly computed here due to the problem of data classification.
12. For the APC method, see Judge et al. (1982), p.603.
13. Chou (1986a) shows that industrial concentration does have a positive influence on profitability, but that this significance exists only in the domestic-market-oriented sector and not in the export-oriented sector (Chou, 1986b).
14. A so-called "dichotomous" market structure is discussed by Chou (1986b).
15. Concerning the heavy role of the government in Taiwan's industrial organization, see Chou (1986a, 1986b).

Appendix

Appendix 9.1
Sources and definitions of variables

Variable	Definition	Source
PRO	Profit before tax divided by sales (%)	(1)
CAP	Capital (million N.T. dollars)	(1)
SALE	Sales (million N.T. dollars)	(1)
TASS	Total assets (million N.T. dollars)	(1)
NASS	Net assets (million N.T. dollars)	(1)
WORK	Number of employees (man)	(1)
OWN	Foreign capital divided by total capital (%)	(1)
RLIA	Liabilities divided by net assets	(1)
EX	Exports divided by sales (%)	(1)
EXA	Exports to U.S. divided by total exports	(1)
EXJ	Exports to Japan divided by total exports	(1)
IM	Imports divided by sales (%)	(1)
IMI	Intermediates imported divided by intermediates used (%)	(1)
KL	Assets divided by total workers (%)	(1)
RD	Expenditure on R&D divided by sales (%)	(1)
CR	Concentration ratio of four largest firms in 1981(%)	(1)
GROW	Annual growth rate of industry sales in 1976-81(%)	(2)
LASS	Logarithm of fixed assets	(1)
CAPIN	Fixed assets divided by sales (%)	(1)

Data sources are:

(1) The original taped data of "the 1983 Survey on Foreign Direct Investment in Taiwan" conducted by the Investment Commission, Ministry of Economic Affairs.

(2) The Committee on Industrial and Commercial Censuses of Taiwan, R.O.C. (1980), *General Report of Industry & Commerce Census of Taiwan.*

References

Caves, R.E. (1971), "International Corporation: The Industrial Economics of Foreign Investment," *Economica*, 38, pp.1–27.

―――― (1982), *Multinational Enterprise and Economic Analysis*, Cambridge University Press, Cambridge.

Chen, E.K.Y. (1983), "Factor Proportions of Foreign and Local Firms in Developing Countries: A Theoretical and Empirical Note," *Journal of Development Economics*, 12, pp.267–74.

Chou, T.C. (1985), "The Pattern and Strategy of Industrialization in Taiwan: Specialization and Offsetting Policy," *Developing Economies*, 23 (2), pp.138–57.

―――― (1986a), "Concentration, Profitability and Trade in a Simultaneous Equation Analysis: The Case of Taiwan," *Journal of Industrial Economics*, 34 (3), pp.429–43.

―――― (1986b), "Concentration and Profitability in a Dichotomous Economy: The Case of Taiwan," paper presented at *the 13th Annual Conference of the EARIE*, West Berlin, August pp.24-26.

Cohen, B.I. (1975), *Multinational Firms and Asian Exports*, Yale University Press, New Haven.

Donsimoni, M.P. and V. Leoz-Arquelles (1981), "Strategic Groups: An Application to Foreign and Domestic Firms in Spain," *Recherches Economiques de Louvain*, 47 (3-4), pp.197–355.

Judge, G.G. et al. (1982), *Introduction to the Theory and Practice of Econometrics*, John Willey & Sons Inc, New York.

Kojima, K. (1973), "A Macroeconomic Approach to Foreign Direct Investment," *Hitotsubashi Journal of Economics*, 14 (1), pp.1–20.

——— (1978), *Direct Foreign Investment: A Japanese Model of Multinational Business Operations*, Croom Helm Press, London.

——— and T. Ozawa (1984), "Micro-and Macro-Economic Model of Direct Foreign Investment: Toward a Synthesis," *Hitotsubashi Journal of Economics*, 25 (1), pp.1–20.

——— (1985), "Japanese and American Direct Investment in Asia: A Comparative Analysis," *Hitotsubashi Journal of Economics*, 26 (1), pp.1–35.

Lee, C.H. (1980), "United States and Japanese Direct Foreign Investment in Korea: A Comparative Study," *Hitotsubashi Journal of Economics*, 20 (2), pp.26–41.

——— (1983), "International Production of the United States and Japan in Korean Manufacturing Industries: A Comparative Study," *Weltwirtschaftliches Archiv*, 119 (4), pp.744–53.

——— (1984), "On Japanese Macroeconomic Theories of Direct Foreign Investment," *Economic Development and Cultural Change*, 32 (3), pp.713–23.

Newfarmer, R.S. and L.C. Marsh (1981), "Foreign Ownership, Market Structure and Industrial Performance: Brazil's Electrical Industry," *Journal of Development Economics*, 8 (1), pp.47–75.

Ozawa, T. (1979), "International Investment and Industrial Structure: New Theoretical Implications from the Japanese Experience," *Oxford Economic Papers*, 31 (1), pp.72–92.

Pangestu, M. (1987), "The Pattern of Direct Foreign Investment in ASEAN: The U.S. vs. Japan," *ASEAN Economic Bulletin*, 3 (3), pp.301–328.

Purvis, D.D. (1972), "Technology, Trade and Factor Mobility," *Economic Journal*, 82 (327), pp.991–99.

Riedel, J. (1975), "The Nature and Determinants of Export-Oriented Direct Foreign Investment in a Developing Country: A Case Study of Taiwan," *Weltwirtschaftliches Archiv*, 3 (2), pp.505–26.

Romer, J.E. (1976), "Japanese Direct Foreign Investment in Manufactures: Some Comparisons with the U.S. Pattern," *Quarterly Review of Economic Studies*, 16 (2), pp.91–111.

Wu, R.I., C.H. Wanglian, T.C. Chou, and C.K. Li, (1980), *Economic Effects of American Investment in Taiwan*, Institute of American Culture, Academia Sinica, Taipei (in Chinese).

Yu, J.J. (1985), "Foreign Investment Policy and Utilization in Taiwan and Its Major Competitors," *Economic Papers*, No.64, Chung-Hua Institution for Economic Research, Taipei.

Index

acquisitions, 210
advertising intensity, 147
aggregate, 205
aggregate approach, 205
Aggregate concentration ratios (ACR), 203
allocative efficiency, 88
American, 4
anti-trade-oriented, 249
Association of Banking Industry, 104
autonomy, 83

bad loans, 91
bad-loan ratios, 96
banking, 127
banking industry, 91
banking system, 243
bankruptcy, 102
bargaining power, 137
basic scarcity, 123
benign attitude, 103
benign policy, 83
bottlenecks, 117
brain-intensive, 259
branches, 95
bureaucratic controls, 28
business group, 203
business groups, 1, 119
business organizations, 210

capacity utilization, 180, 261
capital, 173
capital market, 68
capital requirement, 149
causal relation, 147
censuses, 3

China Credit Information Services, 205
Chow-test, 250
chronological description, 67
classification, 12
collateral, 2, 92
collusive monopoly, 65
collusive pricing, 64
combined effect, 46
common directors, 210
communication, 127
comparative advantage, 235
competition, 15
competitive export market, 3
complementary, 65
concentration, 1, 147
concentration equations, 178
concentration ratio, 12
conglomerate, 4
conglomerate groups, 204
conglomerate groups, 216
conjecture, 83
consensus, 244
conservatism, 67
conservative, 66
consolidated statement, 211
credit allocation, 65
credit information collection, 94
credit information system, 94
credits allocated, 64
critical rate of expected failure, 92
cross-section, 3
cross-terms, 1, 40

decision-making, 66

decompose, 49
decomposed, 48
decomposition, 56
degree of collusion, 138
degree of monopoly, 3, 138
deregulated, 66
deregulation, 69
dichotomous economy, 176
dichotomous market structure, 2
dichotomous sectors, 171, 173
dichotomy, 106, 118
differentiated goods, 152
direct finance, 68
direct foreign investment (DFI, 249
direct investment, 1
dis-intermediation effect, 90
dis-intermediaton, 82
disaggregated approach, 205
discriminate, 31
disintermediation effect, 90
displacement, 66
distribution channel systems, 121
distributors, 132
diversification, 22, 204
domestic-market-oriented, 252
domestic-oriented industries, 2
domestic-oriented sector, 171
dominant firm, 180
dominant firms' models, 162
dual, 34, 64
dual financial system, 2, 64
dualism, 85
dualistic, 85
dualistic financial system, 82
dualistic nature, 80

eclectic theory, 123
economic development, 1

economies of scale, 4
efficiency, 66
empirical, 66
entrepreneurship, 118
entry barriers, 64, 74, 178
evolution, 10
export expansion, 39
export incentive measures, 1
export incentives policies, 120
export intensity, 4, 173, 178, 256
export intensity equation, 148
export performance, 225
Export Processing Zones, (EPZ), 28, 35
export substitution, 19
export-contribution, 243
export-led, 4, 7
export-orientation, 256
export-oriented, 252
Export-oriented industries, 105
export-oriented industries, 2
export-oriented sector, 171
export-processing, 259

failure rate, 92
family groups, 119
Feinberg, R.M., 145, 223
financial activities, 68
financial dualism, 80, 85
financial institution, 64
Financial intermediation, 68
Financial liberalization, 69
financial market, 63
financial reform, 244
financial repression, 64, 107
financial sector, 2, 63
financial statements, 94
financial structure, 63
financing situations, 238

firm size, 225
fixed costs, 150
foreign, 1
foreign competition, 188
foreign direct investment, 147, 173
foreign enterprises, 3
foreign exchange, 118
foreign markets, 237
formal financial sector, 2
funding, 76

government interference, 160
government intervention, 243

Herfindahl index, 150
homogeneous goods, 152

implicit collusion, 151
import controls component, 1
import intensity, 173
import intensity equation, 148
import protection measures, 120
import subsitiution, 39
import substitution, 15
important penetration, 153
incentives, 24
indirect finance, 68
industrial concentration, 176
industrial economics, 149
industrial groups, 124
industrial organization, 1
industrial policy, 30, 243, 244
industrial sectors, 125
industrialization, 1
industry concentration, 150, 173
inflation, 193
informal financial sector, 2
informal sector, 2
input-output, 41

inter-industry, 149
inter-sectoral diversification, 216
interest ceiling regulation, 107
interest liberalization, 107
interest rates, 69
interest spread, 92
interindustry, 43
interlocking, 210
international division of labor, 241
international linkages, 148
international marketing networks, 182
interventionism, 243
intra-industry trade, 15, 163
Inward-orientation, 118

Japanese DFI, 4
joining cross-terms, 46
Joint Credit Information Centre, 104
joint determination, 147

kerb markets, 64
know-how, 242
Kogiku, K.C., 37
Kojima's hypothesis, 249
Korea, 25

Laspeyres, 45
lending, 76
Leontief, 41
Lerner index, 138
liberalism, 243
liberalization, 66
liberalized, 66
listed companies, 76
loan decision, 92
loanable funds, 64

majority ownership, 260
manufacturing, 125
manufacturing stage, 240
market orientation, 118, 121, 250
market size, 149
market structure, 2, 117
market structure dichotomy, 104
market-oriented industries, 105
marketing, 4
marketing stage, 240
marketing systems, 238
mergers, 210
minimum collateral requirement, 96
minimum efficient plant size, 149
minimum profit requirement, 95
minority holdings, 260
money market, 68
monopolistic, 172
monopolistic domestic market, 3
monopoly power, 74, 176
multi-companies group, 203, 217
multi-company firm, 210
multidivisional company, 204
multinational, 152

nepotistic practices, 119, 210
New York, 76
non-performing loans, 83
nontariff, 25
null hypotheses, 250

offsetting, 1
organized, 64
outward-oriented, 7, 63
overdue loans, 95
overestimated, 40
ownership, 4
ownership control, 266

ownership structure, aggregate concentration ratios, 3

Paasche, 45
pattern, 7
PCM, 138, 147
peculiarity, 91
periods chosen, 40
Porter, M.E., 146
post-industrialization, 107
Postal savings, 71
pressure, 68
price discrimination, 152
price-cost margin, 1
price-cost margins, 138, 147, 173
pricing policies, 238
processing, 7
product differentiation, 133
profitability, 3, 147
profitability equation, 179
proportionate, 45
protections, 24
public enterprises, 3

rationing credit, 2, 71
rationing funds, 98
recursive concentration-performance system, 171
recursive structure-performance, 3
recursive two-equation model, 147
red-tape, 28
repression, 64
resistance, 67
retailers, 132
revised measure, 40
rigidities, 83

scale economies, 149, 173
secured loans, 97

securitization, 74
self-sustained growth, 117
selling efforts, 242
service sector, 127
Sheaham, J.B., 146
Shimagughi, M., 146
SIC, 155
Singapore, 25
single multi-divisional corporation, 217
SITC, 156
slanting effect, 42
small-and-medium enterprises (SMEs), 1, 4
specialization, 7
Standard Industry Classification, 155
Standard International Trade Classification, 156
state-owned, 65
strategic group, 193
strategic group hypothesis, 164
strategic industries, 243
strategy, 7
structural change, 1
structure-conduct-performance, 4
structure-performance paradigm, 171
subsidizing, 32
synchronous effect, 42

Taiwan, 2
tariffs, 24
tax holidays, 124
tax rebates, 27
tax reform, 244
technological change, 39
technology intensity, 154
technology-intensity, 173

theoretical, 66
time-series, 3
Tokyo, 76
trade features, 238
trade intensity, 3
trade patterns, 117
trade policy, 117, 244
trade-oriented, 249
trading companies, 133
transfer prices, 152, 261
transfer pricing, 262
transportation, 127
two-equation system, 183
two-regime, 3
two-regime approach, 171
two-regime hypothesis, 183

underestimated, 40
United States, 30
Unorganized, 64
unsecured loans, 97

wave of mergers, 209
wholesalers, 132
Williamson, O.E., 224